Does Everyone Want Democracy?

PAULA L.W. SABLOFF

Does
EVERYONE
Want
DEMOCRACY?
INSIGHTS FROM MONGOLIA

WALNUT CREEK
CALIFORNIA

Left Coast Press, Inc.
1630 North Main Street, #400
Walnut Creek, CA 94596
http://www.LCoastPress.com

ISBN 978-1-59874-565-8 hardcover
ISBN 978-1-59874-567-2 institutional eBook
ISBN 978-1-61132-719-9 consumer eBook

Library of Congress Cataloging-in-Publication Data:

Sabloff, Paula L. W.
    Does everyone want democracy? : insights from Mongolia / Paula L.W. Sabloff.
    pages ; cm
    Includes bibliographical references and index.
    ISBN 978-1-59874-565-8 (hardback : alkaline paper) —
    ISBN 978-1-59874-567-2 (institutional ebook) — ISBN 978-1-61132-719-9 (consumer ebook)
    1. Democracy—Mongolia—Public opinion.   2. Political culture—Mongolia—21st century.   3. Mongols—Attitudes.   4. Mongolia—Politics and government—1992–
    I. Title.
    DS798.84.S235 2013
    320.95173—dc23
                                                                                    2012049078

Printed in the United States of America

∞ ™ The paper used in this publication meets the minimum requirements of American National Standard for Information Sciences—Permanence of Paper for Printed Library Materials, ANSI/NISO Z39.48–1992.

Cover design by Jane Burton

This book is dedicated to my living lines (so far):

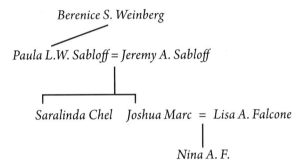

Berenice S. Weinberg

Paula L.W. Sabloff = Jeremy A. Sabloff

Saralinda Chel   Joshua Marc = Lisa A. Falcone

Nina A. F.

CONTENTS

LIST OF ILLUSTRATIONS

FIGURES

TABLES

PREFACE AND ACKNOWLEDGMENTS

I have often advised my students to research topics that satisfy their own emotional needs and interests. In the name of honesty, I feel it only right to share why I have researched democracy in Mongolia. I came to this research after spending years fulfilling a particular psychological need. Although I was not conscious of it when I started, looking back I realize that all of my anthropological writing was about how the little guy—the underdog or the youngest child—achieved some level of self-determination partly by influencing the decisions of the person in charge. My parents and sister had all been oldest children and therefore had little sympathy for my lowly family position as the baby. As a result, I often felt powerless. This deep-seated concern translated into research on patron-client relations (clientelism)—specifically, the ways that clients influence their patrons' decisions. This theme framed my work from Tehuacan and Cozumel in Mexico to New Mexico, Pennsylvania and finally Mongolia.

It only took me until 50 to stop researching the powerlessness of little people and turn to another topic. In 1996 I was working on a short research project to see if I could conduct fieldwork in Mongolia. At that time I met Dr. Mekei, Vice-Rector of the National University of Mongolia. He suggested, "Why don't you come back and do more research in Mongolia? You could study democracy here. It would be most interesting for an American to do." I immediately knew he was right.

The second Soviet-style socialist nation in the world, Mongolia had discarded the communist regime in 1990 and socialism soon after. In 1992, the people ratified a new constitution based on democracy and capitalism. Ever since then, the country has struggled to meet the expectations of the new constitution in everyday life, and it was a topic of great interest to Mongolians.

Mongolian democratization was also of great interest to me, for it really symbolized the next step in my psychological path: a post-Soviet country struggling to institutionalize democracy was really moving from dependency to self-determination. Thus, the study of Mongolian democratization would, in fact, be the logical next step for me. Besides, I was angered by a chance remark made to me while I was exploring the possibility of conducting the research. Someone I interviewed said that anyone over 50 would not understand democracy and would just have to be carried by the rest of society. As I was turning 50 at the time and felt I still had the capacity to learn new things, I wanted to find out which one of us was right. Other comments piqued my curiosity. People said that men and women do not think differently about democracy, yet US pollsters had said that women were responsible for electing Bill Clinton, who was president when I started this work. And some Mongolian academics said that only the educated, the intelligentsia, would understand the principles of democracy. So I decided to study changing democratic ideas in Mongolia partly because I felt that curiosity combined with irritation would be a great motivator for good research.

There is another reason why I wanted to work in Mongolia: I love the people. Professor Richard (Rich) Scaglion, a friend and colleague at the University of Pittsburgh, once told my students that they should work where they like the people, the music and the food. I finally found a place where I loved the first two and tolerated the third.

Mongolians—at least the Mongolians whom I met—are the kind of people I like to be around. They are forthright, telling me what they are thinking on almost any topic. They are solicitous of foreigners. In fact, there are several I have trusted with my life, something I would not do in the United States (well, I can take care of myself in the United States). They have a strong sense of family and community. And they like to laugh. Whenever family, friends or coworkers get together, they join in the conversation until they are laughing together. I think this is a great way to bond.

Their music? Mongolians have a fabulous tradition of throat singing, or two-tone singing. They also have a large repertoire of short songs and long songs, or ballads. They sing as if they were singing against the wind. Their voices are straightforward and honest, like their conversation. When I started researching in Ulaanbaatar, young people were just forming pop-music bands. They combined the Mongolian traditions with Western (including Japan and Korea) phrasing. I think they are neat, and I'm still playing my *Saraa* CD.

To finish Rich's criteria for happy fieldwork, I need to tell you that Mongolian food comes not from the Chinese cuisine but from the nomadic and Russian traditions. They prefer three-year-old mutton and goat rather than lamb or kid. They boil it with rice or potatoes, onions and other vegetables. They also throw a handful of salt into the pot, which practically turned me into a vegetarian while there. Their favorite part of any animal—sheep, goat or cow—is the fat, and they cut the meat to maximize the number of chunks of pure fat. I used to hand off the fatty pieces to any man sitting next to me; I always found him grateful whether he was a teacher or a herder. While this diet is fine for herders who are active all day long, it is heart-attack food for sedentary workers like Mongolian office workers or me. Still, the food was safe because it was boiled. Luckily, there were many foreign restaurants in

Ulaanbaatar where I mostly ate: Korean, Chinese, Japanese, Indian, Mexican, French and German, too. So I could tolerate eating in Mongolia. Since Mongolia met Rich's criteria for a good fieldwork site for me, I decided to work there.

ACKNOWLEDGMENTS

My initial thanks go to the funding agencies and individuals who supported the fieldwork and write-up for this book. The 1998 research was supported by a grant from the National Science Foundation (SBR-9806345, see Sabloff 1999) with additional support from Annette Merle-Smith and Robert and Lois Baylis. The 1999 and 2003 field seasons were funded by the International Research and Exchanges Board (IREX), the University of Pennsylvania Museum of Archaeology and Anthropology and Annette Merle-Smith. The School for Advanced Research kindly provided a summer of analysis through an Ethel-Jane Westfeldt Bunting Fellowship in 2004.

I also wish to thank Mongolian friends and colleagues, especially the research teams: Drs. Baasandorj, Byambadorj, Nyamdavaa, Nyamdorj and Nyamsuren along with students Byersuren and Gantsooj in Khovd; and Drs. Bumaa, Nansalmaa and Olziesekhan along with Ayush, Chinzorig, Enkhtuya, Mongolkhatan,Tsetsegjargal, Tsetseglen and Uyunga in Ulaanbaatar. I could not have accomplished the project without the special organizational and intellectual help of Dr. G. Nyamdavaa Gendenjaviin and Ms. Magsarjav Tsetseglen in 1998. Not only are they wonderful colleagues but they have also become friends. Drs. B. Batchuluun, Regsuren Baterdene and Nyamsuren, Eliot and William Bikales provided extra intellectual stimulation and support. And of course I want to give special thanks to Dr. Bumaa Dashdendeviin of the National Museum of Mongolian History. We started as colleagues and continue as friends, corresponding frequently and helping each other when possible. You will see her name frequently in this book, as she guided me through knowledge and joy of Mongolia. Her constant intellectual support made me confident that the facts in this book are correct.

I never thought this book would take so long to write. It means that I have so many people to thank in the United States. In my University of Pennsylvania years, the following people were kind enough to listen to me and read sections of the book: Drs. Fran Barg, Samuel Freeman, Gautham Ghosh, Maris Gillette, Brian Hackman,Walda Metcalf, Catherine Newling, Brian Spooner and Steve Pinker. Ana Maria Gomez Lopez was always ready to read another draft and comment. At the Santa Fe Institute where I have finally found academic heaven, I have received support from Drs. Christopher Wood, Erica Jen and Paul Hooper as well as Mr. Ramamoorthi Bhaskar and countless others.

My deep love, appreciation and thanks go, of course, to my life partner and pal, Dr. Jeremy (Jerry) Sabloff. Together we have created a stimulating, supportive ride through life together. We have also created two fascinating, wonderful, moral and caring children, Saralinda (Lindi) Sabloff and Joshua Sabloff, which is just what I had hoped they would be. I dedicate this book to Jerry, our children along with their partners and offspring (not the dogs this time) and to my mother, Berenice S. Weinberg, who continues to be an inspiration as she approaches her 100th birthday. Keep exercising! Keep moving!

CHAPTER ONE

Introduction

D o all people desire democracy? Does everyone consider it a universal good? Like many Americans, I assumed that everyone would want to live in a democracy. The World Values Survey brochure states that "Desire for freedom and democracy is a universal human aspiration" (Inglehart, Pura nen, Welzel et al. 2012:8). However, Global Barometer, a network of research organizations that conduct attitude surveys on all continents, finds that only a little more than half of adults interviewed between 2001 and 2006 prefer democracy (Bratton 2009: Table 5). Political scientists started studying the relationship between politics, culture and attitudes in the 1920s, although Pye (1991) credits Aristotle, Plato, Montesquieu and other philosophers with linking political systems to people's values and attitudes. But it was not until anthropologists began integrating anthropology with the new field of psychology that political scientists began to see the relevance of individuals' beliefs, attitudes and values to the study of political systems. Following Gabriel Almond's 1950s study using surveys and interviews to learn people's political attitudes, similar studies burgeoned (ibid.).

These and other surveys are interesting and helpful, but they need to be enriched by case studies that provide in-depth, contextual analyses of people's opinions. We need to find out how everyday people living in democratic and other governments actually talk about democracy rather than squeeze them into boxes devised by Western surveyors. And we need to place their responses in ecological, cultural, historical and circumstantial context. Only then can we learn what people want and why they want it. This book is such a case study.

My impression from years of anthropological research in Mongolia is that once democracy is institutionalized, people no longer consider it a goal or an end in itself. Instead, they see it as a means to an end. They believe that democracy will better enable them to align their deeply held values and personal goals with the lifestyle they desire than other forms of government, particularly communism. Some want democracy to gain freedom from oppression or government control of their lives (see Lukin 2000:195 for the same attitudes expressed by Russians). Some want it for self-determination.

Others believe it will help them and their nation attain dignity. And still others consider it the best way to help them meet family obligations or succeed in the global economy.

Democracy, in other words, is more than a form of government; it is a way of life. Its principles influence how wealth is distributed, where and how people live and what their futures might be. How people define democracy and prioritize its attributes depends on what they think democracy will do for them.

How do I know this? I learned it from the Mongolians, who highly value democracy. Mongolia was the first country to follow Russia into socialism (also called communism) in the 1920s. We might think that Mongolians know little about democracy, as they were completely surrounded by other socialist countries—it was the only Soviet country to suffer this fate. Or we might suppose that they became comfortable living under socialism and would not want to change. Yet Mongolia was one of the earliest Soviet Bloc countries to protest Communist Party control. And in January 1992, its citizens were the seventh of the 28 Newly Independent States (NIS) to ratify a democratic, capitalist constitution.

When I started researching Mongolians' changing ideas on democracy, I thought this would make an interesting case study of how people raised under communist ideology were thinking about democracy. With National Science Foundation support, Mongolian research assistants and I asked a range of voting-age people to name the characteristics of a democratic country (see Figure 1.1). I expected them to mention broad democratic principles such as multiparty elections, a government system of checks and balances, or transparency. This is what my American students had done in class exercises. Instead, I was struck by how personal the Mongolians' answers were. People said that democracy was changing their lives. It brought them free speech, which boosts their personal dignity because now their opinions matter. It gave them valued rights and freedoms that let them—rather than their government—determine how they would live, for they are no longer assigned to education programs or jobs that they do not like.

But they were also appalled by the rising crime rate resulting from the breakdown of strict government control experienced during communism. The collapse of authority forced them to rethink their social relations and frustrated their attempts to succeed in the new market economy. Some people even said that human nature was changing under democracy. They were dismayed that Mongolians are turning from cooperative, caring beings who want the whole society to share a decent standard of living to people

Figure 1.1 Uyuna, a university student, interviewing young herders in Tuv Aimag. Note the intensity on their faces; they really want to communicate with her. (Paula L.W. Sabloff, 1998)

who 'worship money,' that is, become self-centered and even selfish. In other words, they believed that human nature changes with government structure, a concept that echoes the Geneva Enlightenment philosopher Jean-Jacques Rousseau (1755).

In short, the Mongolians interviewed for this project would not answer my question: What is democracy *about*? Instead, they posed (and answered) a different question: What is democracy *for*? How does a democratic government affect their way of life? What do they think they can do in a democracy that they could not do under socialism? How does it limit them?

By examining the Mongolian case, I hope to shed light on democracy's appeal. Do all people desire it? Are some aspects of democracy universally desired but not others? Talking about democracy, Tom Brokaw said on *Meet the Press* (December 7, 2008), "People want to participate in their own destiny." Was he talking only about Americans or all people? While one case study cannot provide a definitive answer, it can move us in that direction, particularly if the people's geographic, historical and cultural backgrounds differ greatly from those in the West.

If people see democracy as a means to an end, as the Mongolian case suggests, then their conception of democracy must vary because they have different goals; the 'ends' change as circumstances change (see also Paley

2002:485; Brink-Danan 2009:6). And because even people living in the same society have different experiences and goals, they emphasize different aspects of democracy. In the words of Ramamoorthi Bhaskar, an artificial intelligence scientist and lawyer, people come to democracy in their own way (personal communication, December 19, 2011).

Mongolia is a wonderful place to conduct research on democracy because of its people and its history. Until the World War I era, Mongolia was a feudal society. More than 90 percent of its people engaged in pastoral nomadism, moving herds of sheep, goats, cows or yaks, horses and camels from one pasture to another in the annual search for fodder. Its princes—descendants of Chinggis Khaan[1]—were vassals of the Manchu Dynasty in China, its southern neighbor. Only the princes joined Manchu officials in making decisions for the rest of the population. In 1921, Mongolia achieved independence from China and soon adopted socialism from Russia, its northern neighbor. For almost 70 years, Mongolians lived under a totalitarian government whose leaders, members of the Communist Party (Mongolian People's Republic Party, or MPRP), made all policy decisions. The state held elections, but there was only one candidate to vote for. People worked for the state and drew salaries from the state, which planned and directed most economic activities. The state told them what to study, what to produce and how much to produce—from the number of lambs to the number of university graduates.

In 1989–90, people all over the country staged demonstrations that destroyed the totalitarian government and command (state-controlled) economy. They immediately started writing a democratic constitution in order to construct a framework for democratic governance and living.

By the time I started to conduct anthropological research in 1996, the adults I met had knowledge of three types of governance. They knew their parents' and grandparents' stories about life under feudalism. They had first-hand experience of Soviet socialism. They had just lived through, and helped foment, a peaceful revolution that destroyed the socialist state in seven months. And they were still adjusting to the transition away from socialism toward their own form of democracy and capitalism. They knew how different types of government directly affect their lives. They were still discussing the pros and cons of living in a democracy when I started my research. As Mongolians' political interest and my research interest coincided, research among them was ideal.

This book represents my thinking based on four extended research trips to Mongolia. The core database is 1,283 interviews on Mongolian citizens' ideas of democracy and market economy collected by Mongolian researchers under my direction in the summers of 1998 and 2003. These interviews are placed in the context of my own experiences living and interviewing in Mongolia in 1996, 1998, 1999 and 2003. Additional material comes from archival materials such as news reports, government and NGO reports, census data, and so on.

THE ALMOST-UNIVERSAL DESIRE FOR DEMOCRACY

A school of thought proposes that people all over the world desire democracy. It stretches back to President Woodrow Wilson or earlier (Ikenberry 1999; Ignatieff 2005; Pagden 2005) and includes policy makers and academics alike (the US State Department 2011 and USAID 2012; Lipset 1959; Huntington 1991; Diamond 2008). This idea is very much alive in diplomatic circles. In his 2012 speech to the American Israel Public Affairs Committee (AIPAC), President Obama (2012) said that Americans and Israelis share "a belief that freedom is a right that is given to all of God's children … that democracy is the one and only form of government that can truly respond to the aspirations of citizens."

There is some evidence that this assumption has merit. The revolutions that freed Eastern Europe and Central Asia from the dying Soviet Bloc started as uprisings for freedom and democracy (Spritzer 2009; Michnik 1998:25). During the 2011 Arab Spring, people called for the basic tenets of democracy, namely justice, rule of law, employment opportunities, personal dignity and the end of corruption. In Egypt's Tahrir Square, men, women and children chanted "freedom, freedom, freedom" (El-Naggar 2011; Fahim and El Naggar 2011). The cry spread to Russia where citizens protested Putin's assumption that he could return to the presidency without opposition, thus subverting the little democracy they had. Like their parents who had staged the 1989–1991 Democratic Revolution, they demanded "dignity, not to be treated like cattle" (Leon Aron quoted in Shane 2012:4).

Related to the assumption that everyone wants democracy is social scientists' search for the conditions under which democracy is attained and sustained (Schumpeter 1975 (1942):269; Lipset 1993; Diamond 2008:20–38; Schmitter 1995:15–22). Some argue that economic development drives the desire for democracy. Once nations reach a certain threshold of economic development, their people want to live in a democratic society (Lipset 1959:56; Lizza 2011:51). Larry Diamond (2008:294) writes:

> Beyond the next decade, the prospects for renewed global expansion of democracy will depend primarily on three factors. One will be gradual

economic development that lifts levels of education, information, and autonomous citizen power and organization. The second will be the gradual integration of countries into a global economy, society, and political order in which democracy remains the dominant value and the most attractive type of political system. As for the third factor ..., before democracy can spread farther, it must take deeper root where it has already sprouted. The new democracies that have come into being since 1974 must demonstrate that they can solve governance problems and meet citizens' expectations for freedom, justice, a better life, and a fairer society.

My data challenge this notion. When Mongolians started protesting for democracy in 1989, the per capita gross domestic product (GDP) in current US dollars was US$664.60 [China was US$307.50, while the United States was US$22,039 then] (World Bank 2012). When they ratified the democratic, capitalist constitution in 1992, the GDP had dropped to US$585.10. Although GDP slipped a bit more (to US$578.70) in 1996, there was still a peaceful transfer of power from the MPRP to the Democratic Coalition. Another peaceful transfer of power took place in 2000 while the per capita GDP fell to US$471.50 (ibid.). So democracy and GDP are negatively, not positively, correlated in Mongolia.

Social scientists propose other necessary factors for democracy, one of which is education. The higher the educational level of a population, the greater the probability that a nation will be able to initiate and maintain democracy. In a statistical analysis of mostly Western nations, Rindermann (2008:320) writes:

Education and cognitive ability favor democracy, the rule of law, and political freedom. In addition to creating material wealth, they improve the quality of life by fostering the development of legal and democratic institutions. During the twentieth century, the rising educational level of the population ... that accompanied the expansion of the school system, have almost certainly been the most important factors for democratization and related institutional improvements, in addition to being the principal cause for technological and economic progress.

The Mongolian data support Rindermann's findings; the country's relatively high education level correlates with a desire for democracy. During the socialist years, Mongolia established secular schools throughout the country. As of 1958, universal primary education had been achieved. And by 1989, Mongolia had an adult literacy rate of 97 percent according to UN standards[2] (Yembuu and Munkh-Erdene 2005:5–6). At that time, the US literacy rate was 99 percent (CIA 2003a) while China's was "over 75 percent" (CIA 2003b). Not only did Mongolia build primary and secondary schools; it also built several universities. The National University of Mongolia (NUM) was established in 1942. Soon after, the medical, technical, pedagogical and agricultural universities were added. Mongolia also sent its brightest students to higher education institutions in the Soviet Union (from Russia to East Germany, Hungary, Bulgaria and so on). Many received a Ph.D., D.Sc., M.D. and other higher degrees abroad. When I asked Nyamsuren and Nyamdorj, history professors at Khovd University, why they had marched for freedom and democracy in 1989 in their undergraduate days, they replied that their history teacher had studied in East Germany and told students what life was like in the West and what was happening in East Germany (July 1, 2003, fieldnotes).

Education was not the only influence on Mongolians' preference for democracy. Another factor long advocated by anthropologists (and noted in Diamond's quotation here) was also operating. That is, people need to be able to relate new ideas, behaviors and institutions to their way of thinking in order to accept change (Cernea 1985; Wulff and Fiske 1987). Even before Ward Goodenough wrote *Cooperation in Change* (1963), anthropologists knew that people would not willingly change their thinking or behavior unless they understood how the introduced behavior, institution or ideology would fit into their worldview and lifestyle. Here, worldview includes people's values, or how they believe people should interact. These beliefs apply to the interaction between a government and its citizens as well as one-on-one relationships (Barber 1998:22).

According to this principle, Mongolians were highly likely to accept democracy because it fit their culture, history and circumstances. Pastoral nomadism, the traditional Mongolian lifestyle, aligned with a desire for national independence, which is the baseline criterion for democracy. While I was conducting research I was also working on a museum exhibition about twentieth-century Mongolia that toured the United States. As I was borrowing artifacts and working with the National Museum of Mongolian History (NMMH) staff to develop the exhibition's themes, I had frequent meetings with Dr. Sanduiin Idshinnorov, the museum's director.[3] He was also an historian and political activist. A constant argument we had was whether Mongolians wanted democracy or independence. I argued for the former; he argued for the latter. Looking back, I think we were both right. In Mongolia, the desire for democracy depended on a desire for independence.

Idshinnorov also said, "We are a horse culture," meaning that the pastoral nomadic lifestyle, given great territorial range by the horse, makes Mongolians feel free and self-reliant. Their sense of dignity derives from this horse culture. The ability to take care of oneself on the steppe matches the democratic principles of human rights as well as political and economic freedoms (see also Mend-Ooyo 2007). They feel that these rights and freedoms would bring them personal freedom and dignity, which they sometimes express as the desires for equality and justice (in the sense of fairness), which are basic democratic principles.

People feel that democracy has the potential to change their historical trajectory of dependence on another nation—first China and then Russia. Democracy would bring them back to the freedom and dignity they enjoyed under Chinggis Khaan, whom they never forgot. By transforming the governance structure from communist to democratic, Mongolia would gain national freedom. It would also end one-party rule and the command economy that they resent so much. Finally, democracy would enable them to join the global market economy, thereby achieving economic self-determination. The desire for self-determination also blends with the old pastoral nomadic lifestyle.

This broad-brush painting of Mongolians' attitudes toward democracy is meant to illuminate their strong association of democratic principles with certain deeply held values. Such values explain why Mongolians would want democracy but not why people in other nations might. My point is that Mongolians' values come from several sources. The first three are Mongolia's culture, history and circumstances. But the fourth, I surmise, is universal values and emotions.

Anthropologists who care about universal human experiences and emotions have been seeking the difference between the particular and the universal for decades. Prominent among them is Donald E. Brown (2000:156). He lists more than 100 "human universals," which he defines as "those (empirically determined) features of culture, society, language, behavior, and psyche found in all ethnographically or historically recorded human societies." Among the 100-plus items are several that resonate with Mongolians' ideas about democracy. These include economic hope and fear, pride, anticipation, a concept of fairness and resistance to dominance or abuse of power (Brown in Pinker 2002:439). Many more have been identified (Berns and Atran 2012).

Some items that are relevant to democracy and are on Brown's list of human universals are also found on Ekman's list of "basic emotions." Ekman, a psychologist and pioneer in determining universal emotions, names 15 that have been tested cross culturally. They are "amusement, anger, contempt, contentment, disgust, embarrassment, excitement, fear, guilt, and pride in achievement, relief, sadness/distress, satisfaction, sensory pleasure, and shame" (Ekman and Friesen 1969; Ekman 1999:55). The data chapters will show the association between Brown's human universals, Ekman's basic emotions and Mongolians' views of democracy. I will argue that their attitudes toward democracy are embedded in basic emotions that are, in turn, combined with particular deeply held values.

I propose that so many people around the world want democracy because they believe that it aligns government ideology and structure with such emotions and values as the desire for human, economic and political rights and freedoms better than more authoritative forms of government. But not everyone wants the same kind of democracy. This is because their culture, history and circumstances cause some universal emotions and values, but not others, to come to the fore of their minds. Almost all of the Mongolians consulted for this study prefer democracy to the communist government they had experienced in the past. They believe that capitalist democracy emphasizes economic freedom and that the role of government is to help citizens succeed in the market economy, just as Adam Smith (1976[1776]:244–47) had. But they prefer capitalist democracy to other kinds of democracy despite pressure from literally thousands of national and international nongovernmental organizations (NGOs) urging them to adopt liberal democracy. Liberal democracy emphasizes the need for politically active citizens, representative government, equality under the law and rule of law in order to maintain democratic governance (Mill 1997 [1869]:931; Diamond 1996:23–25; Plattner 1999:121–24).

The data from Mongolia support the claim that people in different nations choose different ways of practicing democracy because their culture, history and current situation influence their prioritization of universal emotions and deeply held values (see also Schaffer 1998:9–12). But most people do want democracy! Therefore, I propose that the desire for the principles of democracy is almost universal but the kind of democracy desired is not.

RESEARCH THEORIES AND METHODS

How can I convince you that my interpretation of Mongolians' views on democracy and the widespread but not universal appeal of democracy have merit? I turn to the anthropological use of connectionist theory, some methods from cognitive anthropology and comparative analysis in the hope of doing so. When we want to know how people from another society think about democracy, we are really asking them to make two decisions. The first is to decide what their beliefs and attitudes toward democracy actually are. To do this, they have to take into account multiple factors, including what they know about democracy and how they feel about it. The second is to decide what they want to share with the person asking the question. How do they want to present themselves to someone else? Connectionist theory provides a model for understanding these decision processes.

Introduced into anthropology from cognitive science by Maurice Bloch (1991:191–94), connectionist theory recognizes that we humans have more than rational thinking in our mental tool kit. We also have nonlinear thinking, a combination of emotion, intuition, logic, and memory. When faced with a decision, our brains sift through myriad ideas, assigning them different 'weights' (relative values) and then selecting those with the greatest weight (see Bloch 1992:128, 2010:6; D'Andrade 1995:10, 133–38, 150–72; Lakoff 1987; Shore 1996:7, 319; Quinn 2005:35, 2010; Strauss 1992:11–12; Strauss and Quinn 1997:48–51). Some of it is conscious and some is unconscious; often, it is a combination of the two. While this process may sound daunting, it is usually instantaneous.

Connectionist theory is based on the idea that the brain can be a metaphor for how we process information—how we think. Just as neurons in the brain are connected through an elaborate and nonlinear neural network, so influences on our decisions are networked together. These influences, called inputs, may be arranged for analytical purposes into a hierarchy. In this analysis, I group the inputs into three temporal hierarchies. The first is the past, which includes the national history, group history (family, clan, ethnic group) and personal history of each person being interviewed. The information in each of these sections is divided into three parts. One is the historical past, that is, the actual events that affect the present situation. It is the context for current and future decisions. The second is a person's knowledge of the past, which may be different from recorded events. The third is a person's attitudes toward the past. The last two come from stories the interviewee has heard from parents and grandparents. It may also include things learned in school or heard, read or seen (on TV, for example). Figure 1.2 organizes the hierarchy of information about the past that is stored in the brain into a simple tree diagram.

The second temporal dimension is the present. It, too, has three tiers. In the second tier are (a) the current national environment—from the nation's ecology to its internal politics and foreign relations; (b) the group environment, which encompasses the position of the different groups to which the

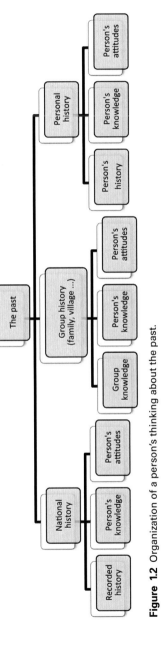

Figure 1.2 Organization of a person's thinking about the past.

individual belongs; and (c) the interviewee's personal situation, that is, her social relations and politico-economic situation. The third tier consists of the same three areas found in Figure 1.2: the objective situation and then the person's knowledge and attitudes toward the current situation.

The third dimension is the future. This has only one referent, and that is a how a person envisions the future and his attitude toward that vision. It is often expressed as hopes and fears. A person's attitude toward the future is based on past history and the current situation as filtered through his knowledge and attitudes.[4]

Connectionist theory models the *process* of sorting through all of the information stored in the brain. Figure 1.3 illustrates the procedure not only of the inputs and outcomes of a decision process but also how the decision is made.

When a new event occurs (such as Mongolia's Democratic Revolution or a researcher questioning a person's political ideas), a person's brain immediately activates all relevant thoughts about the past, present and future. These are the inputs to the thought process. As some thoughts are more relevant or important to the situation at hand than others, the brain assigns relative value (weight) to them. Thus the interviewee prioritizes her thoughts and decides (consciously, unconsciously or both) what she thinks. She then has to decide what parts of those ideas she wants to share with the researcher. This would normally be another diagram of inputs, weights and outcomes, but I have compressed it to save space. The end result, or outcome, is a series of statements (possibly partial or even false) regarding her knowledge and attitudes toward democracy.

I want to make clear that our brains are not neatly organized into temporal categories, although there is evidence that humans "have extensive cognitive capacity for both remembering the past and imagining the future" (Berns and Atran 2012:634). Rather, the mental process looks more like the firing of signals across synapses from one neuron to another, and ideas are joined together in neural networks. Arranging thoughts by temporal and other categories is simply a heuristic device to aid our understanding of the decision process.

People's thoughts about democracy are not neatly organized either. But we can slot them into the boxes in Figure 1.3 to help us understand the decision process. If we think of democracy as a cultural domain, we say that people assign attributes to that domain. That is, they associate certain ideas with that domain. So, for example, a researcher asks a pastoral nomad to characterize a democratic country. The herder immediately remembers how much he

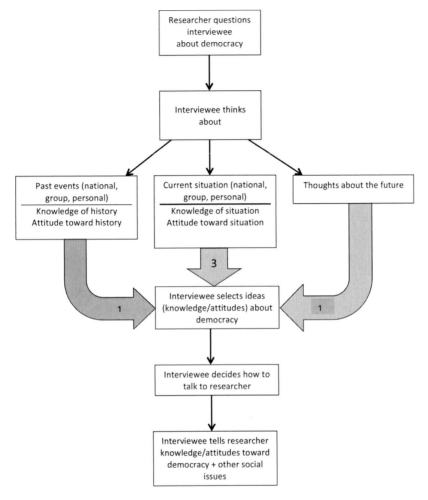

Figure 1.3 An anthropological connectionist-theory model of a person's decision-making process concerning what to tell researchers about democracy.

resents the socialist collective his parents had been forced to join and he had been raised in. He did not like growing up in a dark apartment or having to follow so many rules. He recalls that some people worked harder than others during the socialist years, yet everyone received the same salary. He does not think that was fair. How much happier he is in a capitalist, democratic state! He has returned to the pastoral nomadic lifestyle of his grandparents, which means he is free to be his own boss, to roam the countryside with his herd, and to keep everything he earns from the sale of his animals. He believes that he can succeed in the market economy on his own. Still, he values the education he received in the school at the collective. He is worried about the increasing rate of livestock theft now that there is little policing in the countryside. And despite his optimism, he is somewhat apprehensive that all the economic risk now rests on his and his family's shoulders.

With all these thoughts running around in his brain, the herder has to make one more decision: what to tell the researcher. This person is a stranger but a fellow Mongolian (in this research), so that's good. But what if the stranger is lying about gathering data for an American foreigner and will really report to the government? The herder has to decide whether or not to take a risk and share his feelings honestly.

Connectionist theory is a powerful way to visualize decision-making. However, there are two major drawbacks in applying it to anthropological analysis. It was developed in computer science as a hypothetical model. The weights found in a computer-generated model are assigned by the researcher; they are arbitrary. But anthropology has not yet devised a way to assign weights to a person's thoughts. The numbers 1–3–1 in the arrows of Figure 1.3 are symbolic of the relative value assigned different ideas in the thinking process, but they are not real. That is because the research is not hypothetical; it is based on real data from 1,283 open-ended interviews.

The second problem is that connectionist theory was originally devised to represent the thought processes taking place in one brain. Anthropology works at the level of multiple minds, the minds of people who share a way of thinking (Shore 1996). We can derive the percentage of people who name elections or freedom of the media, for example. But we cannot get into the heads of over 1,000 people and assign weights to their thought processes.

Given these two caveats, we cannot use the model to predict outcomes. But it is still useful for explaining our findings and illustrating how they might have been derived. How did I derive the outcomes? From a long process of fieldwork and analysis. In the summer of 1998, I began fieldwork in Khovd and Ulaanbaatar. Khovd, ancient capital of the Oirad Mongols and a Manchu garrison town, is the capital of a western *aimag* (province) with a mixed population of Oirad and Khalkh Mongols and Kazakhs (see Figure 1.4). Here, people speak Mongolian and Kazakh even though the Kazakh population dates to the beginning of the twentieth century. Buddhist temples and Muslim mosques exist in the same town. There is even a Mormon center on the edge of the university campus. Typical of Mongolia's changing demography, the aimag experienced a decrease in population from 93,000 in 1998 to 87,500 in 2003 (National Statistical Office of Mongolia

Figure 1.4 Khovd from Khovd River. (Paula L.W. Sabloff, 2003)

1999:28, 2003:34). The rural population dropped from 65,565 to 58,188, and the aimag center gained slightly (from 27,400 to 29, 312). These trends fit the national pattern of emigration from rural aimags for education and work, often relocating in Ulaanbaatar.

Ulaanbaatar, the nation's capital since 1911, is mostly Khalkh Mongol but includes citizens from many ethnicities (Figure 1.5). While the primary language is Mongolian, older people also know Russian; younger people are learning English, Korean, Japanese, Chinese and other languages. The majority is returning to Tibetan Buddhism after decades of atheism, but Christian sects are also taking hold. Ulaanbaatar is a cosmopolitan city with several thousand international residents. They are there to implement aid and development programs or establish businesses. The city swelled from 668,700 in 1998 to 893,400 by 2003 as people from all over the country flocked to the capital to find employment and markets for their produce (National Statistical Office of Mongolia 1999:29, 2004:34). The 2010 national statistics report the Ulaanbaatar population at 1.2 million (InfoMongolia.com 2012).

Working through the National University of Mongolia in 1998, I hired two research teams (Figure 1.6a). The first team, led by Dr. G. Nyamdavaa,

(a)

(b)

Figure 1.5 Ulaanbaatar: (a) from Ikh Tenger (Paula L.W. Sabloff, 1994); and (b) showing old kiosks and new construction. (Paula L.W. Sabloff, 2003)

conducted 402 short, open-ended interviews in and around Khovd. The second team, led by Magsarjav Tsetseglen, conducted 465 interviews in Ulaanbaatar and its surrounding province, Tuv Aimag.

The interviews had two parts. The first was basic demographic information. The categories used were location (Ulaanbaatar vs. Khovd), residence (rural or urban), gender, age, formal education completed, occupation and ethnic identity. People had to be citizens of voting age to participate in the study. The researchers found people to interview in the markets, public streets, and among family and friends to meet the quota of 20 interviewees[5] for almost every demographic subcategory (Bernard 2006:187–89).

During all the years of research, I gathered archival and ethnographic data, conducted in-depth interviews with policy makers and foreign workers on site, attended local and international conferences and volunteered in democratization programs in order to gain context and insight.

In the second part, researchers asked respondents to name all the characteristics of a democratic country they could think of and then explain what each item listed meant to them. The same technique was used to elicit ideas on a market economy, or capitalist country. This research strategy allowed the interviewee to use her own thoughts and answer as fully as she wished, which is a method anthropologists prefer over structured questionnaires. Generally, people listed three to eight items and described them in a few sentences.

In 1999 I spent about two months in Mongolia conducting ethnographic fieldwork by volunteering for some democracy organizations. Then I repeated the original study in 2003. This time, I worked with the same interviewers in Khovd but with researchers from the National Museum of Mongolian History in Ulaanbaatar (Figure 1.6b). The researchers were able to meet the requirements of quota sampling with 218 interviews in Khovd and 198 in Ulaanbaatar, for a total of 416.

Back home, I coded the interviews from key words, phrases or ideas, sensitizing myself to the concepts through ethnographic fieldwork and intensive reading in political philosophy—from Rousseau and Smith to Marx, Lenin, Foucault and Bourdieu.

I confess that the work was tedious and often frustrating. While I engaged in a lot of trial and error—which is, after all, basic scientific method—I tried to think of my attempts as a jaunt with the Ulaanbaatar Hash House Harriers. The Hash House Harriers, as I have been told, were nineteenth-century British troops stationed in India who were bored after a day's work. Not having radio, TV, or iPods they decided to set up running trails in the evenings. But the fellows who set up the trails also marked false trails—forks in the

(a)

(b)

Figure 1.6 Researchers (a) Dr. G. Nyamdavaa, then Rector of the National University, Khovd Branch, interviewing a businessman in Khovd Aimag (Paula L.W. Sabloff, 1998); and (b) Dr. D. Bumaa, then Curator at the National Museum of Mongolian History, interviewing in Erdene Sum. (Paula Sabloff, 2003)

road that led to dead ends as well as the actual trail. The faster runners would explore the different paths. When they came to a dead end, they would return to the main trail and tell the slower runners not to take the false trail. In that way, the faster runners would pretty much stay with the slower runners, which was probably safer. The tradition has taken root all over the world; I have heard of it operating from Mongolia to North Carolina. In Ulaanbaatar, the Hash House Harriers meet every Tuesday night to run (or walk) a trail in the nearby countryside marked in chalk by one of its members. I enjoyed many of these jaunts and prefer to think of my research travails as a Hash House Harrier event rather than trial-and-error science because I can temper my frustration with visualizations of the seductive hills of summertime Mongolia studded with edelweiss and other flowers. This helped give me perspective on the research process.

After coding and recoding (and recoding) the interviews and fieldnotes with NVivo software, I felt confident that our research participants talked about democracy in terms of five major subdomains: human rights, political rights and freedoms, economic rights and freedoms, government responsibilities toward citizens and citizens' role in governance. These subdomains form the data chapters for this book.

When people talk about the subdomains, they utilize schemas such as 'Democracy means having _____ characteristic,' 'A democratic country usually has _____ and Mongolia does also' or 'A democratic country should have _____ but Mongolia does not.' Sometimes the schemas are expressed as aphorisms, or set phrases found in several researchers' interviews in both research locations and both years of the study. An example is *songokh songodog erkh* ('choose and be chosen,' sometimes translated as 'elect and be elected').

To be sure that the ideas found in the interviews were not idiosyncratic, I computed the number and percent of respondents who mentioned an idea. I also ran the data through the Pearson's chi-square (χ^2) test using the IBM statistical software package SPSS to learn whether all the people interviewed thought the same or whether they varied by demographic subcategory. And I ran the numbers to see if people felt the same in 2003 as they had in 1998.[6] The concept of variability is directly related to the book's central question: Is democracy a universal value? If people's ideas about a concept such as democracy vary across space (demographic subcategories) and time (from 1998 to 2003), then it cannot be considered universal.

One case study provides a good starting point for evaluating the extent of democracy's appeal. But comparative analysis is even better. As I have not yet been able to conduct comparative analysis myself, I turn to the literature on other former Soviet Bloc countries to find people's reaction to democracy. There is a small but growing body of literature on this topic that I draw from. The works of Caroline Humphrey, Katherine Verdery, Nicolai Petro, Alexander Lukin and Walter Clemens have been particularly helpful.

Another possible comparison is really a mind game I hope you will engage in. Before you read each chapter, I hope you will pause and ask yourself what your ideas on the given topic are before you actually read the material. In that way, you add another comparative perspective to the reading, no matter what your citizenship or ethnic identity is. But do keep in mind that neither your ideas nor the Mongolians' are the right way to conceptualize democracy. Rather, your definition fits your life experience while the Mongolians apply their own experience and hopes for the future to their definitions.

The comparative approach helps us tackle the last question of the book: Is the desire for democracy universal? How do we find out if that is so or not? If people from different backgrounds and with different life goals name the same attributes of democracy, then perhaps this desire is universal. But overlapping attributes are not sufficient. We have to also find out if they overlap because there is a historical link (whereby ideas from one society were adopted in another society), historical accident (similar events cause people in different societies to think the same) or universal appeal. The comparative approach lets us start to explore these distinctions.

ORGANIZATION OF THE BOOK

I have organized the book into chapters that correspond with Mongolians' answers to their question: What is democracy for? Chapter 2 lays the historical foundation for the rest of the book, answering the question: What can you do in a democracy that you cannot do in other regimes? I describe what it meant to live in feudal times (from the late nineteenth to the early twentieth century) and then in the socialist era. While the chapter is organized chronologically, I focus on how the people interviewed perceive socialism—its restrictions and benefits. The chapter concludes with the Democratic Revolution of 1989–90, a nonviolent transition away from socialism and toward capitalist democracy.

Chapters 3, 4 and 5 home in on the three attributes of democracy that our research participants prize most: the human rights guaranteed by their new 1992 constitution (Chapter 3), new political freedoms (Chapter 4) and economic rights and freedoms (Chapter 5). These rights and freedoms have given Mongolians the dignity they so desire, allowing them to change from workers for the state to citizens of the state. Even though Mongolians seem to have always had a sense of dignity, they are able to align their own sense of self-worth with their public behavior under democratic governance. Other deeply felt values, or emotions, are satisfied in democracy. These include the desires for national dignity, self-determination and economic survival or even success in the new market economy.

Letting people speak for themselves, the chapters include many quotations from the interviews, along with historical context and anecdotes. A short statistical analysis found in each chapter suggests that people have modified their ideas about democracy and their life goals since the Democratic Revolution. I hope you will see that people see democracy as the means to an end—their self-worth and life goals—rather than the end itself. And because different parts of the population have different life goals, we would expect to find change over time and variation within the population.

Chapters 6 and 7 illustrate Mongolians' ideas about government responsibilities toward citizens and citizens' (lack of) responsibility toward governance. This pattern aligns Mongolians' ideas more with capitalist democracy than liberal democracy. In Chapter 6 we see that people no longer expect the government to provide health care, although they do want the young, old and poor to have support. More to the point, many believe that the government should help individuals prepare for survival and even success in the new market economy. Chapter 7 explores their attitude toward citizen participation in governance. Those who support active citizenship see it as a right more than a duty. Others feel that people just need to be law abiding to fulfill their duties as citizens.

Chapter 8, the conclusion, revisits the trends noted in previous chapters and revises the model presented in Chapter 1. Here I compare the Mongolian case with that of other post-Soviet peoples to learn whether or not Mongolians' underlying values are found in these countries as well.

Following Caroline Humphrey (2002), I use the Library of Congress orthography for Mongolian words. Mongolian was originally written in its own script, similar to Uighur. It has the grace of Arabic, only it is written vertically and left to right. In the twentieth century, Mongolia along with Central Asia adapted the Cyrillic alphabet to its language. People are moving toward the Latin alphabet now because of the Internet. However, the spelling of words in the Latin alphabet has not yet been standardized. When you see the same vowel repeated, as in *deel,* the word is not pronounced like 'deal.' Instead, the second vowel acts as an accent mark, and the word is pronounced 'dell.'

Finally, I follow the anthropological code of ethics in asking people's permission to use their name or make them anonymous. I have contacted all the people mentioned in this book. I use their real names if they have given me permission to do so or if they had agreed to the formal interview from which I quote. I have given people who wished disguised names and added an asterisk to indicate that they are not real.

CHAPTER TWO

Democracy Means Independence and Freedom

ongolia's history directly affects how people feel about democracy today. While globalized ideals may stimulate interest, reflection on actual experience helps people figure out what they actually want. Mongolians' current views on democracy are rooted in the tales of their national hero, Chinggis Khaan, in stories about feudal life under the Manchu Dynasty, in their parents' or their own experience of Soviet-style socialism and in their personal experience of capitalist democracy. Through positive and negative example, these stories taught them the value of democracy. My point is that some of the ideas that we in the West associate with democratic thinking percolated up from reactions to rather repressive regimes. Why did people caught in a highly structured and controlled society have such thoughts at all? After researching and studying Mongolia for a decade, I believe that the answer lies as much in Mongolia's ecology, history and ancient way of life as it does in Western influence.

I am not a geographic determinist, but it is impossible to understand Mongolia without understanding the country's ecology (see Figure 2.1). Mongolia is huge. If set inside the United States, it would stretch from Washington, D.C., to Boulder, Colorado. Caught between Russia (Siberia) and China (Xinjiang and Inner Mongolia), it is totally landlocked. Yet 4,000 lakes and 1,200 rivers flow across the landscape. The grasslands, or steppe, cover most of the territory; they climb from 4,000 to 10, 000 feet above sea level. Towering above the steppe, the Altai Mountain chain curves from the northwest forest area (the *taiga,* or pine forest) to the southeast, tailing off in the Gobi Desert. About 40 percent of Mongolia's landscape is mountainous.

Although Mongolia is on the same latitude as France, Canada (Montreal), and Washington (Spokane), the climate is very different. Over 200 days of sunshine a year and the ceaseless Siberian winds make a dry climate that resembles Albuquerque more than Spokane. I rented an apartment in Ulaanbaatar in the summer of 1998. After washing my clothes in the bathtub, I would hang them on the balcony clothesline to dry. Several hours later, it took me five minutes to untangle each pair of pantyhose to get it off the line; the wind had simply whipped each one into designs resembling Celtic knots. The temperature varies from a high of 100 or 104F in the summer to a low of −30 or even −60F in the

Figure 2.1 Topography of Mongolia with Ulaanbaatar and Khovd. (Clipart by Michael Schmeling, clipartof.com/91442)

winters. It is not easy to raise herds of animals or even live in this climate. Yet people entered the area in the Upper Paleolithic, somewhere between 60,000 and 30,000 years ago (Bar-Yosef 2003:375; Derevianko and Markin 1997:157).

FROM THE NEOLITHIC TO CHINGGIS KHAAN

People occupied most of the region during the Neolithic, which occurred 8,000 to 3,000 years ago there (Academy of Sciences MPR 1989:88). They supported their families by raising wheat and domesticated animals. They also hunted, fished and gathered wild fruits and vegetables (Salzman 1972:67; Honeychurch and Amartuvshin 2006:259, 2007:46:36–7). The Neolithic economic base meant that people could settle in one place rather than follow game from one area to another. The result was settlements varying in size from hamlets to cities. There is archaeological evidence of incipient trade between settlements at this time.

Pastoral nomadism also developed during the Neolithic. Some people eschewed settled life, preferring to move with their domesticated animal herds several times a year. They would circulate from one rich pasture to another and back again (see Figure 2.2). We often think that pastoral nomads are self-sufficient, but that is not true. The archaeological record shows that pastoralists frequently traded with settled agriculturalists for ceramics, cloth and clothing, flour and so on. Settlers and nomads are really in a symbiotic relationship (Barfield 1989:11–12; Sermier 2002:44).

Figure 2.2 A young herder with his cattle, near Khar Us Nuur (Black Water Lake), represents the Neolithic herding lifestyle. (Paula L.W. Sabloff, 2003)

About 200 BCE (coinciding with the Han Dynasty of China), the Xiongnu nomadic group (Hunnu in Mongolian) formed a confederation of tribes that extended from the heart of Mongolia north into Siberia and south into northern China. While many farmed millet, barley and wheat, others raised herds of cattle, sheep, horses, camels and yaks. Both traded with their neighbors in China and Central Asia. Their leaders also extracted tribute from the territories they had conquered. They built walled settlements and elite burial grounds, evidence that they had formed a sophisticated hierarchical society (Honeychurch and Amartuvshin 2006:262–68).

The Xiongnu polity collapsed about 93 CE, and a series of small kingdoms ruled the area. The pattern of confederation > conquest > trade and tribute > collapse persisted for a millennium.

CHINGGIS KHAAN AND THE MONGOL EMPIRE

In 1206, Temujin (1162–1227), born into the ruling lineage of the Mongols,[1] united the Mongol tribes into a 'nation,' what we would call a confederation. He convened the tribal leaders at an *Ikh Khural,* or Great Assembly. There they named him Chinggis Khaan, which means strong, powerful ruler (Ratchnevsky 1991:89). And powerful ruler he was! His personality and accomplishments have continued to influence Mongolians' identity and ideas about governance ever since. Father Huc, a French missionary who made several visits to Mongolia between 1844 and 1846, reported that the emperor of China was always suspicious of Mongolians because "the memory of his [Chinggis Khaan's] conquests has not passed away from the hearts of this warlike people" (Huc 1931:128). Colwin (1991:157) quotes C. R. Bawden, one of the major twentieth-century Western historians of Mongolia, who wrote:

> Yet a feeling of belonging together, a sense of identity as the subjects and posterity of Genghis Khan [sic], seems never to have deserted the Mongols, and this was one of two internal factors which helped to give them the vision and strength to recover their independence from the Manchus when the last imperial dynasty in China was swept away in 1911.

Even as late as 1998, an old man with little education living in Ulaanbaatar (Ulaanbaatar 1998 Os024)[2] says, "I'm proud of Chinggis Khaan because the world has gotten to know Mongolia because of him."

One of the tribes that joined Chinggis Khaan was the Oirad, which means forest people (Ratchnevsky 1991:81–83; Dr. B. Nyamdorj [chairman of the Khovd University History Department] personal communication, June 28, 2003). They lived in the taiga up around Lakes Baikal (now Siberia) and Khovsgol (in present-day Mongolia). The Khalkh and Oirad are important to our story because they are two of the three major players in Mongolian history (the third is the Buriat from northern Mongolia). And almost all of the people we interviewed for this book are their descendants.

Once Chinggis Khaan united the various tribes, he gained independence from the Jin Dynasty of northern China. The Mongols no longer had to pay tribute to a foreign power, and they could determine their own destiny. Chinggis Khaan, his sons and his generals went on to conquer a good part of Eurasia. In fact, they controlled the largest contiguous land mass ever conquered. Upon his death, the Mongol Empire extended from the Caspian Sea to much of China. His sons and generals pushed the boundaries even further, from most of the land around the Black Sea (present-day Russia, Ukraine and Turkey) south to Iraq and Iran and then east to Southeast Asia.

How did Chinggis Khaan manage these feats? On one hand, he had a strong personality. He was ruthless to anyone who opposed him. He also bound men to him through loyalty and the judicious distribution of spoils of war; when he conquered other peoples, he adopted them into his tribe (Morgan 1986:59–60; Baabar 2000:23–36; Altangerel 2001:26–28; Sabloff 2001:93–102). On the other hand, he had a genius for organizing, taking the best ideas from surrounding peoples and reshuffling them into a new social order. He transformed the Mongolian people from a tribal, or kinship, structure to a military one. He organized the fighting men into units of 10, 100, 1,000 and 10,000. Families traveled with their fighting sons, providing them with food, clothing, horses and gear (arrows, bows and armor). In this way Chinggis Khaan broke the power of the tribal leaders and built a fighting force ready to conquer the world.

While Chinggis Khaan was the epitome of what Asian cultures call 'a strong-hand leader'—one who rules with an iron will—he did institute programs that were later (much later!) identified with democratic principles. He anticipated rule of law when he had his decrees and sayings written down in the *Ikh Zasag*, or *Great Yasa*, and when he established a court system. He punished thievery, adultery, lying and getting drunk more than three times a month (Ratchnevsky 1991:192). He introduced participatory governance by establishing a Council of Wise Men (whose members were not necessarily his kin) to advise him. He granted some personal freedoms. He recognized merit so that even a lowly soldier could rise through the ranks to lead an army. And he encouraged literacy, using the Uighur script to write the Mongolian language. Still, he himself never learned to read.

Almost a thousand years later, Chinggis Khaan's descendants connect him to some principles of democratic governance. A 71-year-old pensioner told us, "[In a democratic society,] all social processes are regulated by law.... This principle was followed in the time of the Great Mongolian Empire founded by Chinggis Khaan" (Ulaanbaatar 2003 Bu055).

HOW THE MANCHU DYNASTY CAME TO RULE MONGOLIA

Chinggis Khaan's empire slowly disintegrated after his grandson Khubilai Khaan's death. Khubilai Khaan (1215–1294), founder of the Yuan Dynasty, had ruled China and Mongolia. In 1368, the Mongols who had ruled China for more than a century abandoned their posts and palaces in present-day Beijing. They trekked across the Gobi Desert to their ancestral home, returning to traditional nomadic life. The great Mongol Empire became a backwater, powerless in world affairs.

As they readjusted to nomadic life, these princes, or *khans*, carved up the vast plains and Altai mountain range into small kingdoms, instituting a feudal politico-economic structure (Baabar 1999:50–56). Families were no longer organized into Chinggis Khaan's fighting units of 10, 100 and so on. Instead, they were assigned to princes and lesser noblemen, Chinggis Khaan's descendants. People lived within the territories assigned to their overlords. At this time, the Oirad moved southwest of the Altai Mountains to the territory now called Khovd. Their royal lineage controlled western Mongolia.

Our image of feudalism is of a medieval village and farmlands radiating out from a stone castle that is surrounded by a moat. The castle houses a lord's family, retainers and soldiers. Inside the castle walls is a chapel for the family's private use while outside, in the village, a small church serves the people. Although the lord of the manor exacts payment from his serfs (the farming families living on his land), he is also responsible for adjudicating conflict and punishing crime. At the same time, he owes fealty to the king who, in turn, is responsible for the manor lord's protection. The king also decides foreign policy; the manor lord does not.

The Mongolian version of feudalism was somewhat different from our mental picture. While a strict hierarchy divided the society into classes (see below), we must keep in mind that Mongolian serfs were not farmers but pastoral nomads. Because most did not grow fodder for the animals or crops for their own consumption (Friters 1949:12), they followed their herds from one pasture to the next, cycling through familiar pastures over the course of a year. Their summer pastures, usually located in valleys near streams, would range anywhere from 26 to 150 miles from their winter pastures (Maiskii 1956 [1921]:278, 281).[3] Families would relocate as often as eight or ten times a year and sometimes even more often (ibid.:281). Not only did the whole family move with the herd, but their homes did, too. I have helped a family disassemble their home, a round felt yurt (a *ger* in Mongolian) on a wooden frame that accordions like a baby-gate but is about five feet tall. It took six of us 50 minutes to take down the ger and load it onto carts pulled by yaks. We then walked it to the next pasture and reassembled it there.

Unlike their European counterparts, Mongolian serfs were mobile within their overlords' territory. Even though they belonged to a prince or noble and owed him corvée labor,[4] they were away from his direct control when out in distant pastures. At those times, they made their own decisions about where to move, whom to live near and what to do each day. They had a certain amount of independence or freedom (ibid.:279–80). However, J. Sambuu (1895–1972), a herder serf who later rose to high position in the communist government, recalls in his autobiography that his overlord would summon him to service by sending a rider to his father's ger (Sambuu 2010:30, 37).

Within this feudal framework, two ruling groups emerged in the fifteenth century: the Khalkh princes in the central and eastern parts of present-day Mongolia and the Oirad princes in the west (Morgan 1986:204; Baabar 1999:56–59; Dr. Nyamdorj, personal communication June 28, 2003). The latter developed their own alphabet that reflected their unique dialect (Khovd Regional Museum exhibit viewed July 1, 2003). The Khalkh and Oirad periodically tried to annex one another and even reconquer China. Every once in a while, a leader would emerge from either camp and unite the Mongol people for a brief time. But mostly the area was divided into multiple small princedoms.

In 1636, a Manchurian clan conquered China, establishing the Manchu Dynasty, called the Qing Dynasty in China. At about that time, the Oirad forged a new empire called Dzungaria (Atwood 2004:419–21). It extended from western Mongolia south into China's Xinjiang Province. Desiring to unite all the Mongols as well, Oirad Galdan Khaan tried to woo or conquer individual Khalkh princes. But many of the latter preferred to submit to the new emperor of China rather than him. In June 1691, the Khalkh princes signed a treaty with the Manchu Emperor of China. By signing the treaty, they became vassals of the emperor rather than a conquered people.

In 1757 the Manchu Dynasty conquered the Oirad, crushing the Dzungarian Empire. China annexed the Oirad lands to northern Mongolia and absorbed what is now Xinjiang Province into China. The Manchus built a fortified town with double walls at Khovd in 1762. It housed the Manchurian administrators and garrison as well as a Tibetan Buddhist temple (Khovd Museum, viewed July 1, 2003). Thus, all of Mongolia became part of the feudal territory of Manchu China.

The Manchu imposed secular and religious hierarchies on the Mongol people. This parallel class division determined how people were treated, how they lived day to day, what their economic situation was and how they were governed. The structure continued into the early twentieth century.

THE SECULAR HIERARCHY OF MANCHU ADMINISTRATORS AND MONGOL PRINCES (KHAN) AND NOBLEMEN (*TAIJ*)

The Manchu placed all Mongol territories under the colonial office (*Li-fan-yuen*) in Peking (now Beijing). It administered southern (Inner) Mongolia as a Chinese province and northern (Outer) Mongolia as a group of separate fiefdoms. It divided Outer Mongolia into four eastern (Khalkh) aimags. Although a Manchu governor (*amban*) oversaw all policy and administration, a Khalkh prince (khan) became the face of the administration. He was selected by the other princes with the emperor's consent (Nakami 2006:48; Campbell 2000:74). The western region, consisting of two provinces, was governed by a Manchu military commander-in-chief (*Tsing-tsiun*) (Prejevalsky 1991:15, 85; Baabar 1999:99). All six provinces of Outer Mongolia were divided into smaller administrative units, called banners (*khoshuun*). Princes (khan), lesser princes (*jassak*) or noblemen (*taij*) ruled the banners. The banners had fixed boundaries that the pastoral nomads were forbidden to cross without permission (Nakami et al. 2005:350).

Because the Khalkh princes were vassals of the Manchu emperor, they could not make foreign policy; only the emperor could. Thus, the princes lost the right to negotiate with their northern and western neighbors. And the presence of Manchu administrators meant that the princes lost the right to administer their territory as they saw fit. They were required to set up administrative gers near their own ger and conduct the business of government: collect taxes, settle disputes, receive petitions and so on. But they usually hired retainers to perform these tasks (Larson 1930:6–8). According to Western travelers, princes and nobles were not subject to any rules or regulations. Most overlords required their serfs to pay their taxes and debts along with the serfs'. They also had a lot of leeway regarding their treatment of underlings (Bawden 1989:144; Rupen 1979:18).

Manibazar, a particularly venal prince, forced the serfs of the noblemen living in his district to perform corvée labor for him as well as for their overlords. He borrowed 81 of his serfs' camels to form a caravan, promising to pay them 11 *taels* (about one ounce of silver) per head. Although the Chinese merchants paid for the caravan, Manibazar never paid his serfs and never returned the camels either (Natsagdorj 1956:15–19). Along with other overlords, he forced his serfs to pay off his debts to Chinese merchants, which could be very large (Larson 1930:8).

Let us keep in mind that most princes and noblemen led a very good life (Figure 2.3). While a few were poor, most had multiple ways of obtaining wealth. They received an annual salary from the emperor (Larson 1930:216). Lieutenant-Colonel Nicholas Prejevalsky of the Imperial Russian Army (the explorer who named the famous Mongolian pony) wrote that in 1873, the emperor annually gave the princes who administered provinces 120,000 *liang* (a unit of Chinese silver money) and 3,500 pieces of silk (Prejevalsky 1991:86). Princes and nobles controlled all the land within their khoshuun

Figure 2.3 Prince Namsrai and his wife, Ikh Khuree.
(National Museum of Mongolian History, early
twentieth century)

(Maiskii 1956 [1921]:276). Thus they were able to raise huge herds for free. Some herds reached 20,000 to 40,000 animals. Since their serfs (*khamjilgaa*) raised these as part of their corvée service, any animal sold was pure profit. The nobility could organize trade caravans to China and Siberia, which the traders paid for. Some of these expeditions consisted of 1,000 camels (Karamisheff 1925:65).

The aristocracy also accumulated huge debts. Princes often maintained a home in their district and a second home in the capital, Ikh Khuree (meaning "Great Encampment") (Larson 1930:6). They bought luxury goods and entertainment on credit, which they then had to pay off at inflated prices (Maiskii 1956 [1921]:430–39). They were expected to give gifts to those who worked for them (administrators, soldiers and serfs). They also gave gifts to the lamas and had monasteries built in their khoshuun. And they spent money paying tribute to the emperor every three to four years and bribing Manchu officials for better titles, as there were six different ranks (titles) for princes and even more for nobles (Prejevalsky 1991:86–87 fn; Campbell 2000:74).

But mostly the nobility became indebted to merchants by buying on credit. Chinese merchants and later Russian traders[5] wandered the countryside buying wool, hides and other animal products while selling goods—basic and luxury. C. W. Campbell, the British Consul in China, traveled through Outer Mongolia in 1902 and wrote that merchants sold "copper vessels, Russian leather boots, hats and caps, drills, cottons, satins, embroidery, silk and woolen braid, Japanese looking-glasses, snuff bottles, cane whip handles, saddles," and so on (Campbell 2000:142). He also noted that Chinese masons and craftsmen built and repaired the nobility's stone houses as well as the Tibetan Buddhist temples and monasteries (Campbell 2000:76).

SERFS (*KHAMJILGAA*), COMMONERS (*ARD*) AND CLASSLESS PEOPLE

Feudal serfs (khamjilgaa) and commoners (ard), about 43 percent of the population (not including the Khovd Frontier Region, writes Maiskii 1956 [1921]:65), formed the 'black bone'[6] or lower classes of society. The feudal serfs were subject to princes and nobles in addition to the Manchu administration, but the commoners owed taxes and labor only to the Manchu. It is sometimes hard to distinguish between khamjilgaa and ard, for Mongolian historians sometimes write that commoners had overlords, which could mean princes, nobles or Manchu administrators (see Natsagdorj 1956:1–13). Those khamjilgaa and ard who were nomadic herders shared the same territory, which adds to the confusion. Furthermore, khamjilgaa would run away from their districts and pass as commoners or 'classless' people in towns or other districts. The father of Sukhbaatar (1893–1923), Mongolia's revolutionary hero, ran away from the nobleman (taij) he served and settled in the environs of Ikh Khuree. There he passed as a commoner and his children were considered commoners (Bat Ochir and D. Dashjamts in Onon 1976:143–44).

Khamjilgaa did not share the good life of their overlords (Figure 2.4). Their overlord could make them raise another overlord's cattle, even though they continued to live in the territory in which they were born (Bawden 1989:14). Thus, they were treated as slaves. Because they owed corvée labor and were responsible for paying their overlord's taxes and debts as well as their own, many were reduced to penury (Karamisheff 1925:290). Any advantages the khamjilgaa had came from their overlords' patronage. By the end of the

Figure 2.4 Mongol serf beating wool into felt. (National Museum of Mongolian History, early twentieth century)

nineteenth century, there were thousands of paupers and impoverished, malnourished and vagrant people roaming Mongolia (ibid.:142–43, 155).

Herder serfs and commoners supposedly had recourse to courts to settle disputes, even disputes with their overlords. But these courts were run by and for the princes, and justice or fair treatment was not always practiced. So serfs depended on the good will of their overlords.

Scattered over the countryside, herder serfs and commoners did not have access to markets. They were forced to buy needed goods at inflated prices from roving Chinese merchants, just as their overlords were. The merchants supplied the lower classes with tea, flour, sugar, rice, vodka (Chinese and Russian), clothing, pots and pans and other household items. People rarely bought these goods with money. Rather, they bartered their animals for the needed imports. When the animals reached maturity (between March and September), herders exchanged them for the merchants' wares. And while they waited for the animals to mature (October to March), they would request credit against next year's livestock (ibid.:35–38). Not only did merchants charge high interest but they also doctored the books. Because the herders could not read and Chinese merchants kept their books in Chinese, it was easy for them to entrap the herders into debt peonage. Lattimore (1949:xxii) writes that at the end of the Manchu era, the average indebtedness to Chinese traders was 540 Chinese ounces of silver, and one Chinese firm collected annual interest payments of 70,000 horses and half a million sheep. What is even worse, Prince Manibazar, like others in his position, conspired with the merchants in his district to raise their prices, thereby assuring that his underlings would remain indebted and therefore unable to flee his district (Natsagdorj 1956:19).

What recourse did the rural serfs and commoners have to such treatment? Their pastoral nomadic lifestyle gave them some freedom, for they were alone with their families and animals in distant pastures during the months they were not performing corvée labor. At those times, they could make their own decisions and roam at will, for the first family to reach a particular pasture had the right to use it (Larson 1930:57). In 1910, Vladimirtsov

> reported that all the Mongols he met stressed that they were the happiest people in the world because they were free and could do whatever they liked on their lands. This feeling reflected one of the dominant themes of the Mongols' philosophy and was amply expressed in songs, epics, and drama. Although life on the steppes is hard and lonely, it is preferred because of its freedom (Hirabayashi, Rupen and Poppe 1956:243).

This was more freedom than medieval European serfs experienced. The nomadic lifestyle also gave them a different relationship with their overlords. Prejevalsky (1991:73–74) noted in 1873,

> Although servility and despotism are so strongly developed among them that the will of the superior generally replaces every law, a strange anomaly is observable in the freedom of intercourse between rulers and the ruled. At the sight of an official the Mongol bends the knee and does reverence, but after this obsequious token of submission he takes his seat beside him, chats and smokes with him. Accustomed from childhood to perfect liberty, he cannot endure restraint for any length of time, but soon gives free rein to his habits. This freedom of manners and equality may surprise an inexperienced traveler.... The very official, who to-day sits beside his inferior and smokes a pipe with him on terms of good-fellowship, may to-morrow punish his companion, confiscate his sheep, or practice any injustice he likes with impunity.

Thirty years later, Larson (1930:9), who spent years in Outer Mongolia and whose account is therefore more trustworthy than Prejevalsky's, wrote, "According to the old common law of Mongolia ... any and every citizen in a state has the right to a personal audience with his ruler; but only in very special cases do citizens take advantage of this right." He added that corvée service forged personal bonds between ruler and ruled, for aristocratic children whom the feudal serfs helped raise became their rulers.

Sometimes serfs and commoners staged protests and revolts against rulers or raids against Chinese merchants. The serfs could also petition the authorities to discipline their overlord. But the emperor was against such petitions, and the cases were usually settled in the overlords' favor (Natsagdorj 1956:2). Also, some petitions never got to court. When Prince Manibazar's serfs realized they would never get their camels back, they sent a delegation to the head of the Zasagt Khan Aimag offices to petition for the return of their camels. But Manibazar caught and tortured them, wrapping their leaders in wet rawhide that shrank as it dried in the sun, causing slow death. He made the families of the prisoners supply the officials who prosecuted the case with flour, tea and sheep throughout their period of imprisonment, a humiliating situation (Natsagdorj 1956:18–21).

Despite setbacks and brutal torture, serfs' and commoners' protests increased in frequency as the Manchu Dynasty weakened at the beginning of the twentieth century, preparing the way for revolution.

THE RELIGIOUS HIERARCHY: TIBETAN BUDDHISM

Tibetan Buddhism took hold in Mongolia in the sixteenth century. Later, the Manchu Dynasty rulers encouraged Mongols to join the religion, for they hoped that it would tamp down their bellicose behavior. *Gelug-pa* (Yellow Sect) Buddhism as practiced in Tibet and disseminated in Mongolia taught that killing and shedding of blood was a sin; pacifism, accommodation to current conditions, and doing good deeds were the right way to live (Larson 1930:216; Rupen 1966:17–18; Baabar 1999:71–72).

Over time, a religious hierarchy of Tibetan Buddhist lamas developed a structure that paralleled the secular hierarchy. They were known as the yellow bone because they were part of the Yellow Sect of Buddhism (Rupen 1966:17–18). By 1918, the lamas formed 44.6 percent of the male population (Maiskii 1956 [1921]:65).

At the pinnacle of the hierarchy was the *Jibzundamba Khutugtu* (Holy Luminescence; Ramstedt 1978:53). He was second to the Dalai Lama and

Figure 2.5 The Jibzundamba Khutugtu, religious leader of all of Mongolia. (National Museum of Mongolian History, early twentieth century)

a reincarnation of the Buddha in his own right (see Figure 2.5). The last Jibzundamba Khutugtu was brought to Ikh Khuree from his native Tibet to rule in 1874 when he was four years old. He lived in a two-story palace that was a present from Czar Nicolas II of Russia. Supposedly he was fond of playing practical jokes, drinking and sex. Larson, who became his friend, noted that he had a penchant for Western goods, including French champagne. As he was not allowed to leave Mongolia, he ordered from catalogues. He bought himself steam engines, an elephant and a whole taxidermy collection that still takes up two floors of his palace (Larson 1930:115). Contrary to the practice of lamas in other parts of Asia, he married in 1902, as Mongolian lamas often did.

The Jibzundamba Khutugtu's lifestyle was supported by over 100,000 *shabi,* or serfs of the religious hierarchy. Many lived in a specially designated territory near Lake Khovsgol; others lived scattered among the commoners and secular serfs (Prejevalsky 1991:13; Maiskii 1956 [1921]:34). Many of these serfs had been given to the higher lamas by the princes (Friters 1949:39). The shabi did not pay state taxes, but they did pay church taxes and gave corvée labor to the monasteries (ibid.).

Between the Jibzundamba Khutugtu and his serfs were multiple ranks of lamas. The wealthy ones had their own herds and shabi. Poorer lamas acted as scribes and general servants to their superiors. While one-third of all lamas lived in the monasteries, the rest lived and worked outside. They often lived among their kin and had their own families, which they supported from the gifts and payments they received from their religious duties or from regular work as many were craftsmen. Ramstedt, a Finnish linguist who went to Mongolia with his wife and daughter (1888–1912) to compare the Mongolian and Finnish languages, writes that all three of his house servants in Ikh Khuree were lamas. One worked with him on Mongolian epics, did the laundry and helped in the kitchen (Ramstedt 1978:65).

URBAN CENTERS

Mongolia's low population density and herding economy produced few urban centers. The major center was Ikh Khuree, known also by its Russian name, Urga. Founded in the eighteenth century but nomadic until 1855 (Baabar 1999:168), it was the major religious, trade and administrative center from the nineteenth century on (see Figure 2.6). Its population reached 100,000 by 1918 (Maiskii 1956 [1921]:259).

Ikh Khuree had three distinct districts. The Mongolian district contained two of the most important religious centers in the country: Gandan Monastery, where future lamas were taught the Tibetan alphabet and religious practice, and the home of the Jibzundamba Khutugtu. While the Ikh Khuree monasteries were constructed in the Chinese style with Chinese labor, there were at least 30 that were shaped like a ger in 1902 (Campbell 2000:95–96). Of the 30,000 Mongols living in the city in 1918, 20,000 were lamas (Maiskii 1956 [1921]:252).

Mongolians came to Ikh Khuree to engage in trade and make pilgrimages. The monasteries gained income not only from people's gifts but also from payment for services, lending money and serving as trading centers (Hirabayashi, Poppe and Kilcoyne 1956:317). Nearby was a market where Mongol men sold livestock and meat or performed specialized labor such as blacksmithing or shoe making. Women sold goods such as saddles, snuff bottles, leather boots and Buddhist pictures (Ramstedt 1978:46; Campbell 2000:96). Sometimes people bartered using brick tea, animals and ceremonial silk scarves (*khadag*) instead of cash; sometimes they used silver measured in Chinese taels or liang. Both the buyer and seller brought their own scales to measure the taels, as they could be shaved and their value lowered (Ramstedt 1978:52–53).

(a)

(b)

Figure 2.6 (a) Naimachin Street, Ulaanbaatar, early twentieth century (University of Pennsylvania Museum of Archaeology and Anthropology); and (b) Camel and owner in Ikh Khuree market, early twentieth century. (National Museum of Mongolian History)

Ikh Khuree was also the seat of government for Outer Mongolia. The head Manchu administrator, the amban, lived there as did most Mongolian princes. Larson (1930:6–7) noted that although most princes had built houses of stone, they preferred to live in their ger and save the stone house for entertaining. Other Mongols also lived in gers enclosed in wooden fences. Erected wherever there was room, the enclosures caused the streets to meander through the town (Ramstedt 1978:40). Foreign travelers remarked on the piles of garbage in the streets, the roaming packs of wild dogs and the great number of beggars and lepers. But the city was also a refuge for runaway serfs who were transforming themselves into commoners and free men.

Three miles east of the Mongol section was the Chinese settlement, Mai-mai-cheng (meaning "place of trade"). By 1918 it contained about 85,000 Chinese merchants and their workers, as well as the skilled laborers needed to maintain a city: masons, carvers, metalworkers, doctors, actors, teachers and some farmers (Maiskii 1956 [1921]:170–81). As the 1691 treaty between the Manchu Emperor and Khalkh princes stipulated that Chinese people could not settle or bring their families to Outer Mongolia, there were no (or few) Chinese women or children in the settlement. The district was a sea of shops and warehouses for merchandise brought from China. From these headquarters, merchants sent traders to all the khoshuuns of Outer Mongolia (Prejevalsky 1991:8; Karamisheff 1925:35–36).

Between the Chinese and Mongolian settlements stood the Russian consulate and a small settlement of Russian farmers and traders (in fur and wool). The farmers had started migrating to Outer Mongolia in the 1850s with their families. By 1918, about 5,000 Russians resided in Mongolia (Maiskii 1956 [1921]:259).

The provincial towns of Khovd and Uliastai also grew in the late nineteenth century. The former first developed as a farming village in the seventeenth century and later became a Manchu fortress. Although Khovd controlled trade for the western regions, it still had only 3,000 inhabitants in 1918 (Maiskii 1956 [1921]:259). Uliastai was also founded as a Manchu fortress but soon became a Tibetan Buddhist center. It, too, had about 3,000 inhabitants in 1918 (ibid.).

WOMEN AND GIRLS

Before leaving the Manchu era, I want to describe the lives of women and girls, for sometimes I feel we are the canaries in the coal mine. We know from travelers' reports that women and girls could be sold or simply given to their overlords by impoverished fathers (Bawden 1989:92). Ma Ho-ti'en (1949:128), who visited Mongolia 1926–1927, reported that 80 to 90 percent of lamas and Chinese merchants had 'temporary wives,' women who received money in exchange for duties and favors but who could be left behind when the merchants returned home or the lamas left Ikh Khuree. Ramstedt (1978:65) was taken aback when a lama offered him dozens of camels for his own tow-headed daughter. He also wrote (1978:54), "I met and talked with three living Gegens [lamas]: … Narobanchin Gegen, who drove around in a carriage drawn by young girls; and Darkin Gegen, who boozed in a hotel in what is now Stalingrad, in company with a lama and a girl he had brought along from Mongolia."

Despite such reports, Mongolian women were rather independent (see Figure 2.7). They were treated as equals at home and were taught the same skills as their brothers: how to ride a horse, tend animals and so on. Marriage needed the consent of the woman as well as the man, and they could divorce their husbands (Maiskii 1956 [1921]:121–27; Campbell 2000:119). According to Larson, in some homes the women "know and keep track of every animal in every flock and herd, and will not permit the men of the family to sell or trade them without their consent. These homes are usually prosperous

Figure 2.7 Women and girls collecting dung for fuel, Bayanhongor Aimag. (National Museum of Mongolian History, 1920s)

because the women are very careful." He continues: "The Mongolian woman is not the property of her husband, but a free and independent personality who can and does do exactly as she pleases. She takes the passing lama or friendly traveler as lover without shame or censure..." (Larson 1930:70–71; see also Campbell 2000:118–19).

Women over 45 could become Buddhist nuns, and women over 60 were free to move about the countryside (Ramstedt 1978:44–48; Larson 1930:109). So it seems that while of lower status than men, women had quite a bit of freedom and respect.

INDEPENDENCE

In 1906 the Manchu emperor reneged on the 1691 treaty and permitted Han Chinese people to settle in Outer Mongolia (Ramstedt 1978:44–48; Larson 1930:109; Nakami et al. 2005:355–57). The Khalkh nobility feared that Outer Mongolia would turn into a backwater province of China with more Chinese than Mongolians, much as Inner Mongolia had (Ramstedt 1978:212). Under such circumstances, Mongolian culture as well as the nobility and higher lamas' power would be compromised. Meeting in secret in July 1911, some decided to seek Russian support for Mongolian independence (Liu 006:6–7; Nakami 2006:48). This was a logical move as Imperial Russia had become increasingly interested in Mongolia during the nineteenth century. Russian traders operating camel caravans between China and Russia wanted safe, tax-free passage through Outer Mongolia. Therefore they wanted to circumscribe Chinese control. The Russian government sought to promote the fur trade with Outer Mongolia by setting up consulates there. And it wanted to protect its long border with China by turning Mongolia into a buffer state between the two (Baabar 1999:109–116). Russians also tried to win Mongolian support by sending doctors and veterinarians, as well as introducing smallpox vaccinations and syphilis ointments (Maiskii 1956 [1921]:234).

Before the Mongolian delegation could reach Russia, the Han Chinese started a rebellion against the Manchu Dynasty and toppled the government. By January 1912, both China and Outer Mongolia were free of Manchu rule (Baabar 1999:126–37). The exception was western Mongolia (the Khovd and Uriankhai frontier regions), which the Manchu controlled until August. At that time, the west joined the east to form the independent nation of Mongolia. Outer Mongolia was now called Mongolia while Inner Mongolia retained its name (Baabar 1999:139–41; Rupen 1979:8).

From then on, Mongolia considered itself independent of China (Baabar 1999:239–41).[7] But China and Russia signed several treaties that assigned Mongolia autonomous rather than independent status. This meant that Mongolia could determine its internal affairs, but China still controlled decisions regarding international relations (Baabar 1999:256–57). Despite these treaties, Mongolia continued to act as if it could determine its own foreign affairs, and its leaders sought recognition [nation status] from Europe and the United States (Baabar 1999:153, 203, 209, 229).

Mongolia's new leaders considered it to be a free state, but how free were the people? The princes simply lopped off the head of the feudal system, replacing the Manchu emperor with the head of the Buddhist hierarchy, the Jibzundamba Khutugtu, now called the Bogd Khan (the Holy Leader). He ruled Mongolia, now a theocracy, along with his council of princes. Although they formed a two-chambered parliament, giving Mongolia the appearance of representational rule, the Bogd Khan appointed its members (Baabar 1999:170). Meanwhile, the feudal system continued (Bawden 1989:190; Haslund 1934:69–71).

We can see the feudal class system in the 1918 census as reported by Maiskii, the first official census to survive. It does not include the Khovd Frontier region, which he estimates at 50,000; the Khovsgol region occupied by the Bogd Khan's shabi (estimated at 16,000) or the resident foreigners (100,000 Chinese, 5,000 Russians and some Westerners) (Maiskii 1956 [1921]:37–38). Maiskii puts the total Mongol population at 542,504 and the total population residing in Mongolia at 647,504 (ibid.). Note that Table 2.1 counts the men and boys as belonging to the same classes as those found in the Manchu era even though it ended at least six years before. The women and girls are not reported. Like the horses, camels, cattle, sheep and goats, women and girls are not counted in the class structure.

In 1919, Chinese troops invaded Mongolia, ending its supposed autonomous status. They removed the Bogd Khan from power in a public ceremony

Table 2.1 1918 census of males in the four eastern aimags, by class

Classes of Mongolians	Number of males	Percent of males
Princes (khan)	205	0.1
Nobles (taij)	13,276	5.6
Commoners (ard)	62,084	26.2
Serfs (khamjilgaa and shabi)	39,389	16.6
Classless	16,915	7.0
Lamas	105,577	44.6

Source: Maiskii 1956 [1921]:65.

that Mongolians still describe as humiliating. Shocked and angered by these events, some revolutionary groups sent a delegation to Russia to request that it help them gain independence from China once again. By then, the Bolsheviks controlled Russia and the Russian consulate in Ikh Khuree (Brown and Onon 1976:696).

When the Mongolian delegation met with Bolshevik officials in Siberia, several agreed to convert Mongolia to Soviet-style socialism. In hindsight, this was not really surprising. Russian influence had been strong throughout the autonomous period (1912–1919); commoners and serfs alike wanted to get out of debt to the Chinese merchants and to abolish the feudal privileges of the nobility and higher lamas.

Given the power of the nobility and clergy, the revolutionaries planned to do so in two stages. Once free of China, they would reinstate the Bogd Khan as a constitutional monarch and replace the aristocratic leadership. Then they would institute a People's Republic along the lines of Soviet Russia. And that is what happened. On September 14, 1921, a new Declaration of Independence was proclaimed. The Bogd Khan set up a constitutional monarchy that continued until his death in 1924 (Bawden 1989:205–37; Baabar 1999:201–25).

ENTERING SOCIALISM

"Do you know the difference between socialism and communism?" Dr. Altangerel asked me. "Why, yes," I replied cavalierly, not knowing at all what the difference was. It was 1998; I was sitting in his living room after a full Mongolian lunch of fresh tomatoes and cucumbers, pickled cucumbers and cabbage, sliced cold cuts, bread, butter and the traditional welcoming dish of *boodz* (chopped mutton and onions wrapped in pasta dough and steamed—the Mongolian version of wonton). Altangerel was the head of the physics department at the Pedagogical University in Ulaanbaatar and the father of Munkhtuya, an undergraduate at the University of Pennsylvania where I was teaching. Munkhtuya had arranged the lunch although she could not be there. Instead, her sister-in-law Byambajav Jagdorj, a young physics teacher in Altangerel's department, interpreted for us. Her English was quite new, but we still managed to have a good conversation. I learned as much as I could about socialism versus communism from our luncheon discussion but then returned to my books to learn more.

Karl Marx and Friedrich Engels proposed that a nation cannot be a true democracy if the capitalist class controls the government and the proletariat—the working class—has no public voice. Capitalists are the owners of the means of production, that is, the things needed to produce new products: land, a factory, machinery and so on. Their goal is to increase wealth so as to continue increasing production. Marx and Engels sometimes called members of this class the bourgeoisie.

The capitalist class gets the government to pass (and enforce) laws that favor its members. Therefore, a capitalist country is a political democracy in name only. The way to ensure true political democracy is for all citizens to have economic equality, which they can achieve only by controlling the means of production (Marx and Engels 1848). Since the capitalist class does not want to share power, the proletariat class—the workers—must wrest control from it by engaging in revolution. Once the proletariat gains control, it will be both worker and owner of the means of production. The proletariat will then decide its own fate.

Once in charge, the proletariat will abolish private property and competition, taking over the production and distribution of goods. And because all workers are equal and in control, national governments will eventually become unnecessary. Instead, workers in all countries will establish an international brotherhood. At that point, true communism will be achieved.

Marx and Engels realized that an oppressed proletariat would not be able to take over governance and production readily. They would need an intermediate step between the overthrow of capitalism and the achievement of communism. They called that step socialism. During the socialist stage, the new proletariat would eliminate the oppressing class (the capitalists), and the state would own the means of production. The state would employ all people and pay them a salary, which would be a living wage sufficient for the needs of the workers and their families. While people's salaries would be used to pay taxes and purchase extras, the state would provide them with free housing, food, clothing, transportation, healthcare, education and so on.

This scheme made sense to a lot of people at the turn of the last century. One of these was a Russian lawyer who called himself Vladimir I. Lenin. He modified the Marx/Engels doctrine to fit feudal Russia. Whereas Marx/Engels believed that revolution could only take place in industrial Europe, Lenin said that revolution did not need an industrialized proletariat; an agrarian society of peasants could also foment revolution if they were led by a vanguard of professional revolutionaries—that is, an intelligentsia scientifically trained to lead the people. He led the October 1917 Revolution and subsequent transition from feudalism to socialism. Lenin promised that this 'socialist democracy' would lead to higher economic and social development than that achieved by the capitalist countries (Tsedenbal 1967:13, Baabar 1999:259–60).[8]

In Russia, Marxist-Leninist political philosophy is described by Lukin (2000:115–16):

> Socialism differed from the final stage of communism by virtue of the continued existence of the state, to non-antagonistic classes (workers and peasants, which were supposed to disappear in mature communism by merging together), commodity—money relations, differences between urban and rural areas, distribution according to labour, crime, and other 'vestiges of capitalism.' Under mature communism all this would die out and communism would be a society of universal public property, of distribution according to needs, of creative labour for everybody, and of a new communist morality. This society was to appear after the victory of socialism all over the world. The Soviet Union, as the strongest socialist state, was seen as the natural guarantor of this process and its fight against imperialism in the world arena was at the same time a battle for the progress of humanity. Within the Soviet Union the Communist Party (CPSU) was the 'organizing and directing' force of the people in its movement along the road of social progress.

Lenin's modification of the Marx/Engels blueprint made socialism feasible in feudal, pastoral Mongolia (Baabar 1999:254, 262). Once the young revolutionaries freed the country from Chinese control with the help of Bolshevik Russian troops and made the Bogd Khan head of a constitutional monarchy, they began the process of destroying feudalism and laying the groundwork for the institutionalization of socialism. The government abolished khamjilgaa status by reclassifying them as commoners (ard). It eliminated corvée labor owed to overlords and canceled all debts to foreign (that is, Chinese) merchants. And it required all princes and nobles to perform the same services to government as the ard, including military service (Brown and Onon 1976:188–89; Baabar 1999:239).

Within three months of the Bogd Khan's death (May, 1924), the revolutionaries convened their third congress and wrote a constitution that formally adopted socialism. With the support of Soviet Russian coaches, it adopted the first constitution, which codified socialist principles for the country (Baabar 1999:261). The congress renamed Mongolia the Mongolian People's Republic, meaning that the ard, not the feudal nobility, held government power. The state was charged with ruling in the interests of the ard, who were granted citizenship. A year later, the new government declared the shabi to be ard and citizens also (Hirabayashi, Poppe and Kilcoyne 1956:347). The congress changed the name of the capital, Ikh Khuree, to Ulaanbaatar, which means Red (as in communist) Hero. And so Mongolia began its transformation from feudalism to socialism.

I want to note that some revolutionaries wanted capitalism, but the power struggle between those who favored capitalism and those who desired socialism was soon resolved when Danzan, one of the revolutionary leaders and spearheads of capitalism, was assassinated during the congress (Sanders 2003:xxxvi; Baabar 1999:262–65).

TRANSFORMING THE CLASS STRUCTURE

While the 1924 constitution elevated the ard, it prohibited the nobility and so-called capitalists from participating in governance. They were not even allowed to vote (Baabar 1999:268–69; Ma Ho-t'ien 1949:119). To reduce the difference between the former ruling classes and the ard, the new government started confiscating the nobles' property (Hirabayashi 1956:211; Friters 1949:23) (see Figure 2.8). Between 1929 and 1932, the property of

Figure 2.8 Confiscating property from a wealthy house. (National Museum of Mongolian History, 1929)

1,136 households was confiscated (Bawden 1989:302). "Everything was confiscated, including animals, houses, gold, silver, jewelry, clothes, religious items, handicraft things, furniture, and so on" (Baabar 1999:305–06). The confiscated livestock were distributed among the new collective farms (*negdel*), modeled after the Soviet *kolkhoz*. Introduced into Mongolia in 1922, the government encouraged the pastoral nomads to live together in settlements where they could herd and farm "scientifically" and where their children could be educated in schools (Hirabayashi 1956:211; Brown and Onon 1976:181). Still, Ma Ho-t'ien (1949:145) noted the class system was strong in 1926. And Hirabayashi (1956:211) thought that remnants of the old class system were still visible in 1955.

The 1924 constitution also limited the authority of Tibetan Buddhism, for the revolutionaries believed that religion was responsible for Mongolia's decadence during the Manchu Dynasty. They also feared it would keep the people from accepting socialism (Ma Ho-t'ien 1949:132). The constitution separated religion from the state, assuring that Mongolia would not return to the theocracy of the autonomous period (Ballis 1956a:510). It abolished the titles and class distinctions of the lamas and forbade them from voting or holding government positions as it had done to the nobility (Riasnovsky 1937:19). In 1929, the state began confiscating monastery property (Hirabayashi, Poppe and Kilcoyne 1956:348–49). It auctioned off the Bogd Khan's property after his death (Ma Ho-t'ien 1949:133).

The new government redistributed most of the livestock to the new collectives. The following year it branded lamas as enemies of the revolution (Hirabayashi, Poppe and Kilcoyne 1956:351). And four years later, the state forbade the construction of new monasteries and blocked them from engaging in lending money or serving as trading centers (Bawden 1989:373).

The republican government imposed a steep graduated income tax to reduce the economic differences between the former ruling classes and the ard (Ma Ho-t'ien 1949:18–19). Revenues from these taxes went to the collective farms (Hirabayashi 1956:211). The government also levied several new taxes on the Chinese merchants: a passport tax, a permit, a business tax and a tax on the goods the merchants bought and sold. Ma Ho-t'ien, a Chinese traveler to Mongolia in 1926, reported that the largest Chinese firm in Ikh Khuree, Ta Sheng K'uei, lost over US$1 million when the government cancelled Mongols' debts. In one district in the Gobi (Baisingto), the number of Chinese trading houses decreased from over 100 to just 5 (Ma Ho-t'ien 1949:18–19). In this way, the government succeeded in reducing the merchant system that had indebted so many Mongolians during the Manchu period.

The government did not limit its transformative efforts to nationalization, confiscation and taxation. It also started a series of 'purges,' or mass murders of the 'feudals'—the elite classes—in the 1930s. Anyone not an ard was suspect and subject to being purged (Baabar 1999:227–28, 293–97, 316–17). It has been estimated that between 1933 and 1953, 36,000 people died in the purges (Bumaa 2001:46). In 2003, archaeologists excavated some mass burials of lamas around Gandan Monastery in Ulaanbaatar. The adults and adolescents had been executed with a single bullet to the back of the head. They discovered several layers of burials, suggesting more than one mass execution (Frohlich and Hunt 2006:4–5).

Despite so many programs to eradicate economic and social differences, social stratification continued as a new elite emerged from the original MPRP membership. While it is said that in socialist countries people from the old ruling elite reinvented themselves as the 'new' elite, Mongolia's former nobles and higher lamas were blocked from joining the MPRP (Ballis 1956b:535). The new elite were drawn from the feudal commoners (ard) and serfs (khamjilgaa and shabi), but they became the elite nevertheless.

There arose three kinds of elite: the governing elite, the urban intelligentsia and the military elite. The governing elite were all party members who were frequently hand-picked by Russians and spoke Russian. How could someone become a MPRP member and join the elite? One had to be recommended by at least two party members and serve a one-year apprenticeship to one of them (Ballis 1956b:534). Party members could appoint people to government and all important positions, awards and so on (Baabar 1999:270). They could help their kin and friends into political positions (Plank 1956c:419–20). "A great indifference to corruption manifests itself, but principally on the local level. Many people know of these improprieties but seem to take them as a matter of course.... [N]epotism has strong roots even within the government" (Hirabayashi, Rupen and Poppe 1956:250).

Members of the urban intelligentsia were the professors, economists and other policy consultants. Many were educated in Russian universities. The military elite staffed the top positions in the departments of defense, security and justice. Rupen (1979:113–121) estimated the national elite at 500 people.

By the 1970s, the intelligentsia had taken over the party and the government (Rupen 1979:101). It had become the elite class within a classless society. Thus Marx and Engels' ideal of the workers leading the country had been subverted.

Other social differences formed: urban versus rural dwellers, industrial versus agricultural workers, administrators versus workers and so on (Rupen

1979:114). Even though political rhetoric stressed equality, Mongolia did not become an egalitarian society. Rather, it achieved the society envisioned by Lenin: a working class governed by an elite intelligentsia that quietly maintained certain privileges.

TRANSFORMING GOVERNANCE

To understand Mongolians' ideas on democracy after 1990, we need to decode the close bond between Soviet Russia and Mongolia and between the MPRP and socialist government. Czarist Russian interest in Mongolia accelerated with farmers and traders in the late nineteenth century. During Mongolia's autonomous period, Russia loaned Mongolia money, treating it as an independent state even while signing treaties with China that placed Mongolia under that country's suzerainty (Holzman 1956:875).

Following the Russian Revolution, the Bolsheviks supported Mongolia's 1919–1921 war for independence from China. They sent consultants to guide the Mongolians through the transition from feudalism to socialism. Mongolia's 1924 constitution was actually written by "Russian legal advisor P. V. Vseviatskii and translated into Mongolian by Elbek-Dorzhi Rinchino. The First Great Khural (November 8–28, 1924) adopted it essentially without change" (Atwood 2004:119). Subsequent constitutions included word-for-word copies of Soviet Russian constitutions (Ballis 1956a:509–18). Ma Ho-t'ien (1949:95)[9] reported that as early as 1926 the "Russians are directing everything." Mongolian historian Dr. Baabar (1999:261) writes that the "Soviet Commissars ... produce[d] the blueprint for Mongolia's future development," and the 1924 constitution made Mongolia a vassal state of Soviet Russia (ibid.:269). Bawden (1989:288–89) wrote that the MPRP followed Stalin into socialism:

> She [Mongolia] now entered a period of total isolation from the world which lasted till [sic] well after the Second World War. Though she maintained her identity as a separate state, the course which her history took during those years, especially during the 1930s, shows such crass similarities, both overall and in detail, with that of the U S S R [sic], that it is hard to credit that she was capable at that time of maintaining her independence of action.

The MPRP and government became tightly intertwined, just as Lenin had advocated. Mongolia's young revolutionaries morphed into the leaders of the new Mongolian People's Party, which they renamed the MPRP in 1924. As they were the heroes who had freed Mongolia from Chinese imperialism, they had credibility with the people. They also gained power in the MPRP by engaging in political assassinations and executions, which continued for decades (Baabar 1999:227–34, 262–65). Once Stalin controlled Soviet Russia, his support was crucial to gaining power in Mongolia (Baabar 1999:352). He hand-picked Mongolia's two dictators. The first, Choibalsan (ruled 1939–1952), took orders directly from Stalin and emulated Stalin's 'cult of personality' (see Figure 2.9). Choibalsan's photographs were everywhere, and he was known as the 'little Stalin' of Mongolia (Baabar 1999:375–82). The second, Tsedenbal (ruled 1952–1984), had the support of later Soviet leaders (Sanders 2003:318).

The MPRP leadership built a tightly controlled hierarchical political organization that reached from a national congress of MPRP delegates down through the aimags to local-level committees, or cells. The government held regular elections, but the people had only one party to vote for.

Although the 1924 constitution constructed a government that resembled the European parliamentary system, it was really a rubber stamp of

Figure 2.9 Choibalsan, the "Little Stalin" of Mongolia. (National Museum of Mongolian History, socialist era)

MPRP policies. The Great Khural (Parliament) only met once every three years. It elected a Little Khural, a subset of the Great Khural, which, in turn, elected a Presidium of five to seven members. The Presidium acted as the cabinet and selected the prime minister from their midst (Ballis 1956a:512).

The two [MPRP and government] are inextricably interwoven so that it is difficult to ascertain where the MPRP ends and the government begins. The same phenomenon occurs in the Soviet Union. As with its model, the Party in the Mongolian People's Republic is the hand, the government is the glove. The fact that all key Mongolian government officials belong to the MPRP and many of them hold leading positions in the party is an indication of the close relationship between the two. Following the example of the Communist Party of the Soviet Union, the MPRP is able from its Central Committee to keep close check on every governmental and administrative organ down to the lowest level of political organization and the most basic unit of economic activity. (Ballis 1956b:541–43)

By the 1980s, the tight totalitarian state began to loosen up. The dictator Tsedenbal was removed from power in 1984 and a more liberal man, Jambiin Batmonkh, became head of the MPRP and the government (Rupen 1979:109–10). This change was influenced by Soviet Union President Mikhail Gorbachev's implementation of *perestroika* (restructuring the government) and *glasnost'* (openness or transparency). Batmonkh followed suit, thus preparing the way for the 1989–1990 Democratic Revolution (Sanders 1991:60–74).

SOCIALIST CITIZENS' RIGHTS AND DUTIES

Ard men and women gained freedom from serfdom along with citizenship in 1924 (Riasnovsky 1937:18). The formerly downtrodden were freed from obligations to their overlords and no longer owed corvée labor (Bawden 1989:258). They gained the right to vote, and even those formerly forbidden to participate in governance (the nobility, capitalists and lamas) were granted that right in 1944. But there were neither electoral choice nor secret ballot until 1949. Instead, there was a voice vote (Ballis 1956a:513–15).

The 1940 constitution included certain rights. Here, citizens were granted the right to an eight-hour work day, an annual two-week vacation in a government-paid sanatorium, free basic education, old-age benefits, religious freedom (that is, the right to practice one's religion or not practice at all), and the right to join a union of workers (Ballis 1956b:528–29).

While these rights sound progressive (they were direct copies of the Soviet Union's 1936 constitution), they were balanced by repressive practices. From 1921 to 1943 the Revolutionary Youth League (Revsomol), the Mongolian equivalent of the Soviet Komsomol, persecuted enemies of the state. In 1934, the MPRP replaced the original secret police with the NKVD (translates as the People's Commissariat for Internal Affairs), a combination public police force and secret police trained by the Russians (Bawden 1989:333). It was responsible for carrying out the purges as well as the arrest and punishment of counter-revolutionaries or feudal sympathizers. Repression of the general population was under the NKVD's purview (Baabar 1999:332; Rupen 1979:3; Bawden 1989:373; Ballis and Hiraga 1956:550–51,560–61). Those who were convicted faced harsh punishments: long prison sentences, forced labor camps and forced labor constructing the Trans-Siberian rail system, apartments, factories and so on (Ballis and Hiraga 1956:562–64).

Another right that we take for granted was also neglected. The socialist state developed a good school system and rewarded smart students by training them in elite schools. Countryside children were brought to Ulaanbaatar to study. Hard-working students could even study abroad in other Soviet countries. But students were taught socialist dogma, as they were in Russia.[10] They were also assigned the subjects they would study (major in); they had no choices. And, after school, students were sent to specific jobs. So even though a true meritocracy developed (with the exception of the privileged children of the government elites), it operated within a system of forced study and forced labor (R. Bat-Erdene and Undrakh, 1994, fieldnotes).

The duties of citizens were pretty limited. According to the 1940 Constitution, citizens had "to observe laws, maintain labor discipline, to promote in every way possible the economic, cultural and political development of the country, to perform their duties honestly and to protect and strengthen public and state property [Article 102]" ("Attitudes and Reactions of the People" 1956:429). Thus the government required that citizens be passive, accepting the dictates of the government (and therefore the MPRP) and producing for the state. They were required to vote in order to show the West that the country was a democracy, but a democracy in the Marxist-Leninist sense—that is, an economic democracy rather than the West's sense of political democracy.

TRANSFORMING THE ECONOMY

The 1924 constitution proclaimed the state to be the owner of the means of production. To that end, it nationalized Mongolia's land, water and other natural resources. It also took control of foreign trade (Riasnovsky 1937:18; Ma Ho-t'ien 1949:139–41; Lattimore 1949:xxvi; Baabar 1999:269). To align its economy with Soviet ideology, Mongolia shifted its exports from China to Russia. In 1925, 86 percent of wool exports went to China, but in 1926, 76 percent went to Russia (Baabar 1999:299). Still, of the 1,700 shops operating in 1928, 1,450 were Chinese; 169 were Russian and 81 were European or American (Bawden 199:290).

The new government restructured the tax system. Previously, government revenues had come from tariffs imposed on imports and exports (including goods that crossed district, or aimag, borders). A lot of government projects had been accomplished through free, or corvée, labor. For example, people had been responsible for staffing the *urton* (relay stations) and providing ponies to the relay stations for free.

In contrast, the socialist government emphasized taxation on consumer goods rather than income tax, in keeping with Soviet Russian policy (Holzman 1956:892).

To build a true socialist state, the government had to build a proletariat of industrial workers rather than remain a nation of herders. Mongolians had engaged in industrial production prior to the socialist revolution. They had produced goods such as felt, sinew and wood poles for yurts. They had bought or traded for other needed products: clothing, pots and religious objects for the family shrine. Most of the crafted items were made by Chinese artisans. These included boots, clothing, metal working and gold and silver objects for the monasteries. The Russians managed and staffed manufacturing plants that prepared animal products for export to Russia; they tanned animal hides, washed wool, prepared gut and melted tallow . Some coal, iron and gold mining operations had existed, but the workers in resource extraction were mostly Chinese (Murphy 1956:828–30).

The socialist government encouraged former serfs and commoners to form cooperative factories or to work in government-owned factories. The first factory opened in 1933 (Murphy 1956:831). By 1939 there were about 10,000 industrial workers and another 10,000 in handicraft operations (Rupen 1979:52). In the 1950s, industry shifted away from small craft shops to factories (Bawden 1989:394–95). These were located mostly in Ulaanbaatar, but they also appeared in other urban centers such as Khovd, Choibalsan and Uliastai (Hirabayashi, Poppe and Kilcoyne 1956:396).

By 1973, the industrial force had 110,000 workers (Rupen 1979:101). During that decade, most industrial employees were also members of trade unions, but trade unions had a different meaning in Mongolia and the Soviet Union than they do in the United States. Because all workers were employees of the state, trade unions did not bargain with capitalists on behalf of the workers. There were no capitalists. So the job of the unions was to disseminate government policy and distribute benefits to the workers (Plank 1956:404).

The socialist government tried to extend the proletariat concept to the countryside. Following Stalin's policy of collectivization of small farms in Russia, Mongolia urged the herders into collectives in order to 'industrialize' herding and agriculture. It wanted to block the former serfs and commoners from becoming petty capitalists (Baabar 1999:293; Rupen 1979:52–53). In 1929–1930, 400 collectives were established, but they were not successful. Rather than collectivize, the herders killed their animals, and the number of livestock in the country dropped by seven million (Bawden 1989:311; Friters 1949:18–19). A revolt in 1932 forced the government to dismantle the collectives (Baabar 1999:322–23). Saving the economy was more important than imposing Marxist-Leninist ideology on the herders (Bawden 1989:352). Cattle stocks recovered within two years.

Although the government tried to revive the collectivization program, 97 percent of the livestock were still privately owned in 1953. In the late 1950s, the government allowed cooperative members to keep some livestock as private property, and by 1960, 99 percent of herds had been collectivized (Bawden 1989:398). This system continued up to the Democratic Revolution.

The new regime also encouraged Mongolians to take up farming. While some Chinese and Russian settlers had grown crops prior to the 1911 revolution, few Mongolians did (Friters 1949:27). During the autonomous period, the government had encouraged the population to plant grains. But the people disdained agriculture as hard work, and the monasteries rejected it as contrary to the religious principle of not disturbing the ground (ibid.:28–29). So to reduce imports of wheat, oats and other grains, the government established some state farms (ibid.:30). I visited one west of Ulaanbaatar in June 1994. After bouncing along a rutted dirt road in Russian jeeps and a Toyota Land Cruiser, we came to the Youth Farm, a collective built in 1977. It was named the Youth Farm because the people who settled it were young and the name just stuck, they said. The state had sent out notices that a new collective would be formed and young herders came to build a life there. They constructed apartments, a school and a meeting house. They poured a concrete basketball court that was still in use. State workers came to teach them farming and lay out fields for wheat, potatoes and other vegetables that stretched for several miles apiece. These were plowed with heavy-duty tractors. The Youth Farm members raised horses, sheep, goats and dairy cattle. One of the veterinarians said that they had 20,000 livestock at the time of our visit. During the socialist era, there was a factory to make animal feed, but it was no longer used. There was also a sewing factory that made uniforms for the collective then (June 23, 1994, fieldnotes).

How did the state get its employees to increase production? Since a socialist economy could not use competition to motivate workers (everyone with the same job earned the same salary), Mongolia adopted the Soviet Union's system of five-year economic plans. Starting in 1948, the government set five-year goals for production that the workers were supposed to meet. All workers were assigned a quota, or goal, for their personal production. The state used a combination of carrot and stick to motivate workers. Incentives included annual two-week vacations and rewards in the form of medals or gifts. Herders could earn silver statues of the domesticated animals they had raised. Disincentives included salary reductions or "corrective labor" (Plank 1956c:421; Rupen 1979:70; Kaser 1991:97).

One more point about the socialist economy: the government, not the market, controlled prices for consumer goods such as meat, milk, heating and electricity (Sanders 1987:118; Rossabi 2005:46).

LIFE WAS IMPROVING

While we might think that socialist life was harsh, it did improve peoples' lives. Under socialism they gained access to education, modern medicine, government support and urbanization. Before the revolution, most learning took place in monasteries or secular tent schools. Boys in the monasteries were taught to read Tibetan texts, or sutras, and so were only literate in Tibetan. Boys in the tent schools were schooled to be scribes for the Manchurian Dynasty and so were taught Manchurian. In 1911, it is estimated that 25–30 percent of the entire school population were studying in monastic schools while only 0.3 percent were in scribe schools (Steiner-Khamsi and Stolpe 2006:33). Anyone wanting to learn the Mongolian script had to study on his own (Sambuu 2010:27). As of 1932, 80 percent of the MPRP members of parliament were illiterate (Bawden 1989:249). Imagine running a government where most policy makers could not read or write!

The first official secular school was established in the autonomous period, but it only accommodated 25 to 50 boys (Hirabayashi 1956:186; Rupen 1964:85). The 1924 constitution guaranteed tuition-free education for all, and the government started a literacy campaign even before then (Krueger, Poppe and Kilcoyne 1956:291). They established a series of primary schools, taught army conscripts to read and write and eventually brought literacy programs to the countryside (Bawden 1989:249).[11] Later, Soviet Russia helped Mongolia establish a National University with a medical school. By 1989, about 80 percent of the population was literate (CIA 2009).

The socialist government introduced modern medicine by separating medical treatment from the Tibetan Buddhist lamas, who used prayer more than medicine to cure. Russian medical workers had entered Mongolia by 1921 (Plank 1956b:407). The first hospital—with 25 beds—opened in Ulaanbaatar in 1925, and small medical stations were built in Khovd and other urban centers soon after (Plank 1956b:408). At first people and lamas resisted Russian attempts to help. But they soon accepted and appreciated Russian medicine for their animals and themselves. In the 1940s the state made universal health care a goal. The government planned to achieve this by employing Russian doctors and Mongolian staff (nurses and such) and by promulgating education programs for the general population. Soon people no longer died of epidemic diseases such as anthrax. By 1987, Mongolia had 423 hospitals (for a population of almost 2 million) and 538 outpatient clinics and health centers (Academy of Sciences MPR 1990:481–82).

The socialist government introduced Western arts and entertainment to the general population. The Mongol People's Cultural Theatre was built in 1931, and a cinema was built in the 1930s (Baabar 1999:303). Early on, people performed plays that recreated the oppression of feudalism and the glory (and relief) of socialism for Mongolian serfs (Ma Ho-t'ien 1949:31–32, 136–38). But soon Mongolians were performing "Swan Lake" and Bach concerts. There is something magical in hearing a stage full of Mongolians playing Bach on native string instruments.

Starting with the 1940 constitution, the government guaranteed citizens and hired foreign laborers the right to social security in old age and illness. The state supplied free medical care, including the care of pregnant women and new mothers (Plank 1956c:421). As the government sought to boost the size of the population, it paid an annual bonus to women having five or more children (ibid.:424–25).

URBAN CENTERS

One of the most dramatic changes was the development and industrialization of urban areas. Ulaanbaatar, once a warren of streets, was laid out in a grid pattern with wide boulevards, the form of a Soviet city. Between the prerevolutionary Mongolian town surrounding Gandan Monastery and the old Russian trading center, a complex resembling Moscow's Red Square was built. A new building that housed parliament and government offices was constructed in the 1950s. In front of it was a large square with an equestrian statue of the revolutionary hero Sukhbaatar in the center. Across the river, factories and housing for workers were constructed. Three power plants delivered electricity and heat to the city.

The Soviet Union helped Mongolia build other industrial cities. Darkhan, Erdenet and Choibalsan were built with foreign labor and supplies. Some of the laborers were World War II Japanese prisoners of war. Once Mao Tse Tung gained control of China, he sent workers to build the cities also. By the 1960s, more than 40 percent of the population was living in urban centers (Bawden 1989:408). By 1970, Darkhan, about 90 miles north of Ulaanbaatar, had several factories that made bricks, cement and building parts and materials, as well as processed fur/skin; Darkhan had a thermal power station, like Ulaanbaatar. Its population had reached 30,000 (Axelbank 1971:71 ff). Choibalsan in eastern Mongolia produced items from animal products (fur coats, saddles, cloth), building materials (bricks, lumber, tiles and so on), printing, electric power plants, metal working (for machinery), wool washing, the handicraft industry (mostly products for local consumption: felt, clothing leather goods, harness, scythes and so on), coal and food (meat, butter, wine, vegetables, soap, sausage) (Murphy 1956:841–55).

WOMEN AND GIRLS

Socialism brought greater equality for women and girls. Although they had always received a certain level of respect because of their economic role in the family (they were responsible for caring for the family, goats and sheep), they gained even more respect and opportunity under a regime that was built around the concept of economic equality. Girls were educated along with boys; women's work was valued in farms and factories; and they became visible in government and unions. Even in 1926 in the Gobi, women voted and could join the Revolutionary Youth League (Revsomol) (Ma Ho-t'ien 1949:33).

Ma Ho-t'ien (ibid.:42–45) describes the girls he met in 1926–1927 as very modern. They had already cut off their long braids and bobbed their hair. They showed no shyness in talking or being alone in a ger with foreign men such as him, which scandalized the Chinese servants who accompanied him. And they continued to practice casual sex, as they had in the Manchu period, he reported.

By the late 1980s, women formed half of all MPRP members, one-fourth of Members of Parliament and 63 percent of the workforce (Academy of Sciences MPR 1990:165). One of the young researchers on the 1998 project told me that she always expected to work because she was raised under socialism. How could she be happy if she did not do her best work and further her career? She was willing to leave her husband for two years of post-baccalaureate training in the United States because, she said, she planned to be with him forever and so they could afford to be apart for a while (August 26, 1998, fieldnotes).

This is quite a rosy picture. It needs to be tempered by private remarks made to me during my visits to Mongolia. In 1999 I brought my friend Brian Hackman, a British doctor of obstetrics and gynecology who was consulting on a project for the World Health Organization (WHO), to lunch at Professor Altangerel's apartment. He asked Myadagmaa, Altangerel's wife and a medical doctor herself, why she thought more women were dying in childbirth now than in socialist times. She replied that people are now reacting to years of socialist domination. In those days, she said, the Area Leader was responsible for knowing everything going on. He (or she) would announce every pregnancy to the public. Since everyone knew when a woman was due, they knew when to send her to the sum center to prepare for the birth of her baby, which was usually three months before her due date. In other words, she did not go voluntarily. Since people want to be left alone now that they are free and since many nomads do not have the money to pay for hospitalization, women do not take themselves or their daughters to the soum center before the birth. As a result, the doctors cannot anticipate problems and thereby stave off death. Altangerel added that under socialism, people were always watching you; everyone knew everyone else's business. No one wants that now, and so the women suffer (August 9, 1999, fieldnotes).

EXITING SOCIALISM

Six months after the Chinese government quelled the June 1989 Tiananmen Square protests, Mongolian university students and faculty began to hold their own public protests all over the country. The first took place in Khovd on December 7. Khovd University history professors Nyamsuren and Nyamdorj recalled that they had joined other students in marching around the main square that day (July 1, 2003, fieldnotes). Several months before, they had petitioned the local MPRP to allow non-MPRP students join the leadership of the local student organization. The petition was refused and the university rector (president) threatened them, telling them to keep the problem within the walls of the university. At that point, they took to the streets wearing masks and Japanese-style headbands. Some had written slogans such as "Chinggis Khaan" or "We want fast changes" on the headbands. When I asked Nyamsuren and Nyamdorj how they knew to protest, they said that their German-trained professors had told their students about the Velvet Revolution in Eastern European countries and the November 9 destruction of the Berlin Wall. This knowledge emboldened the Khovd students to protest. Three days later, a peaceful march to celebrate International Human Rights Day turned into a public protest in Ulaanbaatar (Rossabi 2005:1–2). This time the young people were demonstrating for faster implementation of perestroika and glasnost' as well as a more just socialism. Their demands soon spread to multiparty elections, and by the New Year they were demanding the end of a centrally planned economy and MPRP rule (interview with Baabar [Bat-Erdeniin Batbayar] July 16, 2003).

In March 1990, some leaders of the demonstrations staged a hunger strike at the foot of Sukhbaatar's statue in Sukhbaatar Square, right in front of the parliament building (see Figure 2.10). This caused the MPRP leadership to capitulate to the populace's demands and call for free and open elections in June.

Figure 2.10 The hunger strike at the foot of Sukhbaatar's statue, Ulaanbaatar. (National Museum of Mongolian History, March 7, 1990)

That election was the first time Mongolians had been offered choice at the polls. They kept many MPRP members in government, but there were enough members of new political parties to form a coalition government. Together they wrote a new constitution that combined political democratic and capitalist-leaning principles. Its Preamble foreshadows the political ('unalienable'), economic and socioeconomic rights in the body of the constitution:

We, the people of Mongolia:

Strengthening the independence and sovereignty of the nation,
Cherishing human rights and freedoms, justice, and national unity,
Inheriting the traditions of national statehood, history, and culture,
Respecting the accomplishments of human civilization,
And aspiring toward the supreme objective of building a humane, civil and democratic society in the country,
Hereby proclaim the Constitution of Mongolia.

CHAPTER THREE

Democracy Means Human Rights

W hen I think of human rights, I start with the idea that all people should be treated with dignity just by virtue of the fact that they are born human (see Jones 2006:S105, S105SECT2). I know that human rights include the right to live, free speech and other freedoms. No government should be able to take these away from its citizens; human rights are inalienable. But I don't associate human rights with democracy. To me, they apply to all people of the world no matter what kind of government they live under. Yet over a third of the Mongolians interviewed do make that association. And most of them name human rights as the first or second characteristic of democracy, which means the connection pops into their heads almost immediately. This indicates how important human rights are to Mongolians. Here are just two examples of their thoughts:

> Thanks to democracy, people enjoy their human rights (*khunii erkh*). It is not only about political rights; it is also true for economic rights. The opportunity to enjoy human rights makes it possible for a person to improve his life. In that way, human rights are the main feature of democracy. (Khovd 1998 Bd009)

> I prefer to live in a democratic country because human rights are absolutely ensured. (Khovd 2003 Bj055)

This chapter explores Mongolians' interpretation of human rights and why so many consider it a critical component of democracy. Statistical analysis suggests variability within the sample population. Therefore, the association of human rights with democracy is not universal, even within one country.

'UNIVERSAL' HUMAN RIGHTS

Anthropologists do not like to compare people's interpretation of some abstract concept with universal standards for fear that readers will think the people are subpar. We are more concerned with how people *adapt* an idea to fit their culture, history and situation than how closely they *adopt* a standard definition. Yet cognitive anthropologists talk about 'shared knowledge' or shared understandings as a pool that individuals can dip into and drink from. To describe the water in the dipper—a subset or subdomain of the pool—it helps to know the pool. Because Mongolians did not learn about human rights in isolation from international standards and because the originators of the Universal Declaration intended that it become universal (United Nations 1948; Nickel 2009; Goodale 2007:3), it is logical to start the chapter with a very brief history of human rights in the twentieth century.

Originally designed to protect people from their government, human rights are focused on personal rights to life, dignity and self-determination. On December 10, 1948, the young United Nations (UN) adopted the *Universal Declaration of Human Rights*. It was followed by two UN covenants, the *International Covenant on Civil and Political Rights* and the *International Covenant on Economic, Social and Cultural Rights,* both adopted in 1966. A host of conventions that nations could sign or not were soon drafted (Merry 2001:35). Two examples are the *Convention on the Elimination of All Forms of Racial Discrimination* (1966) and the *Convention on the Elimination of All Forms of Discrimination against Women* (known as CEDAW, 1979).

Underlying all of these documents is the belief that governments have a moral obligation to honor and protect their citizens' rights. By signing on to the Universal Declaration and any subsequent covenants or conventions, governments convert the moral obligations of the Universal Declaration into legal requirements within their territory.

The first group of human rights in the Universal Declaration protects citizens from governmental abuse and guarantees them a decent life. Many, but not all, of these rights are familiar largely because they form the core principles of the *Declaration of Independence, Constitution* and *Bill of Rights* of the United States. While the Universal Declaration lists over two dozen human rights, the main ideas are as follows:

- **Security of person**. All human beings should not be killed, enslaved, tortured or subject to any inhumane or "degrading treatment or punishment" by their government (Articles 1–5). They should not be subject to arbitrary arrest, but if arrested, they have the right to receive a fair, competent trial (Articles 6–11).
- **Equality.** All human beings "are equal before the law and are entitled without any discrimination to equal protection of the law" (Article 3). Neither governments nor international authorities may discriminate

against people based on their gender, race, religion, and so on [sexual orientation was not something that people discussed in the 1940s.] And "Everyone ... has the right to equal pay for equal work" (Article 23).

- **Political freedom.** All people have the right to their own beliefs and to express their thoughts (Articles 18–19). They are free to peacefully assemble and associate with (or dissociate from) whomever they like (Article 20). All have the right to move within and between national borders; and all have the right to political asylum (Article 13). In all of these activities, people have the right to privacy (Article 12).
- **Economic freedom.** All people have the right to make their own decisions regarding their property, work, marriage, divorce and family life (Articles 12–14, 16–17, 23).
- **Political rights.** The Universal Declaration also states that citizens should have a voice in governance (Article 21). Article 15 states that everyone has the right to citizenship in a nation-state.
- **Socio-economic rights.** Governments have the obligation to assure that their citizens can lead healthy, productive lives. Thus, all citizens of a nation-state are entitled to equal access to social security (old-age pensions) and other government services (Articles 21–22). All people have the right to rest and leisure (that is, decent working hours), a decent standard of living, medical care, an education and participation in their community (Articles 24–27).

Even though the document was named the *Universal Declaration of Human Rights,* not all governments were in favor of it. When 48 member-states of the UN General Assembly endorsed it, 8 abstained. Six were part of the Soviet Union (USSR, Byelorussia, Czechoslovakia, Poland, Ukraine and Yugoslavia); the other two were South Africa and Saudi Arabia.

Mongolia could not ratify the Universal Declaration in 1948 because it was not a member of the United Nations. It tried to gain admittance starting in 1946. But nations of the 'free world' like the United States and Great Britain did not want more communist countries in the United Nations to upset the balance of power. So Mongolia's admittance was delayed until 1961. Once Mongolia ratified its 1992 constitution, making it a democratic nation, it signed more than 20 other international human rights covenants and conventions (Rinchin 2010).

The United Nations strengthened the link between human rights and democracy when it ratified the *International Covenant on Civil and Political*

Rights (December 16, 1966). Decades later, I interviewed Douglas Gardner, then head of the United Nations Development Programme (UNDP) in Mongolia. At that 1998 meeting, he told me that the United Nations found it could not safeguard human rights in nondemocratic governments. Such governments do not operate in the interests of the people and often trample their rights in order to stay in power. It is only when people can speak out, when people have freedom of speech and of the press, that they can preserve or demand human rights and dignity. Modern democracies do not always honor human rights, but they remain an integral part of democratic ideals. That is why the United Nations developed and implemented programs that promote democracy along with human rights (June 30, 1998, fieldnotes).

CONCEPTUALIZING HUMAN RIGHTS IN DEMOCRATIC MONGOLIA

Mongolia's last socialist constitution (1960) incorporated many of the human rights and freedoms found in the Universal Declaration. Some were political freedoms. For example, it referred to equality before the law no matter what a person's gender, ethnicity or religion; the right to free speech and assembly; the right to privacy; the right to participate in governance; and the right to asylum (Academy of Sciences MPR 1990:150–52). This list sounds downright Western. But the socialist government maintained a secret police, the NKVD, whose job was to assure conformity to MPRP ideology and directives, so dissent was quashed.

In 1999, I met Zanaa Jurmed, Director of CEDAW-Watch and a coalition of women's NGOs that watches every level of government (see Figure 3.1). At that time, the office was in a dilapidated building, yet the suite looked new. It had just been painted a sweet pink with a white ceiling two months before. The office furniture and equipment were also brand new. Zanaa herself was a beautiful woman with carefully coifed hair, necklace and bracelet of pearls and a delicious French perfume. She had been a Russian teacher but changed occupations after she had become involved in the Democratic Revolution. As Director of CEDAW-Watch, she was responsible for giving the shadow report (what is really happening in Mongolia) to the UN General Assembly.

She started her 1999 speech by recounting some violations of human rights during the socialist era:

> If someone commented or said something against the revolutionary party's policy and its principles, he or she was severely punished. For

Figure 3.1 Zanaa Jurmed, in red shawl, with her office workers. (Paula L.W. Sabloff, 2003)

example, the 'guilty' person could be forced to quit their job and do hard work in difficult living and working conditions, such as herding camels in the desert area or working in a wood processing factory in the countryside. The seven decades under socialism were marked with numerous political assassinations of political leaders who were not in agreement with the policy of the revolutionary party.

Before the democratic changes occurred in the 1990s, Mongolian people had model human rights declared by the Communist Constitution [1960]. However, people's private and social lives were regulated by the Mongolian Revolutionary Party's rules and the resolutions from the party's Political Bureau. (Jurmed 1999)

As an American who was raised during the Cold War, I 'knew' that 'communist regimes' were totalitarian. But when I spoke with some Mongolians, I was a bit surprised to find how angry they were about the socialist era. Perhaps the most poignant quotation is from a middle-aged businesswoman in Ulaanbaatar (1998 Mh054):

Under single-party dominance [one-party rule], people had no rights or freedom in the true sense of these terms. For instance, we believed faithfully in the dogma of the genius Karl Marx that "religion is the opium of the people," so we destroyed our own intellectual culture. The communist ideology advocated by the Soviet Union's Communist Party and [Mongolia's] MPRP resulted in serious breaches in human rights, and our brothers and sisters were murdered and tortured in jails without justice. The main reasons for all of these acts were that [Mongolia] was the vassal [of the Soviet Union] and subscribed to the cult of personality, which means that the population was encouraged to worship and trust the decisions of their leaders. We still see it in North Norea and a few other places. Today, we understand the meaning of freedom and human rights. And although these are unrestricted notions, we understand that rights are restricted by duties and responsibilities, and freedom is restricted by others' freedom [one is not allowed to infringe on other people's freedom]. Human rights and freedom are the kind of wealth that cannot be exchanged for anything. However, they are the products of capitalism.

In the same year, an unemployed young Oirad in Khovd (Gn001) says, "In the former [socialist] system, people had no right to participate in meetings, to speak freely, to publish or express their thoughts freely. It is because at that time there was a commanding system. Now people vote more freely during elections."

The socialist government not only told people what jobs to do but also how to think. There was only one newspaper, *Unen*, meaning 'truth,' and it was an organ of the government.[1] The government also controlled the only radio station. I have been in hotels and guest houses in the Gobi and lived in apartments in Ulaanbaatar that had a blue plastic radio box high on the wall, a relic from the socialist era. If I forgot to turn the sound down, the radio would start blasting martial music at 6:00 AM each day (August 17, 1999, fieldnotes). Its original purpose was to provide government-controlled news and propaganda to each household or hotel guest.

Other interviewees' comments add nuance to the two above. One fellow is a herder with a primary school education (Khovd 1998 Ns007). He is also Kazakh, a member of a small minority that migrated into western Mongolia in the late nineteenth century. While Mongolian Kazakhs maintain their own language and are relearning their Muslim religion (after socialism forbade religious practice), I found their interviews to be fiercely democratic. This herder says,

In the previous society, people had some human rights but they couldn't enjoy them. In socialist times, the commanding mechanism [that is, the authoritarian socialist government] restricted human rights and people had more obligations and responsibilities than rights. Even more, state property was protected more than a man was.

A young woman talks as though she is very old, but she is really in her twenties (Khovd 1998 Ns024). She, too, is Kazakh: "When I was a small child, adults were very careful when they talked with each other. Today people express their thoughts and publish freely. Now it became free to do anything."

A 71-year-old pensioner (Ulaanbaatar 2003 Bu016) recalls past troubles, saying, "During socialism, the young university graduates were sent to work in remote aimags and sumons by the state with no regard to their wishes or requests. Now, the situation is completely different."

A retired herder living on the outskirts of Ulaanbaatar refers to Naadam, the celebration of National Independence Day (July 11). People all over the country celebrate with several days of horse racing, archery and wrestling contests. While the archery and wrestling competitors are adults, children ages 5 to 13 race the horses. The herder also mentions that even a cleaner—someone who sweeps the sidewalks and streets or washes down the staircases in the many apartment buildings—could support his or her family on a socialist salary. The notion that the main breadwinner should be able to support an entire family is found in Adam Smith's *Wealth of Nations* (1976 [1776]:76).

Human rights. Democracy means one can live at his/her own discretion. A herder can have several horses and prepare them for racing at the Naadam horse racing competition. Under socialism, since few herders owned up to 25 horses and camels, many herders were not able to take part in horse racing. On the other hand, a cleaner used to earn 180 *togrog* [Mongolian money] per month during socialism, which was enough to meet the needs of the whole family. Now one's salary can't meet even his/her own needs.

Not only do the Mongolians we interviewed repudiate socialism for blocking their human rights, but they also believe that one needs democracy to have human rights. Chapter 2 of the 1992 Constitution (Mongolia 1992) guarantees the Universal Declaration's political and economic rights and freedoms. All legal residents are "equal before the law" and are protected from discrimination (Article 14). The right to life, citizenship, private property, employment choice and mobility within the country and abroad are specifically named (Articles 15–16). Political rights include freedom of association, fair trial and so on (Article 16). This may look like a laundry list, but the people we interviewed see each right as a rejection of a difficult past and a promise for a future of freedom.

In 1999 I volunteered for Oyunbileg Erendo (nickname Oyuna), National Project Coordinator for the United Nations. She was responsible for implementing the UNDP programs in six of Mongolia's aimags (August 10, 1999, fieldnotes). My reward for helping her was to travel to Mandalgov', the capital of Dundgov' Aimag in the Gobi Desert, with a small group of Mongolian professors working for UNDP. Their mission was to teach the lowest level of government administrators, the *bag* governors, about democracy and market economy.

At lunch on the second day, I asked the bag governors seated with Oyuna and me to explain what people in the bags want regarding democracy (Figure 3.2). Their first answer was human rights. But they added that bag people did not really know what that means. The bag governors were taking this training so that they could explain democracy and human rights to their constituents (August 17, 1999, fieldnotes).

Figure 3.2 Bag governors eagerly learning democracy and market economy in a UNDP training program, Mandalgov'. (Paula L.W. Sabloff, 1999)

Some of our research participants say that human rights are the greatest achievement of democracy or that human rights cannot survive without democracy. The actual numbers are presented in Table 3.1.

The numbers and percentages in the table may look low to you. That is because the interviews were open-ended, not multiple-choice. People had to think of these ideas themselves. Probably the people interviewed value human rights, but they just did not think of them at the time of the interview. Therefore, we would not expect even the majority of the people to say the same thing.

The last column in Table 3.1 is empty. This suggests no significant change from 1998 to 2003 in people's thinking. This makes sense as similar percentages are found in each row. I will explain the last column when we get to Table 3.2 and the column becomes meaningful.

Quotations from the interviews instantiate the numbers in Table 3.1. For example, a young man from Khovd with a high school diploma (Khovd 1998 Bd018) says, "Man has natural [inalienable] rights. Only as a result of democracy can people enjoy their natural rights. Therefore I think that the main feature of democracy is to grant people human rights. You do not need higher education to agree." This 17-year-old high school graduate (Ulaanbaatar 1998 Ch050) says, "In a democracy people are provided with human rights. The state has to protect people's human rights." A Muslim businessman from Khovd Aimag (Khovd 2003 Ns053) says, "Freedom exists to a certain extent in any society. However, I think that democratic society implements human rights in the real sense."

This idea is not unique; in a very interesting book, *Democracy Is a Discussion*, leaders from the former Soviet Union write that one of the purposes of democracy is to preserve human rights (Myers 1998).

Several interviewees believe that democracy cannot survive without human rights. A woman holding a baccalaureate and working for the

Table 3.1 Mentions of human rights attributes, 1998 and 2003[a]

Human rights are:	1998 Total = 867		2003 Total = 416		Significant difference between years
	N	%	N	%	χ^2
Highly valued	330	38.1	142	34.1	
Causally linked to democracy[b]	249	28.7	131	31.5	
Not realized during socialism	62	7.2	20	4.8	
Total (Tables 3.1 and 3.3)	332	38.3	150	36.1	

In a two-tailed chi-square (χ^2) test with 1 df, *$p \leq .05$, **$p \leq .01$ and ***$p \leq .001$.
[a]By number, percent and Pearson's chi-square test.
[b]Either democracy causes human rights to be institutionalized or human rights bring democracy to a country.

government (Khovd1998 Ns019) says, "Democracy won't develop without loyalty to [international] human rights norms." Others remind the researchers (who are fellow countrymen) that human rights are in the 1992 constitution and the laws. Some examples are as follows:

> There is a constitutional guarantee of inalienable human rights such as freedom of speech, of belief, of having personal values and beliefs, freedom to publish, etc. (Ulaanbaatar 1998 Ts010)

> The difference between democracy and socialism is that the laws [in a democracy] secure human rights. (Khovd 1998 Ns048)

> The Constitution has changed. Human rights are [now] guaranteed by law. (Ulaanbaatar 2003 Na058)

Why tell the researchers something they already know? For one thing, people are using the researchers to admonish the government that it has the obligation to uphold human rights. It is clear from a recent report to the United Nations that Mongolia has not yet met international or even national requirements in several areas. According to the 2010 Universal Periodic Review of Mongolia (United Nations 2010), citizens are still subject to arbitrary arrest. The news media are not yet free of political control as journalists are still liable to be subject to harassment, libel suits or even arbitrary arrest. The right to work has not stopped discrimination by gender, age or social status. Several women professionals I interviewed said that women, children, ethnic minorities and others face discrimination and harassment (Zanaa Jurmed interview August 11, 1999; Burmaa Radnaa interview September 15, 2003). Environmental degradation (polluted air and rivers, depleted soil and so on) is causing health problems, especially for neonates born in the mining regions. While no country has a perfect record on these issues, Mongolian citizens expect their government to do better.

I think there is another reason that research participants mention the constitution and laws. They are legitimizing their desire for human rights by saying the Mongolian government is responsible for enforcing laws already on the books. A few also say that other democratic countries enforce human rights laws and Mongolia should also.

What about the rest of the people interviewed? Do they say the same as the people quoted here? I ran the same attributes of human rights through Pearson's two-tailed chi-square test again, this time testing for variability within common demographic categories each year (Table 3.2). The rows with

Table 3.2 Significant differences within demographic categories concerning human rights attributes, 1998 and 2003[a]

Human rights are:	1998				2003			
	Highly valued	Linked with democracy	Not realized during socialism	Total	Highly valued	Linked with democracy	Not realized during socialism	Total
Location	***	*		***	*			
Residence	***	*		***				
Gender	*	*		*		*		
Age group								
Education	***	*		***	***	***		***
Occupation	***	*	*	***				*
Ethnicity		**	*	*				

In a two-tailed chi-square test, *p≤.05, **p≤.01, and ***p≤.001. Location, residence and gender=1 df; age group, education and ethnicity=3 df; occupation=5 df for 1998 and 6 df for 2003.
[a]See Table A.1 in Appendix for details.

stars suggest significant change between 1998 and 2003. Here 'significant' means that when the numbers of people who mention each characteristic are run through a statistical test (Pearson's two-tailed chi-square test), the difference between the 1998 and 2003 numbers is not random. Three stars mean stronger significance than one or two. That is, there is a higher probability that the significance reflects true differences in the population.

I used basic demographic categories, delineating the subcategories with Mongolian colleagues to be sure they were meaningful for the population we studied. They are location (Khovd or Ulaanbaatar), residence (urban or rural), gender, age group, formal education completed, occupation and ethnic identity. I found some variability. For age group, for example, I visited the United Nations advisor to the National Statistics Office of Mongolia in 1998 but found no help. The project researchers, some of whom were faculty, helped me group people by age according to life experience. People over 55 might be working, but they also qualify for a pension from the government. Thus, they have a baseline of security. People 40–55 and 27–39 were educated during socialism but are in the workforce now. The youngest group (18–26) lived through the Democratic Revolution and probably had some education in the post-socialist period.

For formal education completed, the lowest and highest education levels corresponded to 'less than high school' and 'baccalaureate or higher.' We aggregated the people with high school and vocational diplomas because they belonged to the same age group. After eighth grade, students could either go to high school to prepare for university education or to vocational school to train for jobs in skilled manual labor (to become plumbers or electricians, for example). After high school, students could go to university or to technical college, which trained highly skilled workers such as nurses, elementary school and kindergarten teachers, entry-level accounting, construction master and so on. This was the old socialist system. Now the technical colleges have become universities (July 25, 1998, fieldnotes).

The stars in this and the following tables imply significant (nonrandom) variability in 1998 and 2003. I have placed complete tables in the Appendix. These include the raw numbers and percentages of people in each subcategory who mention a particular attribute in the tables. That way, you may see for yourself that people's ideas do sometimes vary by demographic category.

In 1998, the first and fourth columns show significant variability in all demographic categories save age groups. This means that according to Pearson's two-tailed chi-square test, it is reasonable to assume that there is real—not random—variability between demographic subcategories. Therefore, we can say that people do not think alike in 1998. However, there is less indication of variability in 2003, as evidenced by fewer cells with stars (except for education level completed). Perhaps Mongolians are moving toward a more uniform view of human rights in its relation to democracy.

Table 3.2 indicates that we can say with some assurance that people's association of human rights with democracy is not random. But it is not 'universal' either because there is statistically significant variability within certain demographic categories.

HUMAN RIGHTS INCLUDE POLITICAL AND ECONOMIC FREEDOMS, THE RIGHT TO PARTICIPATE IN GOVERNANCE AND EQUALITY

So far, we have examined people's association of democracy with human rights in general. We now turn to the components that have meaning for our research participants. You will see that the categories are the same as the ones used in the Universal Declaration. The first is political freedom. More people mention political freedom in conjunction with human rights than with any other attribute in 1998 (174, or 20.1 percent). In 2003, the number drops (to 42, or 10.1 percent), and economic freedom becomes the most discussed topic.

Table 3.3 shows strong change in people's pairing of human rights with political and economic freedoms from 1998 to 2003. This holds for equality as well. But mention of the right to participate in governance and religious freedom is about the same in both years.

I had the opportunity to interview Khashuu Naranjargal in 2003 (September 9). She had been a TV journalist and deputy director of the government-run station from the late socialist period through the transition

Table 3.3 Mentions of human rights subdomains, 1998 and 2003[a]

	1998 Total=867		2003 Total=416		Significant difference between years
Human rights include:	N	%	N	%	χ^2
Political freedoms	174	20.1	42	10.1	***
Economic freedoms	156	18.0	118	28.4	***
Right to participate in governance	77	8.9	31	7.5	
Religious freedom	35	4.0	24	5.8	
Equality	27	3.1	29	7.0	**

In a two-tailed chi-square (χ^2) test with 1 df, $*p \leq .05$, $**p \leq .01$ and $***p \leq .001$.
[a]By number, percent and Pearson's chi-square test.

to democracy. In 1999 she formed an NGO called Globe International out of concern for political freedoms, especially a free press. During the interview, she said that when someone had requested the list of students studying abroad who had government support, he was told that it is a state secret. She added,

> This is the environment in which such strange stories exist. This is how all information is protected. Our political culture includes the idea that a state is not a state if it can't protect secret information. So freedom of expression is limited, more limited than before because this government doesn't accept information as a human right. This government [MPRP] ignores the opinions of others; it doesn't accept others.

Then she said, "Democratic culture will take time, but it needs a government committed to doing this. The public can't be promoted if the government is against human rights."

While I could have listed pages of people's comments, I give just a few examples. Some interviewees seem to treat freedom as a synonym for human rights. They talk as if 'human-rights-and-freedoms' were one indivisible phrase. And they often name personal, political and economic human rights together.

> In democracy, human rights are highly respected and protected by laws. To mention some human rights: the rights to elect and be elected, to hold meetings, freedom of speech, the right to publish, etc. (Khovd 1998 Nd031)

> I prefer to live in a democratic country because the economic and social system is more progressive than other societies; there is respect for human rights and freedoms; and there is a free market [economy]. (Khovd 2003 Bd057)

> "Human rights" is a broad concept. It means the right to assemble, criticize state bodies and bring such state bodies before the court, education and employment. In a democratic society, freedoms and human rights are significantly ensured. Presently, people are deprived of the right of assembly in Mongolia. (Ulaanbaatar 2003 Bu059)

Following political freedoms, people talk about economic freedoms most. Our interviewees sorely missed economic freedoms during the socialist years, and many considered economic freedoms to be the core of human rights. That is why they named specific economic rights when mentioning human rights. Two Khovd inhabitants say human rights include the freedom to trade, to own private property, to sell their produce and "become rich and not work" (Khovd 1998 Gn019 and Ns047). A pension-age woman in Ulaanbaatar (1998 Mh024) says that the right to travel abroad "is part of human rights."

By 2003, people realized that the government was phasing in human rights at a slower pace than most wanted. The scheduled May (2003) transfer of land from the state to individuals highlighted some of the government abuses. Undarya, then a Mongolian graduate student in political science at Rutgers University, sent an email reporting on an Open Forum of Human Rights NGOs that took place in Ulaanbaatar November 25, 2002 (email December 2, 2002). More than 300 participants met to discuss government violations of human rights, "including the intimidation of farm workers and their families, police attempts to prevent farm workers from entering the city, excessive use of force by the State in dispersing peaceful demonstrations, illegal detentions of citizens, journalists and house arrests of the opposition party office, etc."

The Open Forum "demanded that the President, Prime-Minister and Parliament take immediate corrective measures.... The Petition to the Parliament also demanded that the Parliament enter open negotiations with the members and supporters of the Movement for the Just Privatization of Land on the land privatization law and involve human rights NGO activists as observers and/or facilitators." See Chapter 6 for more details about this period.

What are economic freedoms that are also human rights to the Mongolians? A 40-year-old university graduate working for the government in Khovd (2003 Bd045) says, "The right to work, to be healthy, to be protected [by the state], to study, etc., are human rights." A university student (Khovd 2003 Bj016) suggests a different population that benefits from human rights: "Our women have begun earning money as prostitutes not only in our country but also abroad. They consider it as a human right."

Following political and economic freedom is the right to political participation. Some people associate this right with human rights (77 [8.9 percent] in 1998; 31 [7.5 percent] in 2003). I include in this concept the right to speak out in the press, that is, to publish one's ideas in the press or through other means (radio, TV, books, pamphlets and so on). Two people who mention different aspects of political participation are young city women. The first from Khovd is 17 (1998 Nd025). She says, "The clearest evidence that people enjoy human rights is the fact that one can elect a candidate who is ideologically similar to one's own thoughts." The second (Khovd

2003 Bj057). Unlike the first, she stopped school after primary school. "The human rights of each citizen are fully protected in a democratic country. For example, everyone has the right to ... go on a hunger-strike, take part in public meetings, etc."

A Kazakh, also with a primary school education (Khovd 1998 Ns050), compares the current situation with socialism: "People were forced to vote for one party—for candidates from this party. Today as a result of democracy the electoral system has changed fundamentally. To elect and be elected became a human rights issue."

One freedom we would consider highly important is the right to privacy. Among our research participants, no one associated the right to privacy with human rights in 1998; only one did in 2003. A 71-year-old woman with a high school education (Ulaanbaatar 2003 Bu022), said, "Basic human rights were seriously violated during socialism. Now the state doesn't meddle in the personal life of an ordinary citizen."

Although only a small percent mention religious freedom at all (4.0 in 1998 and 5.8 in 2003), religious practice is on the rise in Mongolia, and some consider it a human right. One is a young professor at Khovd University (Khovd 1998 Nd038), who describes human rights by saying, "Now it became possible to enjoy human rights such as ... the right to practice one's religion. In the former society [socialist period], human rights depended much on political ideology. [But human rights] are one of the conditions for building a just society." Another young person, this time a government worker and probably a professor also (Khovd 2003 Bd029), says, "A person is free to practice any religion without violation to their human rights."

When a government discriminates against someone because of race, gender, income and so forth, equality becomes a human rights issue. Liberty Center, a Mongolian human rights organization, reported such discrimination in March 2003. Just as the government had authorized the occupants of state-owned apartments to be the private property of the occupants in the early 1990s, so it was getting ready to convert parcels of state land in and around urban centers into private property in May 2003. In 1992 citizens did not have to pay for the apartment or the land; they simply had to prove long-term occupation. In 2003 a person needed a certificate of occupation from the local authorities to claim a house or ger plot. The Liberty Center wrote that a Mr. Saintogtoh, a poor man whose family ger had stood close to the center of Ulaanbaatar for years, had been denied a certificate since 2000, although no reason had been given for the rejection.

"I did not have any failure in my registration or documentation or something else which would disqualify my application for land permission. I built up my dwelling according to the written permission of city architectural and planning authorities. Since September 2000, I have been constantly applying for getting the final permission form the district governor's office," said Saintogtoh in his second complaint to the MHRC.

Although 23 other families were allowed to keep their land in the area around Saintogtoh's, he was not. In February, the police and authorities kicked the family of 10 out of their ger and removed it from the area. Saintogtoh appealed to the Mongolian Human Rights Commission. The Commission then wrote to the local authorities, stating that this case was "a serious breach of basic human rights of Mr. Saintogtoh and they should reimburse his loss and give" him permission to the land. While the Liberty Center does not tell us the outcome, it does speculate that Saintogtoh was refused the certificate because the officials expected that particular plot to sell at a high price. (Liberty Center March 5, 2003)

Given people's concerns about equality, I am surprised that so few associate it with human rights. Only 27 (3.1 percent) in 1998 and 29 (7.0 percent) in 2003 mention them together. Still, each of the concepts (equality and human rights) is well represented, as you will see in Chapter 6. Even though she prefers socialism, a young unemployed woman with a high school diploma (Ulaanbaatar 1998 Ch029) says, "People have been given their human rights. They are equal before the law." An older man, an unskilled laborer (Ulaanbaatar 1998 Os038), adds, "Human rights mean ... no one may be discriminated against on the basis of gender, origin or religion." And another young woman includes the political dimension in her description of human rights by saying, "All members of society ... must not be discriminated against on the basis of ethnic origin, social status or sex. Everyone has the right to file a complaint to the state's ruling bodies and officials as well" (Ulaanbaatar 2003 Bu005).

Table 3.4, which presents the results of the chi-square test on demographic variables within years, shows less significant variation than is found in Table 3.2. Here, the biggest difference seems to be according to location. Perhaps this fits the US pattern that people 'within the Beltway' of Washington, D.C., are more involved in politics than people in the rest of the country.

78

Table 3.4 Significant differences within demographic categories concerning subdomains of human rights, 1998 and 2003[a]

Human rights include:	1998				2003			
	Political freedom	Economic freedom	Right to political participation	Equality	Political freedom	Economic freedom	Right to political participation	Equality
Location		**	*	**	*			
Residence								
Gender						*		
Age group		*				**		
Education		*						
Occupation								
Ethnicity	*		*					

In a two-tailed chi-square test, *p ≤ .05, **p ≤ .01, and ***p ≤ .001. Location, residence and gender = 1 df; age group, education and ethnicity = 3 df; occupation = 5 df for 1998 and 6 df for 2003.
[a]See Table A.2 in Appendix for details.

The final human right people discuss is what the Universal Declaration calls 'security of person.' In August 1999 I interviewed Chinchuluun,
Executive Director of the Women Lawyers' Association, an NGO working
for women's rights. She estimated that about half of the NGOs are women's
organizations concerned with women's issues. This is partly because women
are always active in social issues and partly because women suffer most from
injustice. Therefore, her NGO organizes training sessions for women lawyers
all over the country; these sessions range from human rights and women's
human rights to specific concerns such as domestic violence, child abuse and
sexuality (August 6, 1999, fieldnotes).

Zanaa Jurmed told me that the responsibility of CEDAW-Watch is to
make sure that discrimination in employment, economic opportunity and
human rights is not perpetrated against women—purposefully or inad-
vertently. It polls women and conducts training workshops. It also writes
recommendations to the government. She felt that the government was run
by men who don't understand that the laws they are passing violate women's
rights. For instance, the 1999 labor law prevented women from hard jobs and
allowed them the opportunity to care for their children. But the law also
restricted women's employment rights and political freedom. It stipulated
that mothers are responsible for the care of children less than two years of
age. Therefore maternity leave (with pay) is for two years per child. But men
are not responsible for their children. The result is that women are stuck at
home cooking and cleaning, with no status in the family. I learned from one
university rector that he tried not to hire young women because he didn't have
the funds to pay them for two years of maternity leave and also pay someone
else to teach their courses (August 11, 1999, fieldnotes).

Whereas the women heading NGOs were passionate about women's
rights (especially their 'security of person'), only a few interviewees discuss
the topic. One is a young woman in Khovd working for an NGO (Khovd
2003 Bj004). She says, "Under democracy, human rights are honored very
much, especially the right to security of life—in other words, the right to
exist." Another young woman, a government worker with a university degree
(Ulaanbaatar 2003 Bu001), agrees: "One must not harm the rights of others
when exercising his/her rights."

The last human rights mentioned are the socio-economic rights found in
the Universal Declaration but not in the US Constitution. Like other socialist countries, Mongolia's 1960 constitution promised its citizens the right to
work (and fair compensation for one's work), leisure and old-age pensions
and the right to free health care and education (Academy of Sciences MPR

1990:150–51). These rights were part of the Soviet ideology—the Marxist-Leninist philosophy that laborers control the government and therefore should benefit from the state's economic success (Lenin 1970 [1917]:111). The socialist government gradually bestowed these socio-economic rights on the people as the country's standard of living rose and the government could afford to give citizens free health care and education, daycare for infants through school-age children and summer camps for school-age children (Academy of Sciences MPR 1990: 256; Prof. Dr. Baysakh Jamsran, then Chair of the Department of International Relations and the Founding Dean of the College of International Relations in the National University of Mongolia, personal communication, on his visit to the University of Pittsburgh, 1994). Of course the 1960 constitution did not tell people that the government would determine the type and level of education they would receive or that they would have no choice of employment. A few people in 1998 said that they miss those benefits, especially universal free education, but no one did in 2003.

The 1992 constitution includes such socioeconomic rights as 'a healthy and safe environment,' humane working conditions, good health and medical care, education, financial assistance when old or disabled and the right of mothers and children to state protection (Article 16, §§2, 4–7). In the early 1990s, circumstances caused the government to pull back on socioeconomic rights, a reversal of its former socialist priorities (see Chapter 6). Other Soviet countries stopped sending aid, and the trade network among the Soviet socialist nations (Council for Mutual Economic Assistance, called COMECON or CMEA) collapsed in June 1991 (Rossabi 2005:133). The government could no longer support the health, child-care and other programs that it had run during the last years of socialism. The food and clothing that had flowed from the former Soviet Union stopped. Grocery shelves were still practically bare when I visited in 1994.

When Western advisors recommended and the Mongolian government adopted economic 'shock therapy'—the replacement of the socialist command economy with a market economy by the immediate removal of all price controls and state subsidies as well as immediate trade liberalization, people had to stand on bread lines to feed their families (Tuya Altangerel 2001:6). Western advisors also encouraged the government to privatize as many industries as possible (William Bikales, personal communication 1998). By privatizing industries such as cashmere, cattle and copper, the government would gain immediate revenues and would soon be able to collect taxes from successful businesses. The result was that workers' income dropped precipitously. When hospitals and medical clinics also privatized, people who could no longer pay did not receive treatment. I heard of cases where women walked around with broken arms because they did not think they should take money away from their family to get the bones set.

The extreme deprivation and poverty resulting from a crashing GDP and shock therapy caused people to rethink their relation to the government, to each other and to survival. This new relationship is reflected in their characterization of human rights and their relation to democracy.

When discussing socio-economic rights, a few people use phrases that are holdovers from the socialist era, namely 'humane society' or 'generous, caring society.' These people miss the rights they had during the last years of socialism. Two interviewees separated by years and location reflect this perspective. The first is a young businessman with a baccalaureate (Ulaanbaatar 1998 Ts002). He says, "It seems as if human rights are always violated to some degree. There is no guarantee of medical treatment, food or health services [now]." The other is a young woman living in the countryside near Erdene Sum (Ulaanbaatar 2003 Bu039). She says, "One has the right to health and medical care, personal liberties and safety. However, human rights are not protected and honored in accordance with the laws in Mongolia" (Ulaanbaatar 2003 Bu039).

The most frequently mentioned socio-economic human right is access to education, which will be analyzed further in Chapter 6. The Mongolians I met considered education the best way to prepare for a capitalist economy, and so I found that many suggested education as a human right. For example,

People should enjoy the human right to be educated, to work and be healthy. In short, they should enjoy all political and economic rights as stated in the Human Rights declaration [the Universal Declaration]. (Khovd 1998 Nd039)

Human rights are limited. During socialism, the right to an education and to choose the place of residence was restricted. On the other hand, such rights may be restricted in a capitalist society due to financial constraints. (Ulaanbaatar 2003 Bu059)

HUMAN RIGHTS SATISFY DEEPLY HELD VALUES

Most of the quotations in this chapter intimate that the speakers highly value human rights. Why is this so? I believe that they see human rights resonate with deeper values. These include the desire to maintain their personal dignity, gain national dignity in the eyes of the international community and gain self-determination.

Mongolians' desire for personal dignity comes in part from wanting the right to self-determination. This is the underlying goal of the Universal Declaration and a major cultural theme for Mongolians. It motivates their anger toward socialism and their appreciation of democracy.

Table 3.5 suggests significant variation from 1998 to 2003 in personal dignity and self-determination. In the former, the numbers drop significantly, while in the latter, they rise. One would think the two ideas are related, but they do not seem to be.

This chapter has already covered people's attitudes toward human rights. However, I include a few more examples to emphasize the point that people use these freedoms to attain and maintain their personal dignity. I should make explicit that no one uses the term dignity, but you can see the idea behind the words. A 27-year-old Oirad on a fixed income (government worker; Khovd 2003 Bd034) says, "As a result of democracy, people have the opportunity to enjoy their human rights. That leads to a free state [i.e., free in one's body; a person controls his/her own self]." Another Khovd resident, this time a 40-year-old man in business for himself (2003 Gn022), adds, "Anyone can express himself through the mass media. It is one of the evidences of people enjoying human rights. In the former system, people couldn't publish and couldn't even speak freely." Finally, an unemployed Oirad woman with a high school diploma (Khovd 2003 Ns013) says, "Before we followed the guidelines of the higher institutions [the Communist Party and government officials]. Now under democracy we not only express our own attitudes freely but we also enjoy human rights."

Table 3.5 Mentions of deeply held values associated with human rights, 1998 and 2003[a]

	1998 Total = 867		2003 Total = 416		Significant difference between years
Human rights bring:	N	%	N	%	χ^2
Political freedoms	174	20.1	42	10.1	***
Personal dignity	220	25.4	72	17.3	***
National dignity	99	11.4	51	12.3	
Self-determination	26	3.0	30	7.2	***

In a two-tailed chi-square (χ^2) test with 1 df, *$p \leq .05$, **$p \leq .01$ and ***$p \leq .001$.
[a]By number, percent and Pearson's chi-square test.

To value personal dignity and freedom is not unique to Mongolians. Writing about the Russian 'democrats' (people dissatisfied with the Soviet government) he studied in the late 1980s, Lukin (200:183) writes,

> The authoritarian regime, or totalitarianism, in their view, began to distort the personality, depersonalized the human psyche, and transformed human individuals into slaves, slaves not only in terms of their social status, but conscious slaves who were satisfied with their subordinate position and considered it quite normal.

There is another cultural theme that crops up in the interviews. It is the idea that Mongolia will gain international stature or at least acceptance by upholding human rights. The argument goes like this: Human rights are associated with democracy and are, perhaps, the greatest achievement of democracy. Therefore, the practice of human rights is a sign that a country is democratic. Mongolia has human rights written into its 1992 constitution and laws. Therefore Mongolia is a modern democratic country and deserves the respect (and support) of other modern democratic countries.

Several people connect human rights and national dignity, but the person who stands out is Rinchinnyamyn Amarjargal. When I interviewed him (May 22, 1996, fieldnotes), he was president of the Economics College in Ulaanbaatar. He became a Member of Parliament, so his words have special import. Toward the end of the interview when we were just chatting, he said that democracy is the key to maintaining Mongolian independence, partly because he thinks the Western countries (Germany, France, Denmark, Great Britain and the United States) would not be interested in helping Mongolia if it did not turn toward democracy.

Some interviewees took Amarjargal's idea even further, saying that Mongolia has proven itself a modern, democratic nation because it subscribes to international standards of human rights. Therefore, it belongs in the international community. A middle-aged fellow with a baccalaureate and a government job (Ulaanbaatar 1998 Mh001) says, "Democratization of a country is measured by how the state respects human rights. The Mongolian Constitution states 18 rights of the people. It is in complete accordance with the International Human Rights Convention."

A young woman with a high school degree (Ulaanbaatar 1998 En033) says, "Democratic countries respect human rights. Our country is developing according to the democratic way. The law has already guaranteed human rights." In a similar vein, a pensioner with a university degree (Ulaanbaatar

Table 3.6 Significant differences within demographic categories regarding the association of deeply held values with human rights, 1998 and 2003[a]

Human rights bring:	1998			2003		
	Personal dignity	National dignity	Self-determination	Personal dignity	National dignity	Self-determination
Location		*	***	*		
Residence	*	**	*			
Gender	*					
Age group			***			
Education	*	*		*		
Occupation		*	***			
Ethnicity						

In a two-tailed chi-square test, *p≤.05, **p≤.01, and ***p≤.001. Location, residence and gender=1 df; age group, education and ethnicity=3 df; occupation=5 df for 1998 and 6 df for 2003.
[a]See Table A.3 in Appendix for details.

2003 Bu060) says, "I highly appreciate that a Human Rights Committee already exists in Mongolia."

The more I read through the interviews, the more I felt that Mongolians' real desire for democracy is to attain self-determination, the right to make their own decisions for their family and themselves. Here, a few people (26 [3.0 percent] in 1998 and 30 [7.2 percent] in 2003) consider self-determination to be a human right. One university student (Ulaanbaatar 1998 Tj030) sums up the sentiment when he says, "Human rights mean having freedom of choice when doing things. There is no control and no pressure over one's feelings and thoughts." Interestingly enough, all the respondents who invoke self-determination are university-educated and younger than 36.

Table 3.6 focuses on the deeply held values that correspond with human rights. The greatest variability occurs in people's desire for human rights in 1998. Again, location, occupation and residence exhibit more variability than other demographic categories in that year. And there is less variability in 2003 than in 1998.

HUMAN RIGHTS AND DEMOCRACY: DOES EVERYONE WANT THEM?

In her very interesting book on human rights, Alison Renteln reminds us that a concept can only be universal if everyone shares it (1990:51, 80–82). The quotations in this chapter show that Mongolians carve out their own sections of the Universal Declaration. For example, no one talks about women's rights as a human right. Among the people interviewed, there is some variability by demographics and by year. In short, the people interviewed do not share one view of human rights, even though Mongolia is a nation with a rather homogeneous population. Therefore, we have to conclude that people's ideas about human rights are not universal, even within one country.

The Mongolian case suggests that knowledge about human rights has the potential to become closer to universal than it is. Our interviewees' concept of human rights already closely corresponds to the Universal Declaration. They name the same attributes (for example, security of person and political freedoms) found in the Universal Declaration. And they do not add any new rights or freedoms, although the Universal Declaration is pretty comprehensive. Just as the Universal Declaration emphasizes personal and political freedoms and views human rights as a moral imperative, so do the Mongolians.

The tables in this chapter propose that there is more agreement among respondents in 2003 than 1998. This inclination toward a more 'universal' approach to human rights suggests two things. As international contact increases, people have the opportunity to learn more about international standards of human rights, especially the United Nations documents. And if it is true that people swing back and forth between universalism and relativism (culture-specific human rights; see Dembour 2001:56), then the Mongolians we worked with were clearly swinging toward universalism in reaction to the gap between socialist and democratic practices they had experienced.

What is the appeal of human rights? Renteln notes that although specific rights in the Universal Declaration are not universal, certain moral principles underlying these human rights seem to be so. She (1990:131–37) analyzes the human right of 'right to life' in view of the universal moral principle that life is, indeed, precious. Most preindustrial societies take only one life to replace one lost. If a member of one tribe kills a member of another, often the murderer's tribe pays 'blood money' in recompense or the victim's tribe has the right to kill only one member of the murderer's tribe.

In this chapter, I have found that Mongolians' attitudes toward human rights are deeply rooted in some underlying moral values. Especially important to our respondents are the desires for personal dignity, self-determination and national dignity. It is these deeply held desires that make human rights valuable to our research participants.

CHAPTER FOUR

Democracy Brings Political Freedom

There is an apocryphal story that after decades of psychoanalyzing women, Sigmund Freud asked on his deathbed, what do women want? I am tempted to start this chapter by asking, what do Mongolians want—from democracy? In 1998, 358 (41.3 percent) wanted political freedom; in 2003, 258 (62 percent) said the same, a significant increase from the base year of the study. The chi-square tests in Table 4.1 suggest that people's thinking is not uniform, even in Mongolia.

The numbers and percentages in Table 4.1 are much higher than the percentages for human rights (see Table 3.1). But political freedom *from what*? *To do what*? The quick answer to these questions is that people believe democracy brings freedom from oppression and government control. Democracy is like a *Star Wars* force field; it gives citizens a protective shield that government cannot penetrate. With democracy, citizens can speak their minds, practice their religion and stand up for their rights.

Political freedom also satisfies some underlying values or emotional needs. Just as human rights bestow personal and national dignity and self-determination on citizens, so political freedoms offer them personal dignity, self-determination and national democratic development. I think that the rising percentage of people who like democracy (178 [48.6 percent] in 1998 and 170 [72.6 percent] in 2003; see Sabloff 2012:60) means that it is satisfying some of these underlying values.

This chapter concerns Mongolians' answer to the question, *political freedom for what purpose?* Philosophers and political scientists split this question into two parts: *freedom from* and *freedom to* (Wenar 2005; Carter 2003); Mongolians do the same. After analyzing our research participants' desire for freedom from oppression and government control, we will look at some of the key political freedoms they mention—namely, free speech, religious freedom and the right to protect or defend one's rights. By examining each subdomain by people's hopes and fears and by placing them in historical-cultural context, we will be able to ascertain the underlying values people associate with political freedom. The statistical data will help us judge whether or not their attitudes toward political freedom are 'universal' even within Mongolian society.

THE DEMISE OF SOCIALISM ENDS OPPRESSION, WHILE THE RISE OF DEMOCRACY BRINGS POLITICAL FREEDOM

Personally, I don't often worry about oppression or think about democracy in that context, but 42 (4.8 percent) Mongolians do in 1998 and 14 (3.4 percent) in 2003 (Table 4.1). These mentions are lower than what I expected because Mongolians greatly value their freedom. It became a slogan of the early postsocialist years. Young people especially would challenge their parents or teachers by shouting, "Don't take away my freedom!" or "Don't repress me!" (Altangerel 2001:59). It got to the point that some people wondered if anarchy would replace Soviet-style repression. That is why I was surprised that few research participants mentioned freedom from oppression in conjunction with political freedoms.

How repressive was socialism? One evening in 1998 I met Seth Spaulding, an American professor who had spent more than a decade working for UNESCO, and two colleagues, a professor and a senior from the University of Osnabruck, Germany. All three were here to help revamp the Mongolian education system, which needed to prepare teachers and students for capitalism and democracy instead of socialism. Over a dinner of batter-fried fish at Oscar's, a German restaurant in Ulaanbaatar, Seth said that he first visited Mongolia in 1986. While in Khovd, he sat around a table with local MPRP leaders and others, and all were complaining about the government. So, he said, things were not as repressive here as Westerners think. Theodor Sander, the German professor, interrupted. Starting in the latter half of the 1960s, he said, people throughout Eastern Europe could see that repression was no longer as effective as before. By the 1980s—especially once Gorbachev introduced *glasnost'*—almost everyone in the communist countries was speaking out without fear. Theodor added that the multimedia communica-

Table 4.1 Mentions of political freedom attributes, 1998 and 2003[a]

	1998 Total=867		2003 Total=416		Significant difference between years
	N	%	N	%	χ^2
All political freedoms	358	41.3	258	62.0	***
Freedom from oppression	42	4.8	14	3.4	
Democracy brings political freedoms	79	9.1	60	14.4	**

In a two-tailed chi-square (χ^2) test with 1 df, $*p \leq .05$, $**p \leq .01$ and $***p \leq .001$.
[a]By number, percent and Pearson's chi-square test.

tions flowing through the Iron Curtain by then helped in breaking down the Berlin Wall (June 13, 1998, fieldnotes).

The Mongolians I talked with do not feel the same. They greatly resent the repressions and limitations imposed by the communist government and enforced by the NKVD, the secret police. Dr. Damdin Natsagdorj, the head of the Manba Datsun monastery and university of traditional healing, showed me the beautiful drawings of medicinal plants found in Mongolia. They were of the same quality as Audubon's birds. I asked him how he had learned herbal healing during socialism. He interviewed old people, the ones who held such knowledge in their heads, he replied. Then he said, during communism they were afraid to speak, so they would whisper to him (June 15, 1994, fieldnotes).

Some quotations from the interviews provide further evidence of repression. A woman between 27 and 36 (Khovd 1998 Bj016) compares communism and democracy, saying,

> A characteristic of democracy is life without purges or persecution. In a democratic country, people are not repressed. In socialism anyone who had attitudes different from the Communist Party's policy and protested their leadership was repressed severely. In the1930s these people were shot; later they were dismissed from their posts and sent to the countryside.... Now as glasnost' develops, people are provided with the right to express their own thoughts and attitudes freely.

An older Khovd herder (Khovd 1998 Bs046) emphasizes repression of speech when talking with one of the researchers. He remarks, "There were things we were allowed to say and things we were forbidden to say. It was forbidden to speak about Chinggis Khaan."

Not everyone feels that free speech is a good thing. A pensioner with a university degree (Ulaanbaatar 2003 Na002) says, "In the sessions of the Great Khural [Parliament] no one used to criticize others. But today members of parliament are practically quarrelling because of their different attitudes and opinions."

People say that freedom came not when the socialist system disintegrated but when democracy was institutionalized (79 [9.1 percent] in 1998; 60 [14.4 percent] in 2003; see Table 4.1). Causality is often hard to prove in social science. So many variables contribute to an outcome! But that does not stop people from believing that there is a direct causal link between two events. For our research participants, that link is between the advent of democracy and citizens' political freedom. Mongolians especially value free speech. One day, I was lunching with an academic friend, and he asked me the question that no foreigner wants to be asked: "What do you think of Mongolians?" I thought a bit and then replied, "Everyone is very smart and knows exactly how to fix the country's problems. And everyone knows that everyone else is wrong." "That's us!" he exclaimed. How frustrated people must have been during the socialist era when they had to guard what they said.

The phrasing of the next set of quotations suggests that people believe democracy causes political freedoms, especially free speech. A middle-aged Khalkh woman with a baccalaureate but not working (Khovd 1998 Bd038) simply states, "Thanks to democracy, we started to express our attitudes openly." A young Kazakh living in Khovd (Khovd 1998 Ns012) stresses the legal aspect of democracy, saying, "Democracy legally confirmed freedom of speech and the right to publish. That is the main feature of democracy." And another Kazakh, this one with a primary education and engaged in agriculture (Khovd 2003 Bj065), compares communism with democracy: "The right to freely express one's opinions and views was introduced into Mongolia by democracy. I used to be afraid of the Communist Party and state officials, and I could not freely voice my opinions when the communist regime was in power. Now, I have the right to criticize officials of any party or government organization."

Corollary to the idea that democracy causes political freedoms is people's view that the nation that secures political freedoms is truly democratic. We can see this in the frequently repeated phrase, 'political freedoms are an essential part of democracy.' A middle-aged businessman who only completed primary school (Khovd 1998 Bd017) says, "As a result of democracy, everyone has the right to express his own attitudes anywhere and anytime. Therefore I consider freedom of speech to be the essential feature of democracy." An unemployed youth (Khovd 2003 Ns072) echoes the businessman's sentiment, relating it to a deeper philosophical issue when he says, "A society that honors and respects the opinions of its citizens is a real democratic society."

Table 4.2 is a breakdown of some political freedoms by demographic category. It shows little variability by demographic category for 'freedom from oppression.' The 1998 exception is location. In 2003, people differ by occupation. Herders do not seem to associate political freedom with freedom from oppression, while NGO workers—usually young women—most frequently do.

Oddly enough, people under 40 connect democracy with freedom from oppression even more than older people, even though the difference is not

Table 4.2 Significant differences within demographic categories concerning attributes of political freedom, 1998 and 2003[a]

	1998			2003		
	All political freedom	Freedom from oppression	Democracy brings political freedom	All political freedom	Freedom from oppression	Democracy brings political freedom
Location	*					
Residence	***	*	*	**		
Gender						
Age group				**		**
Education	***			***		
Occupation	***				*	
Ethnicity			**	**		

In a two-tailed chi-square test, *p≤.05, **p≤.01, and ***p≤.001. Location, residence and gender=1 df; age group, education and ethnicity=3 df; occupation=5 df for 1998 and 6 df for 2003.
[a]See Table A.4 in Appendix for details.

statistically significant. Why would the young bring this up when they had grown up under a democratic government? Perhaps a contributing factor is that Mongolian children are often raised by their grandparents. Sometimes their parents study abroad. People told me of parents and kin studying art in Hungary, physics in the former East Germany and engineering in Irkutsk or other Russian cities. I think that some children whose parents were not educated abroad were raised by their grandparents while their parents worked in Ulaanbaatar and other industrial centers. So the children heard their elders' stories and internalized them.

DEMOCRACY MEANS FREE SPEECH AND FREE THINKING, RELIGIOUS FREEDOM AND THE RIGHT TO PROTECT ONE'S RIGHTS

Our respondents consider free speech the most important political freedom by far; it is the most mentioned of the political freedoms. In fact, there is a wide gap between free speech and religious freedom, the second-most mentioned freedom. In 1998, 334 (38.5 percent) mention free speech; 243 (58.4 percent) do so in 2003.

To our research participants, free speech includes the right to publish or just form one's own opinions. Free speech is a major indicator that the socialist era is over. It means that the secret police, the NKVD , can no longer limit the right to think or speak as people wish. Several pension-age people mentioned free speech as a right of everyone from basic citizens to the president (for example, Ulaanbaatar 1998 Mh016 and Khovd 2003 Ns070). One pensioner with a primary-school education (Khovd 1998 Bj070) said, "Today even I, a herder, can speak my thoughts about the government." A young businesswoman in Ulaanbaatar (1998 Mh050) added a legal dimension, saying, "Under democracy, everyone has the freedom to express his

Table 4.3 Mentions of major subdomains of political freedom, 1998 and 2003[a]

	1998 Total=867		2003 Total=416		Significant difference between years
	N	%	N	%	χ^2
Free speech	334	38.5	243	58.4	***
Freedom of religion	65	7.5	61	14.7	***
The right to protect one's rights	9	1.0	5	1.2	

In a two-tailed chi-square (χ^2) test with 1 df, *p≤.05, **p≤.01 and ***p≤.001.
[a]By number, percent and Pearson's chi-square test.

opinions. One can discredit the president and the prime minister in the newspapers and get away with it without any punishment."

Aside from the formal interviews, several people told me that they were not allowed to talk about Chinggis Khaan during socialism. The *Secret History of the Mongols* was taught as literature but not as history. In Khovd, Dr. Baasandorj, then Chairman of the History Department, said that Chinggis Khaan was totally taboo as a political subject because communism is completely against nationalism and Chinggis Khaan is the one who made Mongolia a nation. To avoid trouble, parents and grandparents rarely spoke of him to their children (July 8, 1998, fieldnotes).

Free speech becomes valuable when you do not have it. It affects so much of your behavior. When I first met Mongolian officials visiting the United States and tried to interview them in 1994, they spoke under their breath as if they were afraid to speak out loud. I feared that I would never be able to hear what they said or record their language so that I could learn it (at the time, I could not find books or recordings in the United States). But by 1996 I found that people spoke freely even in their home country. One example is from a middle-aged businesswoman (Ulaanbaatar 1998 Mh050): "In a democratic country, the law must protect people from oppression or discrimination based on their views and opinions."

Closely related to free speech is the notion of a free press, meaning all forms of media (television, radio and now phone and the Internet). The MPRP controlled the media during socialism (see Chapter 2). But the new constitution and a 1998 law guaranteed freedom of the media (see Article 16§10). The people interviewed that year discuss the importance of free media as a political freedom. For example, a 40–55 year-old Oirad with a baccalaureate (Khovd 1998 Bd015) said, "Thanks to democracy, the mass media became free. As a result, people can now obtain necessary information. Therefore I consider freedom of the mass media a feature of democracy." Comparing the press under socialism and democracy, another Khovd resident (1998 Bj011) says, "Before we had very few newspapers like *Unen,* which published articles on government policies. And it was impossible to express your own attitudes and thoughts. But today people are provided with the right to publish freely."

Of course, some point out that free media are not always a good thing. Some, like a young Oirad businesswoman (Khovd 1998 Bj003), denigrated the newspapers. She said, "Now we have many newspapers. I think they write what they wish. But it seems to me that they publish too much inappropriate material." An even younger person, a 17-year-old student (Khovd 1998

Bj027), complains, "Nowadays newspapers publish false and slanderous materials. I think it is wrong."

One day I was lunching at Millie's, the major gathering place for expats (ex-patriots—people from other countries living in Mongolia). Tuya and Clyde Goulden joined me at my table. Tuya is a native but lives in the United States as she is married to Clyde, who is the Director of the Institute for Mongolian Biodiversity and Ecological Studies at the Academy of Natural Sciences, Philadelphia. They return to Mongolia every summer where Clyde carries out ecological fieldwork near Lake Khovsgol. Tuya works on the project and visits with her family. At lunch they both remarked that the Mongolian press is too fragmented to help build democracy. Instead of a few good papers, there are so many that there are not enough reporters to go around or money to pay them well. As a result, they publish rumors and never check their sources (July 23, 1998, fieldnotes).

The situation grew worse by 2003. When the MPRP regained control of parliament in 2000, it stifled the media. During those years, I was lucky to meet with Khashuu Naranjargal (interview conducted September 9, 2003; see Figure 4.1). After years of working for the government TV station and after some time studying in England, she founded an NGO, Globe International, in 1999.[1] The NGO's purpose is to help Mongolians transition from seeing themselves as serving the government (as they did under socialism) to seeing the government as serving the people (as people do in a democracy). She is doing this by helping to strengthen the media and arts. "Mongolians need information to make them powerful, active citizens," she said. "This will not happen as long as the political parties own and control the news."

She went on to say that a group of lawyers found that 51 of the 91 laws related to the media need to be amended so that they no longer restrict freedom of expression and the media. Instead of a free press, the current MPRP government was suing 83 journalists for defamation of particular government officials. Another NGO, Liberty Center, wrote about one such case to its email list (2003):

Mr. Dashrentsen Gombo, 42, a journalist who investigated where did 400 million tugriks [togrog] go from [the] state budget is now accused [of the] crime of "defamation and libel" according to the complaint submitted by the Mongolian People's Revolutionary Party and some state officials. His case [was] created by the Police three months ago and now the case is at a Prosecutor. Mr. Dashrentsen anticipates 6–8 months of imprisonment or [a] fine. In

Figure 4.1 Naranjargal Khashkhuu, President and CEO of Globe International. (Tsogtbayar Namsrai, 2000)

addition to it he is threatened to pay 300 million tugriks—equal to his salary of 300 years which ruling ex-communist party demands from him. . . .

In September 2002, while curiously investigating where millions of togrogs from the state budget went, Mr. Dashrentsen concluded that the non-interest loan of 200 million [togrog] each provided to few companies could have been used for private interests of company owners including Vice Minister of that time. And he wrote a lengthy article "Wholesale Network meant to be Wholemoney Bribary" [sic].

Government control of the media does not seem to influence the ideals of our 2003 respondents—just their disgust. Some compare the 2003 situation to an ideal democracy. When a pension-aged government worker in

Ulaanbaatar (2003 Bu014) says, "The mass media are not subject to any form of censorship in a democratic society," he is stating a democratic ideal. Other people limit their comments to the situation in Mongolia. An 18-year-old herder from Chandmani Sum (Khovd 2003 Ns046) complains, "The press is not sufficiently free today; one-party propaganda dominates. The power of the MPRP is overwhelming." Meanwhile, another Khovd fellow, a businessman (2003 Bj028), mentions the problems of an open press, just as people in 1998 had: "A person has the right to publish anything, but sometimes it is too open. I don't like it that tabloids are on the increase because they propagate mostly crime, theft and gossip."

After the desire for free speech, including free media, people mention religious freedom most (65 [7.5 percent] in 1998 and 61 [14.7 percent] in 2003; see Table 4.3). In Mongolia, Tibetan Buddhism was encouraged during the Manchu Dynasty, but religion was suppressed in socialist times. The socialist government destroyed almost all of the monasteries and banned public religious ceremonies. It executed the upper-class lamas and dismissed the lower-class ones, dispersing them into the general population. Despite great pressure, many people maintained their religion secretly at home. When I asked one interviewee how she knew Buddhist customs, her simple answer was, "Granny, and my great-granny" who lived to 94 (April 26, 1996, fieldnotes). Others also learned Buddhism or even shamanism from their grandparents, said Baasandorj (July 8, 1998, fieldnotes; see Figure 4.2).

Figure 4.2 A shaman performs a curing ceremony at Mother Rock. (Paula L.W. Sabloff, 2000)

With the advent of democracy, religion was allowed once again. Some people remained atheists, but others started practicing Tibetan Buddhism again. In 1994 I visited Gandan Monastery in central Ulaanbaatar with some American colleagues. It was the only monastery allowed to stay open during socialism. Sitting on a little orange-painted stool in front of a small ger was an old lama with a large round lump on his forehead (see Figure 4.3). He was collecting money to rebuild an 80-foot-high golden statue of Avalokiteshvara-Janraiseg. The original statue had been melted down for bullets in World War II. Along with my American colleagues, I made a contribution. Two years later, the new statue was in place. By 2003, several new monasteries had opened in Ulaanbaatar.

In Khovd, the Kazakh people practiced Islam. Nyamdavaa, then Rector of the Khovd branch of the National University of Mongolia, took me to visit a Kazakh ger just outside of town in 1998. It was taller than the Mongol gers and the inside walls were lined with embroidered hangings made by the women, something Mongolian women do not do (see Figure 4.4). The family members greeted me and sat me on pillows in the place of honor opposite the door. The father told me that during socialism they had been given a copy of

Figure 4.3 Lama collecting money to rebuild the central statue of Migjid Janraisig (Eye-opening Avalokiteshvara, the Buddha of compassion) in Gandan Monastery, Ulaanbaatar. (Paula L.W. Sabloff, 1994)

Figure 4.4 A Kazakh family in their ger, Khovd, 1998. The father was working for the government. (Paula L.W. Sabloff, 1998)

the Koran translated into Russian. But now they were truly free to practice Islam. In fact, his nephews were studying the Koran in Istanbul, Turkey (July 8, 1998, fieldnotes), supported by Turkish funding.

Some Mongolians, especially the young, accepted Christianity. I think that its attraction was three-fold. First, some believe that in order to succeed in the globalized market economy it makes sense to adopt the whole Western package—not just capitalist ideology but Christian theology, too. They associate Christianity with economic success. Second, proselytizing religions such as American Mormons and Korean Protestants sent missionaries to Mongolia immediately following the Democratic Revolution. Not all, but some posed as English-language teachers and entered the schools. They provided services that the state had once supplied but no longer could: after-school care, English-language training, sports programs and so on. One distraught parent said that his fifth-grade child came home from school one day and said that a missionary group had come to his elementary school. The Americans told the students that anyone who converted would become rich (May 6, 1996, fieldnotes). In a poor country, that is hard to pass up. I do not know the motivation of one 19-year-old Ulaanbaatar resident (2003 Na050), but his conversion seems sincere, for he says, "Anyone is free to choose any religion. I have believed in Christianity since 2001. My brother and sister also believe in Christianity."

Yet another perspective on the adoption of Christianity comes from religion scholars who have said that in Asia, people borrow from many religions to 'hedge their bets.' That is, to be sure that you are covered, you pray to the deities of several religions rather than just one. So the Mongolians simply added another religion to their mix. This concept is reflected in the interview of a 28-year-old businessman (Ulaanbaatar 2003 Bu028): "Although Buddhism is the traditional religion of Mongolia, nowadays, one can practice Christianity and Islam in the country. For example, I am a Buddhist, but I can practice Christianity if there are some teachings that attract me. This means that any religion may have some good teaching."

Buddhists and even atheists sometimes interweave shamanist practices with their religion. Shamanism is the ancient worship of natural objects such as mountains and wild animals combined with the belief that shamans (women and men) have the ability to resolve life's problems, especially illness, when they contact the spirits through trance. Along the roads are shrines, called *ovoo*, at the top of every hill. An ovoo is a pile of loose stones shaped in a cone (see Figure 4.5). It is usually decorated with the *khadag*, the long sky-blue scarf in silk or polyester that symbolizes respect. I have seen money, sticks and crutches placed on ovoos. These shrines are shamanic in origin but have been incorporated into Tibetan Buddhist practice in Mongolia. Sometimes even atheists will exit their car at an ovoo and walk around it three times in a clockwise direction. When I asked some atheist friends why they do this, they have said they do it to thank the spirits for getting them from one place to another. But I could never decide if they were sincere or if they were showing the foreigners a Mongolian custom.

I have not separated people's attitudes toward religion into the 'freedom from' and 'freedom to' categories, as they frequently appear together. However, this structure is evident in the interviews. The first comment associated with religious freedom, of course, is how much better democracy is from socialism. A 40-something Oirad with a primary education (Khovd 1998 Bd026) implies the contrast between socialism and democracy: "Democracy respects religion; it doesn't repress religion, and it respects the right to practice religion in reality. Therefore, the most important trait of democracy is respect for religion." A herder living in the Khovd countryside (1998 Bs046) is more specific, saying, "During socialism we were afraid to invite the lamas to pray for us. Now we can. We can also worship a mountain openly." Five

Figure 4.5 An ovoo draped in silk ceremonial scarves. These ceremonial rock piles usually sit alongside a road between two valleys. This one sits beside a natural spring in Khovd. Notice the permafrost ground behind it. (Paula L.W. Sabloff, 2003)

years later, a pensioner (Ulaanbaatar 2003 Ay031) adds, "In the old days, we hid if we wanted to see a lama. It was especially forbidden to members of the Communist Party."

Another recurring theme regarding religion is that a democratic government must honor people's rights, including the right to practice religion as they wish. An older businesswoman in Ulaanbaatar (1998 Os060) says, "The constitution provides for freedom of religion, and the government respects this right in practice. Because of democracy, many different religious groups exist. The law does not prohibit proselytizing."

After religious freedom, very few people mention the right to defend their rights. I doubt that I would think of adding the defense of personal rights to my list of democratic attributes. Most of the people interviewed did not include it either (1.0 percent in 1998; 1.2 percent in 2003). But the very mention of having the right to protect one's rights made me think that it is a critical part of democracy, especially for a former satellite of the Soviet Union. They are still concerned that their rights might be taken away. Most of the quotations I found come from 1998. I present them here so that you know they are not idiosyncratic or limited to one demographic group. However they are all from 1998:

> Any party, force or individual has the right to hold a demonstration in order to protect their own interests. (Khovd 1998 Gn040; a 27–39 year-old urban Khalkh, a government worker, with a baccalaureate)

> Human rights. The realization of free speech, the right to express one's own thoughts and the right to protect one's own rights according to the United Nations is a feature of democracy. (Khovd 1998 Ns052, a Kazakh woman of the same age and education working in agriculture)

> People have the right to freedom of speech and the right to defend their interests. (Ulaanbaatar 1998 Ch026, a 20-year-old Buriat with a high school diploma still studying in the capital)

> By taking part in elections, people choose the delegates who protect their interests and rights. (Ulaanbaatar 1998 Tj023, a student, age 20, working on her baccalaureate)

In Table 4.4, people vary by residence, age, education and occupation for free speech in both years. Again, the younger people, who cluster in the urban

Table 4.4 Significant differences within demographic categories concerning major subdomains of political freedom, 1998 and 2003[a]

	1998			2003		
	Free speech	Religious freedom	Right to protect one's rights	Free speech	Religious freedom	Right to protect one's rights
Location		***				
Residence	***				**	
Gender						
Age group	*				**	
Education	***				***	*
Occupation	***					
Ethnicity			*		**	

In a two-tailed chi-square test, *p≤.05, **p≤.01, and ***p≤.001. Location, residence and gender=1 df; age group, education and ethnicity=3 df; occupation=5 df for 1998 and 6 df for 2003. [a]See Table A.5 in Appendix for details.

centers and often have higher levels of education than the older interviewees, seem more attuned to free speech than their elders.

Religious freedom and the right to protect one's rights exhibit little variability, partly because the counts are so low. Often only one person in a category talks about this right.

WHAT ARE POLITICAL FREEDOMS FOR? ALIGNING UNDERLYING VALUES WITH BEHAVIOR

Obviously, political freedom is an end in itself. So are its subdomains of free speech, a free press, religious freedom and the right to defend one's rights. But Mongolians add another reason for wanting political freedoms. The underlying values—the desires for personal dignity, self-determination and living in a true democracy—are partly satisfied by the practice of political freedoms.

Political freedoms bestow dignity on people. I found the notion of personal dignity in 273 (31.5 percent) of the 1998 interviews and 215 (51.7 percent) of the 2003 quotations regarding political freedom. Personal dignity is visible when people talk about doing things 'without fear,' such as an unskilled worker in Khovd (1998 Bs027): "Now at any meeting people can express themselves without fear from their bosses."

Table 4.5 denotes a significant rise in the association of political freedom with personal dignity but not with self-determination. National dignity is not included here, as it is in the preceding chapter, because so few people link it with political freedom. Instead, I included the development of democracy, which seemed more relevant to political freedom.

Personal dignity also means that people respect each other and the government respects them as well. A young teacher (Ulaanbaatar 1998 Ch032) gives voice to the former, saying, "People have a right to get educated, to their beliefs, etc., and they must respect others' thoughts and opinions." While

Table 4.5 Mentions of underlying values associated with political freedom, 1998 and 2003[a]

	1998 Total = 867		2003 Total = 416		Significant difference between years
	N	%	N	%	χ^2
Personal dignity	273	31.5	215	51.7	***
Self-determination	18	2.1	11	2.6	
Democratic development	17	2.0	9	2.2	

In a two-tailed chi-square (χ^2) test with 1 df, *p≤.05, **p≤.01 and ***p≤.001.
[a]By number, percent and Pearson's chi-square test.

another young woman (Ulaanbaatar 2003 Bu005) mentions the latter: "The dignity of every citizen must be respected by the state."

Mongolians imply the desire for personal dignity when they talk about 'no discrimination.' An example comes from a 17-year-old student who had recently completed high school (Ulaanbaatar 1998 Ts041). A member of the majority ethnic group, the Khalkh, he still said, "The state shall show no discrimination based on which religion one belongs to."

Political freedoms also give people the space for self-determination. I asked Burmaa Radnaa, the founder of the Mongolian NGO, Women for Social Progress, what she thought of democracy in Mongolia (interview conducted September 15, 2003; see Figure 4.6). She explained the connection between political freedoms and self-determination, saying:

> We have so many private newspapers now. Ten years ago we had only the state newspapers. Now we have NGOs, a multiparty system. These are indicators of democracy. We can go abroad without permission from the state—this is all new. Now Mongolians are traveling a lot to the West and between the aimags. In the past we needed permission to go to other aimags. Now we have more freedom than then. If you were divorced then, the Party would discuss the issue even if you were not a Party member. All offices had a Party chapter that controlled the office, including the private life of people. Now we have more freedom. Now we can talk freely, too, like now I can talk freely about the government with you, a foreigner. Under socialism, you would have to report to the Party that you talked with a Westerner.

Did everyone choose their political candidates independent of each other? One day in 1998 Nyamdavaa and I stopped at a ger to conduct one more interview in the Khovd countryside. We entered the home of a 60-something-year-old businessman. With the help of his adult children, he imported Chinese goods from just over the Mongolian-Chinese border below Khovd City. He proudly told us that he votes for the MPRP. And, he added, he makes sure that his children vote the same. "Is it a secret ballot?" I asked. "Yes, of course," he replied. "Then how do you know how they really vote?" I quietly retorted. Anthropologists are not supposed to interject their own feelings, but sometimes I just couldn't help it.

Self-determination often means the right to make one's own economic decisions, and many of our research participants define it thus. An older government worker (Ulaanbaatar 2003 Ay053) says, "I prefer to live in a

Figure 4.6 Burmaa Radnaa, Women for Social Progress. (Paula L. W. Sabloff, 2003)

democracy because people work as they want. They fix prices for their labor. The right to worship is free; all rights are guaranteed."

But some interviewees consider self-determination to mean the freedom to make any and perhaps all of their own choices. This includes choice of religion and the decision to speak, write or read what one wants. In 1998, 18 people (2.1 percent) associated political freedoms with self-determination. By 2003, 11 (2.6 percent) made the same association. Again, these numbers are low, but they show that more than one person thought to talk about the issue. An unskilled worker in Khovd (1998 Bd032) exhibits the connection between self-determination and free speech. "Democracy," he says, "provides a man with the possibility to speak his thoughts and accomplish his plans freely. Therefore freedom—living in a free state—is the main feature of democracy." Five years later, a young man in Khovd working for an NGO (2003 Bj069) says, "All citizens of a democratic country are free from autocracy and political pressure. One can be a master of his destiny and achieve personal goals there. There are favorable conditions for improving and mastering gifts and talents in a democratic society as well."

A small group of people believes that political freedoms will also lead to the institutionalization of democracy in Mongolia (17, or 2.0 percent in 1998; 9, or 2.2 percent in 2003). Most are urban dwellers with a high school or university education and under 40 years old. I found their responses particularly interesting because they contrast with my ideas as an American citizen. Perhaps we differ because the Mongolians live in a new democracy while the United States is considered old. A young Khalkh man working in business (Ulaanbaatar 1998 Os041) says:

Men and women enjoy their rights in the political and social arenas. Without the right to express an opinion, to free speech, to free press, to organizing and to participating in demonstrations and assemblies, there is no way to build a democratic government.

A wise young businessman with a high school education (Khovd 1998 Bd012) expresses the nuances of this idea, saying, "As a result of democracy, a man becomes free in all aspects of life and has the opportunity to think freely. As a result, pluralism comes into existence and democracy develops. In that way, a person's free state [state of freedom] is the main feature of democracy." In the same year, a 20-year-old businesswoman in Ulaanbaatar (1998 En035) focuses on the relationship between a free press and the development of democracy: "A free press is very important for developing democracy. Therefore, it is necessary to have the law of freedom of press."

Five years later, another Khovd high school graduate, this one a Kazakh (Khovd 2003 Ns072), expresses moral certainty, saying "The right of free expression of opinions. A society that honors and respects its citizens is a real democratic society."

Table 4.6 analyzes the relationship between underlying values and political freedoms mentioned. Like the other even-numbered tables in this chapter, it suggests decreasing differences in opinion by 2003. In 1998, personal dignity shows significant variability by residence, age group, education and occupation. In 2003, people's mentions vary by age group and education but not by residence or occupation. Now ethnic identity shows differences between groups. For self-determination and democratic development, there is little variability in 1998 (by occupation only) and none in 2003.

Table 4.6 Significant differences within demographic categories concerning the association of underlying values with political freedom, 1998 and 2003[a]

	1998			2003		
	Personal dignity	Self-determination	Democratic development	Personal dignity	Self-determination	Democratic development
Location						
Residence						
Gender						
Age group				*		
Education	***			***		
Occupation	***	*	*			
Ethnicity					**	

In a two-tailed chi-square test, *p≤.05, **p≤.01, and ***p≤.001. Location, residence and gender=1 df; age group, education and ethnicity=3 df; occupation=5 df for 1998 and 6 df for 2003.
[a]See Table A.6 in Appendix for details.

CONCLUSION

It is no longer acceptable to talk of the former Soviet Bloc countries as being "in transition" (Carothers 2002; Hann 2006:2). Political scientists, anthropologists and others feel this terminology is forcing a unilineal development model on nations that are not necessarily changing from totalitarian rule to open, democratic rule even if they are moving from socialism to capitalism. But 'transition' works for Mongolia. Here, people clearly *want* their country to travel that path. They especially value their freedoms, be they political, economic or human rights. This is evident not only in these interviews but also in the 1992 ratification of a constitution that champions Western democracy and capitalism. And the government structure is democratic even if the political competition sometimes is not.

Mongolian interviewees frequently speak in terms of *freedom from* and *freedom to,* as do some scholars (see, for example, Nugent 2008:26). But the Mongolians use these frameworks to refer to historical events, not just abstract principles. *Freedom from* usually refers to the socialist period of repressive government. *Freedom to* or *freedom for* can only be realized in the new democratic age.

The statistical tables show that people's thoughts about political freedoms are not universally shared within Mongolia. The percentages are rather low, meaning that most interviewees did not think to mention particular attributes. They also vary within the sample population and change over time. Therefore, everyone does not necessarily want—or think of—political freedom within democracy in the same way. However, among those who do mention political freedom, the attributes of free speech, free media, self-determination and so forth remain the same.

CHAPTER FIVE

Democracy Brings Economic Freedom

T he Mongolians we interviewed in 1998 cared more about political freedoms than economic freedoms (358, or 41.3 percent, to 303, or 34.9 percent). But in 2003 the reverse was true. That year, 258 (62.0 percent) listed political freedoms while 315 (75.7 percent) mentioned economic freedoms (see Table 5.1). As one old woman herder said to Nyamsuren, a university history teacher collecting data on the outskirts of Khovd,

> Our knowledge of democracy is very basic, sonny. We herders are not able to watch television, listen to the radio or read newspapers regularly, as we always heat in the sun and numb in the cold [a Mongolian expression regarding the life of herders]. I just heard that in democratic countries, the human rights of all citizens are equally respected and the laws are scrupulously observed. In Mongolia, economic democracy is developing faster than political and social democracy. (Khovd 2003 Ns073)

This chapter describes how our interviewees associate economic survival or success—the opportunity to 'live a good life'—with economic freedoms. To Mongolians, these mean the right to private property, to run a business or engage in trade, to choose one's employment or education and to have geographic mobility. Lukin (2000:211–12) tells of the Russian 'democrats,' who believed that prosperity as well as honesty and freedom could only be achieved in a democratic state. Therefore, Russia should become democratic, like the West. In Mongolia, the desire for economic survival/success in a capitalist, democratic political economy became a deeply held value, as did personal dignity, economic survival/success, economic opportunity and self-determination. We will see these underlying values in the following interviews, first in peoples' relief that they are free from socialism and then in the sections on particular economic freedoms, starting with private property.

More and more, Mongolians realized that they would need economic freedoms in order to survive the collapse of socialism or even succeed in the global market economy. In the mid-1980s, President Gorbachev knew that the USSR was in financial trouble and could no longer support a military all over the world. He started pulling troops out of Mongolia and curtailed loans and aid as well. In the process, Mongolia lost about 30 percent of its GNP (Bruun and Odgaard 1996:26). In 1991 the CMEA (Council for Mutual Economic Assistance, a Soviet Bloc trade organization also called COMECON) trade network—Mongolia's socialist trading partners—fell apart. This and rapid privatization wreaked havoc in many Soviet Bloc nations (Grant 1993:35; Hann 2006:57–58, 133). Hann (ibid.:71) attributes the collapse of the Soviet Bloc market and privatization of vineyards for the destruction of Hungarian wine production and sales. The Mongolian economy, which had shown signs of trouble back in the 1980s, fell into recession (Asian Development Bank 1992:12–24; Goldstein and Beall 1994:116; Bruun and Odgaard 1996:22; Sanders 1996:xlii–xlvi). By December 1990, the lower house of parliament called for rationing of food and other consumer goods. People stood on bread lines in bitter-cold Mongolian winters (the temperature could fall below –11F in Ulaanbaatar and even lower in the countryside). Tuya Altangerel (2001:6) recalls standing on one breadline for her grandmother while her brother stood on another for the family's ration of bread.

About that time, foreign advisors including the Asian Development Bank counseled the implementation of Jeffrey Sachs's shock therapy to transform Mongolia from a socialist to a capitalist economy (Goldstein and Beall1994:116; Rossabi 2005:45–53). Shock therapy was the term used to urge the former Soviet Bloc to change from socialism to capitalism in the shortest possible time by adopting a three-pronged economic strategy: privatization of state-owned production properties such as negdels and industries; removal of government price controls and reduction of government. Because the economy lacked the proper supports for this program—markets and international trading partners, as well as a banking system based on capitalist principles and legal supports—the Mongolian people experienced severe shortages and hyperinflation (Rossabi 2005:49–53).

Within a few cold winter months, families became responsible for their own economic welfare. The state gave people a start by distributing 10 vouchers called blue tickets (worth 10,000 togrogs, or less than US$10) to everyone born before May 1991. In the countryside, people could use them to buy shares in the newly privatized industries and collectives (the old negdels), making them shareholders in the cooperative (agricultural or industrial). Those who did not want to remain in their collectives (now converted to cooperatives) could use their vouchers to purchase animals or start small enterprises, thus becoming entrepreneurs (agricultural, industrial or trade).

In the cities and towns, the state privatized apartments by allocating them to their occupants, although people continued to pay for heating and electricity. Mongolia had constructed huge apartment buildings in the urban centers with the help of Russia and China as well as Japanese prisoners of war (World War II). The early apartments were three- or four-story apartment complexes the size of a city block. They surrounded a courtyard that held playground equipment so that the children could play in a safe environment. Later, 9- to 12-story buildings rose on the outskirts of the old-style apartments. Here the playgrounds were not as protected as the original apartments, but there was some room to construct basketball courts, for basketball was a favorite sport.

The government had originally assigned people to apartments as they were constructed (Figure 5.1). Now it gave the occupants ownership. Those living on the ground floor could convert them to shops. I watched many do so in 1998. They began to sell tourist goods such as original or antique art and modern trinkets that Mongolians could decorate their homes and gers with or foreigners could take home. I'm still wearing the cashmere sweaters I bought in 1994. People also sold basic household items (such as bread, candy and detergent), liquor and clothing from these newly converted storefronts.

Figure 5.1 My first apartment building. People guessed it was built by the Chinese because of the Chinese-style bathtub. (Paula L.W. Sabloff, 1996)

DEMOCRACY BRINGS FREEDOM FROM GOVERNMENT CONTROL OF ECONOMIC LIFE

To our interviewees, freedom from oppression often means freedom from extreme government regulation of their economic life. People, like a Kazakh herder who had moved near Ulaanbaatar to be closer to the country's major market (2003 Ay065), often express this as the freedom to participate in the market: "After the democratic reforms, machinery, technology, mines, buildings, livestock, industries were transferred to private hands. Livestock production—in particular milk, meat and wool—is sold according to the owner's will [decision]."

Others focus on being free to make their own decisions about their newly acquired private property. A pension-age herder living outside of Ulaanbaatar (2003 Bu043) explains the contrast between the old socialist system and the new market economy:

> Under socialism, herders could purchase one sheep for 120 togrogs only with prior permission from the collective farm director. Nowadays, if herders manage to increase the size of their herds, they can sell or slaughter the oldest and weakest animals for food. The only negative phenomenon that took place around here [during the transition] is that many state-owned cattle barns, enclosures and fences were destroyed or looted. Now, some herders are talking about restoring them.

Mongolia had just come from a system where practically everyone worked for the state (Bawden 1989:394–95). Imitating Soviet Russia, Mongolia's Council of Ministers developed five-year plans of production starting in 1948. The relevant ministries (agriculture, forestry, industry, mining and so on) apportioned the quotas established in the five-year plans to the provinces (aimags), and the provinces then allocated portions of the quotas to their factories, towns, state farms and negdels. On the negdels, administrators assigned quotas to the work teams (*suur*)—see Figure 5.2(a) and (b). These work teams drew workers from a few households. Workers 16 years old and older were responsible for meeting individual production quotas. In exchange, they lived in permanent settlements that had schools, health services, electricity and shops. They received cash wages, free education, free medical services and pensions (social security) upon retirement. The government—not the market—controlled prices for consumer goods such as meat and milk, heating and electricity (Sanders 1987:91–95, 110–18; Rossabi 2005:46).

(a)

(b)

Figure 5.2 Milking cows: (a) during socialism, a negdel woman milks in a lab coat (National Museum of Mongolian History, socialist era); (b) in democracy, a herder milks his horses himself. (Paula L.W. Sabloff, 2000)

Socialist government control extended to pressure on women to birth big families in order to increase the native workforce. It is ironic that the government purges of the 1930s–1950s greatly reduced Mongolia's already sparse population numbers and then forbade abortions. Women told me that bearing many children was considered a patriotic act that was rewarded with medals and extra income (July 18, 1998, fieldnotes). As of 1971, mothers received extra allowances for the fourth, tenth, and subsequent children (Sanders 1987:118). But two life stories illustrate the stress of having such large families.

The first Mongolians I ever met were higher education officials visiting the University of Pittsburgh (1994), where I was teaching. They were responsible for converting an entire higher education system from preparing students for socialism to preparing them for a democratic market-economy society. They had come to the United States to stimulate their thinking about restructuring the higher education system, just as they had done in Europe. With the delegation was a teacher at one of the smaller colleges. Although she had been a Russian teacher just two years before, she was acting as English translator for the group. One evening she told me her story to show how much the socialist government had controlled her life. Listening to her government's call for more babies, she had 9 or 12 children (I forget the actual number). Soon after they were born, they entered a full-time daycare center provided by the state. Still, so many children plus a full-time job took its toll on her, she said.

The second story is sadder. In 1998, the Ulaanbaatar research team and I took a trip to Tuv Aimag Center to find herders to interview. We found two ger camps on the hilly slopes outside of town. The people in the first camp were happy and upbeat. Although they had come from the center to live outdoors for the summer, they had scattered their gers on the hillside the way a traditional nomadic camp would. When they learned that we wanted to interview them, they enthusiastically shared their thoughts with the researchers and carefully listened to each other when it was not their turn.

The people in the second ger camp appeared very depressed. They had lined up their gers in two rows, as if they living were on a city street. They turned out to be from the aimag center also. They lived in gers in the summer to save enough money so that they could pay their electricity, gas, trash and water bills in the winter. The arrangement of gers suggested that the wished to be in the town even during the summer. Tsetseglen Magsarjav and I went into the last ger in the row, which was occupied by a small, grey-haired woman. It was very neat and clean. The interior lattice walls were hidden behind cheery royal blue cloths that were bordered in red. *Ulzii* designs decorated the corners.[1] When I admired the work, she told me she had made the panels herself. She then pointed to some embroidery along the bottom borders of the beds that she had also made. Still, there was no fire in the stove, and the ger was chilly.

Tsetseglen tried gently to get the old woman to answer our questions, but she had her own agenda. She said that she was old and tired, with heart problems. She added that life was easier under socialism. In those days 1,000 togrogs bought a lot of things. Now even though the government raises the pension by 1,000 togrogs a year, it doesn't keep up with inflation. She actually has less to live on now than at the beginning of democracy. Part of the problem is that she bore 13 children during socialism, when the state wanted to increase the population. Now, under democracy, they cannot get higher education because they cannot afford it under the new system. To make matters worse, half of them cannot find jobs. So several of her children and their families are living on her pension. She is very worried about her family's future after she dies, she said. When I asked her if she saw any benefits to democracy, she said no. The life decisions she had made during socialism (producing a large family and relocating to Tuv Aimag Center where her extended family could not help her) was causing her too much economic hardship.

Despite these tales from pension-age women, snippets from the interviews that follow illustrate how happy most interviewees are to have the new economic freedoms and the opportunities that democracy brings. Young people seem especially glad to be free of socialism. A 20-year-old in business for herself (Ulaanbaatar 1998 Os046) says, "No more dictatorship. Now people have the opportunity to have a job that lets them live however they like. The person who is smart, cultured, educated and skilled has a great opportunity to work in any business. Enjoying a better life depends on an individual's effort; democracy guarantees it." Also in business, an older man (40–55) with a primary school education (Khovd 2003 Bj006) says, "Everything is allowed within the limits of the law. In former times, everything was limited and under government control. With the advent of democracy, this is changing. Now I have a side car [motorcycle] so I can do everything with it."

THREE MAJOR ECONOMIC FREEDOMS

The foundation for all the other economic freedoms is private property. In 1998, 121 (14.0 percent) mention private property. In 2003, 124, or about twice the percentage (29.8 percent) do, which is a significant change (see Table

Table 5.1 Mentions of some subdomains of economic freedom, 1998 and 2003[a]

	1998 Total = 867		2003 Total = 416		Significant difference between years
	N	%	N	%	χ^2
Private property	121	14.0	124	29.8	***
Own business or trade	76	8.8	90	21.6	***
Employment choice	74	8.5	103	24.8	***

In a two-tailed chi-square (χ^2) test with 1 df, *p≤.05, **p≤.01 and ***p≤.001.
[a]By number, percent and Pearson's chi-square test.

5.1). During socialism, people could own goods (for example, their clothing and household items) but not 'the means of production'—that is, property that could be used to produce goods for the market. This included land to pasture the livestock or grow crops; domesticated animals to produce milk, meat and skins; buildings and equipment for manufacturing boots, carpets and craft items and so on. Of course people were allowed to keep some livestock. According to Sanders (1987:95–96), families living on negdels could keep 10 head of livestock per person or 50 head per household in mountain and steppe regions. Those living in the Gobi could keep 15 per person or 75 per household. Townspeople could keep up to 25 per household, depending on the size of the town.

As part of the Democratic Revolution, the government started to allow people to own the produce they grew and goods they produced. The historian and activist Baabar describes the process of privatization in our July 16, 2003, interview:

> The Law of Privatization had been passed on May 24, 1991. This was so important that it was noted in the world chronology book. However, when we (the Democratic Coalition) gained power in '96, only 15 percent of state property had been privatized—a very limited amount. From 1996 to 1998, we carried out more than 50 percent privatization of state properties. We were working on the big items—the power stations, Erdenet [mining company], etc., when we experienced a 'crisis of power' starting in 1998 [when the parliament went through a series of prime ministers and their cabinets].

Many, like a 40-something woman herder (Khovd 2003 Bj003), seemed to be happy to be able to own private property, partly because it gave them a sense of control, of self-determination, and partly because they could make a living from their property.

Now I can give my livestock products—meat, wool, cashmere and milk—to my siblings or sell them to others. This is just my own right to do that. A person can also increase the number of livestock. In former times, the number of livestock was fixed and extra livestock were not allowed. Now, he who can increase his cattle has multiple heads of livestock. My family has 740 head of livestock, but I think that it is better for me to have a few good livestock within my means. A lot of livestock cannot endure the *dzud* [harsh winters when the ground freezes and livestock cannot break through the ice to graze].

An older businesswoman with a baccalaureate (Ulaanbaatar 1998 Mh054) is more philosophical: "Before, state ownership of property was supreme. This led to the loss of personal ownership [that had existed in the feudal era], which made us brutal and lazy [had she read Hobbes?]. Today we have multiple forms of ownership: private companies, cooperative properties and state property. People became enthusiastic and their lives became meaningful."

Some others connect private property to economic development. One is a young Oirad woman with a high school degree (Ulaanbaatar 1998 Tj025). She says, "People have the right to own their own property. It is very significant for the country's economy because if people could live well, it is important to the country [that is, Mongolia could experience economic development]."

People associate private property with certain underlying values. A 20-year-old university student (Khovd 2003 Ns012) connects private property with hope for the future, remarking, "The Communists confiscated private property by force and made it state property and so they made people's lifestyle communal as suggested by Thomas More. Thanks to democracy, this was changed and gave us confidence in the future."

A 69-year-old woman living outside of Ulaanbaatar (2003 Ay035) says that private property provides self-determination and a better life: "I moved from Uvs Aimag five years ago. I have 12 children. Their life is tending to get better. Privatization provided us with some state livestock as private property, and now we are selling the herd's milk and meat. We are living on it. People are selling to each other."

In 2002, the MPRP-controlled government wrote and passed another land privatization law, the Law on Allocation of Land to Mongolian Citizens for Ownership. This law took effect on May 1, 2003. Urban and suburban plots and agricultural fields became eligible for privatization. When I first visited Ulaanbaatar in 1994, I saw family gers interspersed among the apartment buildings, factories and government buildings. I found this odd. It seemed that people had the right to plunk down a ger anywhere they wanted, and they did so during socialism when all land belonged to the state. The 2002 land law would assure the ger occupants the right to remain where they were.

In anticipation of the new land law, urbanites began settling and claiming suburban plots that they could access by bus or car. They built summer houses (*dachas*) within the perimeters of the wooden fences they had erected (Figure 5.3). I visited my friends' house one day. In the new neighborhood, each enclosed plot contained a house and outhouse, as there was no sewage piping in the suburbs. (They did have electricity, though.) Byambajav took me for a walk in the family's new neighborhood so that I could see the rather fanciful designs of the new houses. I think my favorite was the one completely covered in baby blue and pink square bathroom tiles.

Figure 5.3 Dachas outside of Ulaanbaatar. The one in the forefront reminded me of bathroom tiles. (Paula L.W. Sabloff, 2003)

With privatization came concern for its just distribution. A herder in 1998 (Ulaanbaatar 1998 Ch055) thought that the 1991 distribution of animals and apartments had been problematic. He said, "The old agricultural communities (negdels) are now dispersed. People are getting their own property. But we countryside people have less property than city dwellers."

In 2003, a 22-year-old university student (Ulaanbaatar 2003Ay027) talks about the advantages and drawbacks of the recent land law:

Apartment buildings and livestock were privatized and, just like those, the government is now privatizing land. Land privatization is somehow going the wrong way. Because of land privatization [that is, how the law is written and implemented], maybe people would argue and we can expect the worst. But it is good that people now own specific property. In land privatization there are advantages. For example, people will grow veggies, build their house and undertake enterprises there.

Once people could own their produce and manufactured goods, they needed the right to engage in business and trade in order to sell them. Although this sounds so obvious, it had been forbidden under socialism. Then, people had to shop in state-owned stores that sold the same quality of goods to everyone. The exception was a special store for government officials, which occupied the top floor of the State Department Store in Ulaanbaatar (Sanders 1987:122). Nergui*, an Ulaanbaatar professor I met in 2003, recounted the day he was getting ready to study abroad and was allowed to enter the special top floor and select suitable clothes for his trip. He remembers being shocked by the high quality of goods, quality not available to ordinary workers.

Between 1994 and 2003 I watched free enterprise spring up in Ulaanbaatar (Figure 5.4). In my first visit, there were no store signs or advertising. You had to know where the stores were in order to buy food or clothing. I saw people on the sidewalk selling one cigarette at a time. I passed a man shining shoes and even repairing them on the sidewalk outside a shop. I patronized small kiosks that dotted the sidewalk corners. They sold bottles of soda, bars of soap, boxes of cookies and chocolate—one at a time. We had to drink the soda right there so that the kiosk could recycle the bottles, as there was no glass bottle factory in Mongolia.

There were also small 'black markets,' which resembled the black markets of Soviet Russia. Caroline Humphrey writes (2002:60) that during socialism people would take goods from the factories they worked in and surreptitiously

Figure 5.4 Shops such as these are built into people's first-floor apartments in Ulaanbaatar. (Paula L.W. Sabloff, 2003)

sell them in the back streets and alleys (Humphrey 2002:60). When I asked Mongolians why they called it the black market, they said that is because vendors do not pay taxes. Several black markets were operating in 1996. I even found one for exchanging foreign currency. People there offered much better exchange rates than the banks (May 3, 1996, fieldnotes).

By my 1998 visit, the government had recognized the black market as a legal way of conducting small business and prepared an enclosed area about the size of a football field east of Ulaanbaatar to control this trade. Vendors set up tables or stalls, displayed their wares and made sales. Visitors had to pay an entrance fee, but it was only a dozen togrogs (about US$12). Once inside, they could shop for anything from antiques, wooden saddles and horse blankets to meat and vegetables. I found the same arrangement in Khovd.

In 1994 and 1996 there were no supermarkets. Instead, the Mercury Market, a large domed building similar in shape to an airplane hangar, contained small stalls. People sold household goods and food from these stalls, often duplicating the same goods in side-by-side stalls. There you could buy one egg at a time. By 2003, Ulaanbaatar had real supermarkets, complete with refrigerated shelves, shopping carts and checkout registers. To transition from selling one cigarette at a time to running supermarkets, people needed the right to engage in commerce.

People seemed happy to engage in the free market, either as sellers or buyers, and the number of interviewees who mentioned this increased from 76 (8.8 percent) to 90 (21.6 percent)—a remarkable trend (see Table 5.1). I present some quotations from the interviews so that you can see for yourself the demographic variability in similar answers. In other words, people do not have to be alike demographically to think alike.

Anyone has the right to compete in the market. Before, there was no competition in the market because everything was centrally regulated. That limited [national] development. (A young professor living in Khovd City, 1998 Nd038)

Democracy means human rights. This means that it is now free for a person to sell milk, to become rich and not to work. (A Kazakh herder of pension age, with a primary school education, Khovd 1998 Ns047)

Before, everything was closed and tied down. But now things have changed. For instance, business people can set their products' prices themselves; they can increase or decrease prices; they just think about how to sell them fast. (A 20–26-year-old university student who is also a Christian, Ulaanbaatar 1998 Mh069)

Everyone has an opportunity to engage in business and sell products equally in the market economy. He who works well will live well. (A 27–36-year-old student with a baccalaureate, Ulaanbaatar 1998 Tj028)

There are equal rights in Mongolia. Everyone has the right to start a private business and support his family in this society. Under social-ism, the state assigned people to jobs and paid fixed salaries. Now, everything is up to the individual. I used to work as a mechanic on a collective farm (negdel) during socialism. Now I am running a pri-vate business specializing in crop farming, vegetable gardening and haymaking. At the same time, I am engaged in livestock breeding. I planted vegetables on a 3–4 hectare plot and barley on a 10-hectare plot. Besides that, I prepare hay for my livestock on an 80-hectare plot of land. We fenced the plots to protect the vegetables and hay from the grazing herds. (A 60-year-old Buddhist living in the countryside, Ulaanbaatar 2003 Bu047)

The transition from working for the state to owning a business or engaging in commerce is not always easy. Three people from the 2003 Ulaanbaatar interviews talk about the unemployment and poverty that accompanied marketization. The first is a 28-year-old woman with a high school education (Ay047). At the time of the interview, she was unemployed.

Under one-party rule, we were not free to choose our employment. Now under democracy, people enjoy the freedom to engage in any business or trade. That is why people have some money now and life is getting better. Still, poverty, alcoholism, robbery and theft are occurring because people do not have education and a profession. Also, even if some people have a profession, there are no jobs.

An older woman who is also unemployed (Bu019) faces a different problem, saying "It is impossible to start a business if one doesn't have the required financial resources. A mortgage is required for taking a bank loan." And a 59-year-old pensioner (Bu054) describes the problem of learning wise investment. He still supports private property, however:

I am a shareholder of the NIC Petroleum Concern. Unfortunately, the concern did not pay our dividends because it suffered extensive losses during the last few years. It is becoming unprofitable for ordinary shareholders to possess shares. Still, the decision to privatize state-owned property was a correct decision. Herders received livestock, and urban dwellers own their apartments. Now, every property owner is entitled to sell it at his/her own discretion.

Not everyone could or wanted to own a business. Many lacked the capital or the will. They were used to working in state mining operations, farms or big factories such as the Gobi Company, which produces cashmere. So they continued to be employees. But now they wanted to choose their own employment rather than be assigned a job by the government, which is what had happened during socialism. Like the right to run a business, the number of respondents who mention free choice of employment leaps—from 74 (8.5 percent) in 1998 to 103 (24.8 percent) in 2003.

While employment choice was the major issue, some also appreciated employee rights—the right to strike, to change jobs and to simply control their working life. In 1998 a 27-year-old Oirad woman with only a primary education (Khovd 1998 Bj003) says, "Freedom means that people can do what they want. For example, before if you were trained as a teacher, you could only work as a teacher. But now regardless of your training, you can do anything." A 17-year-old student (Ulaanbaatar 1998 Ch028) sees a broader picture when she says, "Democracy is the freedom to work and relax (*ajillakh amrakh cholootei*). People have the right to choose their jobs. If they have the opportunity, they may even stay at home without a job."

Five years later, another young woman, this time in agriculture (Khovd 2003 Bj068), equates democracy with "the right to do what one does best. In a democratic society, one is encouraged to do what he/she does best. I only have an eight-year compulsory education and do not have a profession. In spite of this, I support my family by growing vegetables with my father. I also can grow vegetables on my own." Also discussing agriculture, a 46-year-old farmer (Ulaanbaatar 2003 Na023) suggests, "Anyone is to work according to his own skills and potential. Today, it is not necessary to be a member of a cooperative (negdel) as it was in socialist times."

I did not find anyone speaking against employment choice, but a few people allude to problems associated with that right. Some, like a young fellow just graduating from technical college (Ulaanbaatar 1998 Tj077), associate employment choice with chaos. He tells us that "People can do whatever they like for a living. However, everything must be regulated under law; otherwise, social disorder will occur." Others are concerned that the political parties still control employment. That is, the political party in power tends to dismiss workers who belong to a different party in order to place their own people in bureaucratic positions: "Opportunity for members of the opposition party is limited under the MPRP government" (Khovd 2003 Ns046). Finally, one woman (Ulaanbaatar 2003 Bu036) complains about the effect of democracy on women, saying, "Although we are freely engaged in raising livestock, the women tend to bear the brunt of the hard work. We do not have time to visit hospitals and receive proper medical treatment."

According to Table 5.2, there is some significant variability among the demographic categories in 1998. Reference to the right to private property (first column) in 1998 suggests slightly significant variability by location, education and ethnic identity. People's education level is higher in Ulaanbaatar than in Khovd. Kazakhs, I was told, speak their own language until they go to school. They frequently drop out before completing high school.

Table 5.2 Significant differences within demographic categories concerning people's mention of some subdomains of economic freedom, 1998 and 2003[a]

	1998			2003		
	Private property	Business or trade	Employment choice	Private property	Business or trade	Employment choice
Location	*		**		***	
Residence			*			
Gender						
Age group						
Education	*					
Occupation						
Ethnicity	**					*

In a two-tailed chi-square test, *p≤.05, **p≤.01, and ***p≤.001. Location, residence and gender=1 df; age group, education and ethnicity=3 df; occupation=5 df for 1998 and 6 df for 2003. [a]See Table A.7 in Appendix for details.

Therefore, we should expect that if education level shows significant difference, then ethnic identity and location will, too.

The ratio of people who mention the right to trade or own a business to those who do not is fairly constant. However, the right to employment choice varies by location and residence. Herders, farmers and townspeople all value the right to trade or own a business, as that is how all but government workers are living now. Employment choice may not be as valued for those who remain in the countryside because they are replicating the lives of their parents and grandparents.

Pearson's chi-square test on the 2003 data suggests significant differences between Ulaanbaatar and Khovd for the right to engage in business or trade. There is some variability regarding the right to employment choice by ethnic identity, but it is not nearly as strong as it was in 1998.

ECONOMIC FREEDOMS WE DO NOT THINK ABOUT

There are two economic freedoms that we take for granted but people freed from feudalism or socialism do not. The first is the right to mobility—to move about the country and live anywhere, even abroad. The second is the right to choose one's higher education and therefore prepare for the future one wants. The rate of mentions of these two freedoms grows significantly, from 38 (4.4 percent) in 1998 to 114 (27.4 percent) in 2003 (Table 5.3).

It goes without saying that pastoral nomads value mobility.[2] They need to be able to move their livestock in order to keep them fed and watered,

Table 5.3 Mentions of other subdomains of economic freedom, 1998 and 2003[a]

	1998 Total = 867		2003 Total = 416		Significant difference between years
	N	%	N	%	χ^2
Mobility	38	4.4	114	27.4	***
Education choice	56	6.5	96	23.1	***
Total (Tables 5.1 and 5.3)	303	34.9	315	75.7	***

In a two-tailed chi-square (χ^2) test with 1 df, *p≤.05, **p≤.01 and ***p≤.001.
[a]By number, percent and Pearson's chi-square test.

especially since Mongolian nomads do not grow fodder for their animals. This right was denied during the socialist years (Bruun 2006:68). People had residence cards that limited them to a particular aimag or *sum*. Farmers and herders attached to collectives could only relocate with permission from the government. And people could only go abroad for government business, which included diplomatic missions and advanced education. But in the new market economy, people need the freedom to travel and relocate in order to maximize their earning potential. In 1998, people like this university-educated businessman (Ulaanbaatar Mh049) express appreciation for the newfound ability to move abroad: "The right to travel abroad was guaranteed by law in 1992. Anyone holding a passport can travel to any country freely. It became like a life vest for Mongols. Seeing other nations with our own eyes convinced us about the goodness of democracy; foreign travel enabled us to bring home our new experiences." A young herder (Khovd 1998 Bs049) suggests another valued aspect to foreign travel: "It became free to travel abroad even for people who haven't been to the aimag center."

One of the reasons for the increase is that between 1998 and 2003, parliament passed a law that gave people the freedom to relocate within the country. As a result, we see people talking about moving within Mongolia in 2003 but not in 1998. The 2003 interviews include examples of families from Uvs Aimag in the northwest corner of the country. They had moved their herds to the pasturelands around Ulaanbaatar to be close to the country's major market for beef, skins and other animal products. Because there were no highways or trains connecting the northwest with the capital, it was not cost-effective to raise animals in Uvs and sell them in the capital. A 52-year-old Dorvod herder (Ulaanbaatar 2003 Ay063) tells Ayush, "In Mongolia it is possible to move and live everywhere. Our family arrived here from Uvs Aimag to improve our life. Many Mongols go abroad to study, to work, and to make commerce. There they have a US$1,000 salary a month. Half of this amount is sent back to support the family."

An NGO worker (Ulaanbaatar 2003 Bu048) lauds internal mobility even while she notes a problem: "As a result of the right to choose where to live, the population density in urban areas is rising. Mongolia is becoming an increasingly urbanized country. Although excessive urbanization generates numerous problems, it is an indication of freedom. One should not have to reside in rural areas against his/her wishes. Employment opportunities and various services should be created in rural areas in order to attract people there."

People still talked about the freedom to travel abroad. In the following quotation, a 32-year-old unemployed resident of Ulaanbaatar (2003 Ay058) describes the benefits of travel, saying, "People travel abroad a lot. Mongols frequently travel to South Korea, England, America [United States] and Japan. People go in order to work to improve their lives, to study, to make business and trade. Previously people had been traveling almost only in Russia."

Some people found reasons to worry about this new freedom in 2003 but not in 1998. A 40-year-old Oirad woman living in the town (Khovd Bj009) says, "Now that people can live where they want, wealthy people live anywhere. But lately, with land privatization, poor people can't live anywhere that they want."

Table 5.4 continues the analysis of economic freedom's subdomains by demographic category. While variability is greatest by location and residence (reading across the table) in 1998, it is also significant for education level. Reading down the table, there is no significant variability for mobility. Choice in one's education appears to have the most significant instances of variability (location, residence, education level and ethnic identity).

The third column—total economic freedoms—refers to all the subdomains from Table 5.1 and 5.3. This column suggests significant variability by location, residence and ethnic identity. People living in or near the capital have already taken advantage of economic freedoms just by relocating near Mongolia's biggest market, so they would be aware of economic freedoms. Those already living in Ulaanbaatar would need employment choice to work two jobs to make ends meet. I knew several professors at the National University of Mongolia who also taught classes at the new private universities so that they could feed their families. In 1998, public university professors were making about US$90 a month. Yet a computer disk (floppy disks in those days) that they needed for work cost US$1. The chi-square test also suggests significant variability in residence (rural versus urban) and ethnic

Table 5.4 Significant differences within demographic categories concerning people's mention of other subdomains of economic freedom, 1998 and 2003[a]

	1998			2003		
	Mobility	Education choice	Total economic freedoms	Mobility	Education choice	Total economic freedoms
Location	***	***			***	
Residence	**	*				
Gender						
Age group						
Education	**					
Occupation						
Ethnicity	**	*			***	*

In a two-tailed chi-square test, *p≤.05, **p≤.01, and ***p≤.001. Location, residence and gender=1 df; age group, education and ethnicity=3 df; occupation=5 df for 1998 and 6 df for 2003.
[a]See Table A.8 in Appendix for details.

identity. As the Buriats ("Other Mongols") and Khalkh interviewed live in Ulaanbaatar, while a mixture of Kazakhs, Oirad and Khalkh live in Khovd, ethnic identity coincides with location in this case. Thus, three of the eight demographic categories vary significantly in 1998.

In 2003, variability drops (as it did in Table 5.2). However, significant difference remains for education choice according to location and ethnic identity. All the subdomains taken together (third column) suggest differentiation by ethnic identity. Still, looking at this table, we might say that people's thinking about economic freedom seems to be coming together toward a universal desire for economic freedoms.

Along with valuing mobility, our research participants appreciate education choice (Figure 5.5). I assumed that people would want to continue the socialist system where everyone had tuition-free schooling up through the university years. In those days, student hostels (dormitories) accommodated students who were studying far from their parents. The very bright students were selected to go to special schools in the capital where they were prepared for higher education and trained for specialist jobs. The school system was one of the high points of socialism.

After World War II, the government launched a literacy campaign for children and their parents. By 1989, the country was 98 percent literate according to UN standards. Such a high literacy rate made it easier for Mongolia to make a successful transition from socialism to democracy.

The socialist education system was not problem-free. The universities maintained places only for the number of people needed to fill specific jobs

Figure 5.5 High school students in Darkhan, 1994. This was the day their examination scores were posted. Huge apartment complexes form the background. (Paula L.W. Sabloff, 1994)

(Steiner-Khamsi and Stolpe 2006:43). Students were assigned subjects (majors) that they might or might not have any interest in. Once they graduated, they were assigned jobs that they were expected to do the rest of their working lives.

The people we interviewed seemed much happier in the democratic system where elementary and secondary education is free but students pay for higher education. What is different? People have options. In the lower grades, parents can even keep children from going to school.[3] On the university level, the expansion of state universities and proliferation of new private universities are enabling more people to study. Most people believe that education is the surest path to economic success, so the more one has the better. In 1998, most of the examples contrast socialist and democratic education policies, pointing out the problems in the former. For example, a teaching lama (Ulaanbaatar 1998 Mh002) says, "It is possible now to get an education in the field one is interested in. Previously, we had no right to choose; there was obligatory training in the fields that weren't attractive. So, the right of choice in education is essential." A young university-educated woman (Ulaanbaatar 1998 Os048) suggests, "In the last regime, students who couldn't succeed were sent to herd livestock. Now, people decide for themselves where to go and what to learn." And another young woman says, "Democracy guaranteed the right to have an education. Before, people couldn't advance their career or education unless they were members of the MPRP, had social status (that is, the privilege of being the children of high-ranking officials) or had a family of good standing. Now it depends on one's own efforts."

In 2003, fewer people referred to socialist education policies, but they still appreciated the freedom to make their own decisions (96 [23.1 percent] as opposed to 56 [6.5 percent] in 1998). An exception is this young woman living in Erdenet Sum (outside of Ulaanbaatar: Bu039) who says, "Unlike the socialist education system, one can freely choose one's profession and field of study from many higher education institutions. This is the main achievement of democracy."

More typical is a 40-something woman with a high school education (Ulaanbaatar 2003 Bu011), who said, "Everyone can specialize in any profession as long as the person is intellectually capable to attain the profession. Acquisition of a good education will enable the person to freely converse on many subjects."

People seem genuinely pleased with the new expanded access to education. However, a few are concerned that the cost of education is keeping children and youth from attending school. A 60-year-old herder (Ulaanbaatar 2003 Bu047) says,

School dropouts. The herders are not able to send their children to secondary schools as they can't afford the hostel fees. [Nomads place their children in hostels while the parents move around the countryside with their herds.] The herders' only source of income is selling livestock products. A lack of financial resources deprives their children of an opportunity to study at higher education institutions. Most of them face unemployment after graduating from secondary schools. Under socialism, our children were able to study at universities and colleges as long as they passed the entry examinations.

UNDERLYING VALUES TIED TO ECONOMIC FREEDOMS, OLD AND NEW

Four underlying values accompany people's mention of economic freedoms. The first two, the desires for personal dignity and self-determination, are also found in human rights (Chapter 3) and political rights (Chapter 4). The last two—the desire for economic survival/success and the desire for opportunity—are new.

Table 5.5 Mentions of deeply held values associated with economic freedom, 1998 and 2003[a]

	1998 Total=867		2003 Total=416		Significant difference between years
	N	%	N	%	χ^2
Personal dignity	368	42.4	216	51.9	***
Economic survival/success	264	30.4	227	54.6	***
Opportunity	143	16.5	169	40.6	***
Self-determination	79	9.1	81	19.5	***

In a two-tailed chi-square (χ^2) test with 1 df, *$p \le .05$, **$p \le .01$ and ***$p \le .001$.
[a]By number, percent and significance according to Pearson's chi square test.

Table 5.5 presents the underlying values that people associate with economic freedoms. By comparing Tables 5.5 and 4.5, you will see that in 1998 a greater number of people associate personal dignity with economic freedoms (368 [42.4 percent]) than with political freedom (273 [31.5 percent]). However, the numbers are practically the same in 2003 (216 [51.9 percent] for economic freedoms and 215 [51.7 percent] for political freedom).

You may find that the quotations I have selected are a bit of a stretch in this section, especially the ones from 1998. But I believe that behind the expressed desire for equality, minimum government interference and respecting—or at least not harming—others, interviewees are expressing a desire for personal dignity. Here, people want and appreciate economic dignity, a form of personal dignity. In 1998, a young woman (Ulaanbaatar 1998 Mh046) says, "the right to have private property and manage it as one desires should be protected, and the state shouldn't infringe on these rights. The state may deploy private property in specifically determined emergency situations only. In such a case, sufficient compensation should be guaranteed."

In 2003, a man close to retirement age (Ulaanbaatar 2003 Ay003) adds, "Everyone now has the right to their own thoughts, to undertake any enterprise, to express their opinion to the government, to have free contact with foreign countries, to study abroad, and to work abroad." And a 19-year-old with little education (Ulaanbaatar 2003 Na054) suggests, "Bosses and common people both have equal rights. People are allowed to travel wherever they like. People are independent of others [in making decisions]."

After personal dignity, the desire for economic survival/success is mentioned the most. This is not unusual for people who are in transition from socialism to the market economy (see Giordano and Kostova 2002). In 1998, 264 (30.4 percent) link economic freedom and economic survival/success; by 2003, 227 (54.6 percent) do (Table 5.5). The major difference between socialism and market economy is not the introduction of trade and letting the market determine value but the fact that economic risk passes from the state to individuals (Beck 2006; Sabloff 2012).

Mongolians did not have to worry about economic risk under socialism, for they all had jobs. There was no need to work hard as they were paid the same wage as everyone else in their position. They received free education and health care as well as a pension when they retired. Therefore they did not have to think about economic risk. All of this disappeared between 1989 and 1991. Mongolians were told that they would be responsible for their own welfare. They received livestock and apartments through the state's privatization program, and the government stopped controlling the price of basic goods such as bread. But there was no market infrastructure in which to conduct trade, except for the black market. People relied on their networks of kin and friends for mutual support. Dr. Bumaa Nasan Dashdendeviin, a curator at the National Museum of Mongolian History in Ulaanbaatar, explained that some friends were raising her and her husband's herd of animals in the countryside. In exchange, she and her family would bring gifts of clothing, candy and urban foodstuffs such as flour and sugar. It seemed as if every time I spoke with her, some family member was camping out in her family's small two-bedroom apartment. Humphrey (1998:445, 459, 470–71) repeatedly describes the critical need for rural-urban ties in the early years of transformation.

I was pulled into the Mongolian social network in 1996 by Dr. Chuluunbaatar, a scholar of the Mongolian language and old Mongolian script (which has always looked like vertical Arabic to me). He was Dean of International Studies and teaching English at the National University of Mongolia. He was 44, small and round and very friendly. When I first met him and described my research, he said he would help me any time. But I ended up helping him, too. He introduced me to people I needed for my research and translated for me in meetings with university officials. In exchange I proofread a manuscript he had written in English (April 28 and May 9, 1996, fieldnotes).

Market development took years, even with the support of the international NGOs that had come to teach people how to function in the market economy. One of these was Mercy Corps. Sponsored by a 1999 USAID grant, Mercy Corps established the Gobi Regional Economic Growth Initiative, which taught herders in six Gobi aimags how to treat their herds as businesses, build markets and connect to international markets. Realizing that there was a missing piece to the market cycle, Mercy Corps soon established the Khaan Bank so that the herders could borrow money at decent interest rates to tide them over from one season to the next (US Embassy Ulaanbaatar, Mongolia, 2003).

While some became poor, others became rich. A few politicians amassed fortunes through corrupt dealings. Other people used the knowledge and connections they had developed while acting as government officials in embassies abroad. I met a very nice man at a barbeque on the hill slopes outside of Ulaanbaatar in 2003 (July 26, 2003, fieldnotes). He told me that he had worked abroad for Mongolia's Ministry of Trade and Finance in the waning years of socialism. There he made connections, learned to handle foreign currency and other skills necessary for an importer and distributor of paper products such as paper towels, napkins and bathroom tissues. Soon after the Democratic Revolution, he opened his own import business and was beginning to manufacture supermarket-type products when I met him. Starting in Ulaanbaatar, he soon was distributing paper products to other urban centers (July 26, 2003, fieldnotes).

A good number of people talked about the possibility of getting rich under democracy. One is a pension-age herder woman (Ulaanbaatar 1998 Tj057): "People's property was limited before, but now they have the opportunity to have property of their own. If a person has a good job, he/ she could be rich and own property." A young businesswoman (Ulaan-baatar 1998 Os46) qualifies the previous remark, saying, "The person who is smart, cultured, educated and skilled has a great opportunity to practice any business. Enjoying a better life depends on an individual's effort, which is guaranteed by democracy." A young government worker with an elementary school education (Ulaanbaatar 2003 Na069) uses a phrase I found in several interviews: "I prefer to live in a democracy because the freedom to work exists. If you can work, you can enjoy a beautiful life."

The ability to seize economic opportunities allowed people to be optimistic about the future. In another analysis (Sabloff 2012), I found that 95 (29.1 percent) in 1998 and 68 (41.0 percent) in 2003 were optimistic. I met a couple in 1996 in Ulaanbaatar, Dorj-Bat* and Tseltal*. They were somewhere around 40 years old. Tseltal* was a Russian teacher who had taken the government's one-year course that prepared Russian teachers for teaching English. Now she was teaching both languages. Dorj-Bat had a degree in engineering. He owned a driving school that was thriving as more people wanted to learn to drive. He also owned a travel agency that made arrangements for Mongolian students to study English in California. He wanted to open a car repair shop and a hotel, too. He was very entrepreneurial, jolly and optimistic although not blind to the problems ahead. He pointed out that all kinds of cars were being imported into Mongolia—European, American, Korean and Japanese. How do you stock parts for all of them? He also wondered how you counteract the damage from potholes, as there are so many (May 7, 1996, fieldnotes).

Dorj-Bat reminded me of Don Eduardo Ruiz on Cozumel Island, who used to take the Merida, Yucatan (Mexico), Yellow Pages to figure out what businesses to start on the island (May 7, 1996, fieldnotes). When I returned to Mongolia a few years later, I ran into Tseltal* behind the State Department Store one day. She was in a rush because she was starting her own business. Dorj-Bat* and Tseltal* were living proof that there were many opportunities in the new economy.

The downside of capitalism was the possibility and fear of becoming poor. In 1998, 71 (8.2 percent) remarked that living standards were falling, while 135 (15.6 percent) said the gap between rich and poor was rising. In 2003, 54 (13.0 percent) mentioned dropping living standards, and 41 (10.0 percent) worried about the growing gap between rich and poor (see Sabloff 2012). Despite the efforts of the government and international NGOs, many people became impoverished. In the early 1990s, some were so poor that they deserted their children on the streets of Ulaanbaatar, hoping someone would pick them up and care for them. These children became known as the street kids of Mongolia. They lived in the steam pipes under the city and begged for food. My 1998 neighbors worked for World Vision, a Christian NGO dedicated to saving children all over the world. They said that most of the street kids—boys as well as girls—had been sodomized by the age of 7. World Vision gathered up as many street kids as possible, housed them in apartments, cleaned and fed them and gave them education.

One 66-year-old Kazakh herder living on the outskirts of Ulaanbaatar (Ulaanbaatar 2003 Ay067) talked about the rise in living standards but then expressed concern that Mongolia was experiencing a growing gap between rich and poor. In fact, 15.6 percent in 1998 and 9.9 percent in 2003 say the same thing. He says, "We now have the right to sell the dairy and livestock products such as animal skins and wool in any market place. In towns and small centers of settlement small businesses and shops were opened. Living standards are slowly improving, thanks to them. But in the city and countryside, everywhere there are many poor people. Why there are so many poor people, I don't know well."

Although a few people are worried for their fellow citizens (very few doubt their own success), the interviews on the whole suggest that people saw opportunity when talking about three new rights. This was despite the fact that Mongolia had a GDP per capita of US$460.70 in 1998 and US$527.80 in 2003 (World Bank 2012).[4] First, they talked about the right to own property that can be used to make money (Marx and Engels's 'means of production'). A young man in business (Ulaanbaatar 1998 Os040) said, "Privatization brought many advantages. People now own properties such as farm animals, houses and land that make them enjoy being owners. Since people have ownership rights to the land, for example, they have the opportunity to start their own business."

Our research respondents also discuss the right to start a business or engage in trade. One 27–36 year-old graduate student (Ulaanbaatar 1998 Tj028) used a common expression found in the interviews: "Everyone has the opportunity to participate, make business and sell products equally in the market economy. He who works well will live well." But perhaps he was a little naïve. A pensioner (2003 Bu049) described the catch-22 to Bumaa, "If one starts a private business, the person can improve his/her living conditions. Under socialism, one was assigned a job and was paid a fixed salary. Engaging in any form of private business or trade was strictly prohibited. Now, people who wish to start a private business can take loans from a bank. However, their initiatives are hamstrung by the need to pay a mortgage in order to receive the loan. Therefore, people without property cannot start private businesses."

The third right that has the potential to lead to opportunity is the right to higher education. It enables one to receive the training needed to make money and live well. The first example comes from a 48-year-old government worker with a high school education (Ulaanbaatar 2003 Ay002). He said, "Due to open relationships with other countries and freedom of access to up-to-date information, the opportunity to learn and get an education opened up for us."

Regarding self-determination, the ability to make their own economic decisions, some Mongolians want what we want. To them, self-determination means deciding what work to do and how to prepare for that work, what to own and what to buy. Even under feudalism, the pastoral nomadic tradition enabled serfs (khamjilgaa and shabi) to make some decisions (see Chapter 2). In Jamsrangiin Sambuu's autobiography (Sambuu 2010:27–28, 35), he tells how his father, a serf, would decide when and where to pasture his livestock. Each animal—horse, camel, cow, sheep and goat—had different grazing needs. His father also selected his breeding stock:

> My father carefully selected his cattle by their color, and his few horses were all brown in color. Just from looking at the horses' coats, people

knew which ones were missing. And, likewise, the cows were speckled black, and the sheep had no horns, and were pure white with black eyes and a white patch on their foreheads. The goats were of a dark color, and the camels were mainly yellow with white cheeks. He explained to me that when the black and white sheep's wool turned brownish gray, its quality declined, making it unsuitable for felt.

During the socialist decades, the state made all decisions on production and education. Once freed from socialism, people realized that they needed economic freedoms to make their own decisions in order to gain the self-determination that their pastoral-nomadic ancestors had enjoyed.

To our interviewees, self-determination comes in several forms. A young unemployed woman with a technical college degree (Khovd 1998 Bd010) links political with economic self-determination: "Democracy provides a person with the possibility to organize his life freely. In other words, as a result of democracy every man became free in all aspects—political and economic. And he could organize his private life in accordance with his labor and talents. Therefore, I consider freedom of a man as the main feature of democracy." Stating a more succinct position, a university student (Ulaanbaatar 1998 Uy031) sees both sides of the issue: "People can do the things they want and not do the things they don't want."

That about says it all, I think. Still, it is valuable to note the words of a pension-age herder (Khovd 2003 Bj066): "Democracy has enabled people to live at their own discretion. A herder's household was allowed to raise only one type of livestock at an agricultural cooperative [negdel] under the former [socialist] regime. Now, herders are allowed to raise herds of all five types of livestock."[5] Finally, an Ulaanbaatar university student (Ulaanbaatar 2003Bu042) mentions another aspect of economic choice: "One has the right to freely choose anything from consumer goods to the president of the country."

The Table 5.6 matrix summarizes the significant differences within demographic categories for 1998 and 2003. In 1998, people significantly vary by occupation in all four values. It is followed by education, age group and residence.

For 2003, location and education exhibit variability. Personal dignity (column 2) varies significantly in these categories, too. Even without knowing the history or current situation of Mongolia, we can see from this and other tables that our respondents are not homogeneous when discussing the value of economic freedoms and its subdomains. Still, they seem to come closer together in their thinking by 2003.

Table 5.6 Significant differences within demographic categories concerning the association of certain deeply held values with economic freedom, 1998 and 2003[a]

	1998				2003			
	Personal dignity	Economic survival	Opportunity	Self-determination	Personal dignity	Economic survival	Opportunity	Self-determination
Location					***	*		**
Residence	**			*				
Gender								
Age group	**			***	*			
Education	***		*	*	***			*
Occupation	***	*	***	***				
Ethnicity		***			*			

In a two-tailed chi-square test, $*p \leq .05$, $**p \leq .01$, and $***p \leq .001$. Location, residence and gender=1 df; age group, education and ethnicity=3 df; occupation=5 df for 1998 and 6 df for 2003.
[a]See Table A.9 in Appendix for details.

CONCLUSION

In this chapter, our interviewees talk about economic freedoms in terms of the right to private property, to own a business and engage in trade. They also speak of the freedom to make their own decisions regarding employment, education and travel/residence.

People's thinking changed significantly between 1998 and 2003 (Table 5.1) and varied within certain demographic categories both years. One contributing factor is changes in the laws. The 2002 Land Law gave people the right to relocate within Mongolia. People had not mentioned internal migration in 1998, but they did in 2003 because they now had the right to move about the country. Another is being five years more removed from socialism and experienced in capitalism. I don't have empirical evidence, but I think that Mongolians had settled into capitalism by 2003 and understood what they would need to survive if not thrive: ownership of the means of production, the right to relocate near markets and preparation for the market economy through access to higher education programs. So economic freedom supports the argument that people's attitudes toward economic rights and freedoms reflect history and culture; they are not always universal.

CHAPTER SIX

A Democratic Government Is
Responsible to Its Citizens

Anger surfaces when people speak of Mongolia's new government. They have clear expectations and know that their government is falling far short of them. They want the government to be honest and transparent, but they have seen that transparency varies with the political party in charge. They believe that a truly democratic government would honor their rights and freedoms, but they feel the Mongolian government does not. They expect fair and equal treatment in government offices (and courts), but they need to bribe officials to get things done. Finally, they want their government to support them in their transition to the market economy, but their expectations of law and order, access to education and so on are infrequently met. Mongolians are not alone. People in other NIS express disappointment concerning the gap between the democratic ideal and their new reality (Petro 1995:151; Verdery 1996:223; Humphrey 1998:461).

Foreign advisors and the Mongolian intelligentsia recognized that the government would need support to transition from communism to democracy. On my first visit in 1994, a group of us attended a concert and reception sponsored by the US Embassy. There I met Bill Nance, the head of USAID. He told me that his organization had three missions in Mongolia. The first was to teach the political leadership more about democracy by letting them observe US democracy in action. The second was to keep the Ulaanbaatar power plant running until next year when the Japanese would take over. Without the power plant, Ulaanbaatar would have no heat. And the third was to help build the economy (June 25, 1994, fieldnotes). Delegations from many nations—the United Kingdom, France, Germany, India, Norway, Sweden and so on—took on different projects to help Mongolia democratize and join the international market economy.

In this chapter, people talk about the characteristics of a democratic government and its duties toward its citizens. Regarding the former, it should not be corrupt. Its officials and administrators should promote rule of law and consider themselves subject to the rule of law. And a democratic government should be transparent, partly to reduce corruption.

A democratic government should also guarantee people's rights and freedoms, promote justice and equality, provide a healthy environment and access to health care and help its citizens survive or succeed in the new capitalist economy. Government should provide a social safety net for those who cannot succeed on their own.

People place all these ideals in the context of the past, present and imagined future. Concerning the past, their views are partly a reaction to the socialist decades when they knew they were working for the government and not vice versa. Despite rhetoric to the contrary, the socialist government operated for the benefit of its political elites. In 1998 Regsuren Bat-Erdene (then State Secretary of the Ministry of Science, Technology, Education and Culture) and his wife Tsetseglen Magsarjav took John Weidman and me to the Mongolian Circus. My childhood experience of a circus was the Ringling Brothers and Barnum & Bailey Circus in Madison Square Garden. There were lions, tigers and bears as well as horses, clowns, high-wire acts and so on. There were three simultaneous performances in side-by-side rings. It was simply huge to a child (and a bit confusing). My expectation of the Mongolian Circus was that it would only use horses in the animal acts and there would be one big ring. The round building with the blue circus-tent roof it was housed in seemed appropriately large from the outside. But when we entered, I saw that the ring was about the size of the stage in a provincial American theatre. I couldn't imagine how the horses would make the turn in that space. And instead of rows of seats surrounding the oval circus ring, there were rows of desks. What was going on? Bat-Erdene explained that the Mongolian Circus was built during socialist times as entertainment for the MPRP members only. In fact, we were sitting one row down from the last dictator Tsedenbal's desk. The desks were not for paperwork so much as they were for the vodka bottles, shot glasses and platters of food consumed during the show.

Mongolians share with other postsocialist people the worry that the negative aspects of communism will spill into the future. David Cerny, a Czech artist, expressed disgust toward the socialist government when he told *New York Times* reporters Bilefsky and Krcmar (2009:10), "The Communists ruined this country and oppressed freedom and yet here they are 20 years later in our Parliament…. It is a national disgrace. The Communists are endangering the country. The Czechs need to wake up."

Because our research participants remain idealistic, they phrase their responses as complaints ('this is the ideal and Mongolia is not meeting it') or as 'ought' phrases ('the government should be doing X but it is not'). They do not feel that their government is of the people, by the people or for the people, as they believe a democratic regime should be.

People tap into certain underlying values when describing a democratic government. The values I found were the desires for personal dignity, justice (in the sense of fairness), equality and economic survival or even success. While a later section of the chapter focuses on these values, you can see them in many of the quotations and anecdotes that follow.

A DEMOCRATIC GOVERNMENT SHOULD BE ...

Mongolians want a government they can trust. That is why they fomented the Democratic Revolution. A 27- to 39-year-old with a university degree (Khovd 1998 Bd030) espouses this ideal: "In a democratic society, the state works for the people; people trust the state." Yet by 1998, they already knew that their government was not trustworthy because it was neither free of corruption nor transparent (Figure 6.1).

What exactly is corruption? Bill Frej, a new friend who had years of experience in Asian countries as a member of USAID, thought it would be

Figure 6.1 Government House, where the Ikh Khural and government offices are located. Note the mausoleum in front of the building. (Paula L.W. Sabloff, 2003)

fun to write a paper on corruption together. "Good idea," I said. And we sat down to discuss what approach we should take. Within the first five minutes we realized that we were using different definitions of corruption. While his was comprehensive, including bribery and anything unethical a government could do, mine was more circumscribed. This naturally led me to think about how Mongolian research participants see corruption.[1] Is it limited to government officials and administrators? People had said, for example, that two of the most corrupt parts of government in Mongolia at the time of research were the customs officials and the judiciary. Corruption and bribery give current officials and administrators extra income. While I have no record of this, friends would point out the fancy homes purchased by politicians.

While working on the museum exhibition, I went to the National Archives with a film crew to obtain historical photos and film for the exhibition. After spending hours with us, the person in charge that day named a price for the copies. But, she added, I will give you a low price on the copies and you can pay the difference (between real cost and the lower price) directly to me. Although I was sympathetic to the fact that her low government wages could not support her family, I refused.

Not everyone was corrupt. I was lucky to be working with people who were not corrupt as I collaborated on the museum exhibition. When the National Museum of Mongolian History was helping me send artifacts for an exhibition in the United States, I got so frustrated with customs that I turned to the museum director, Dr. Idshinnorov, and asked him whom I could bribe to get the shipment out of Mongolia. "I don't know," he replied, and, having known him for several years, I believed him.

Still, bribery and corruption were real in the decades after the Democratic Revolution. In 1998, some people (63, or 7.3 percent) seemed upset by it (see Table 6.1). In that year, the Democratic Coalition was in power. Led by academics in their early 40s, it maintained a policy of openness but exhibited the same secretive behavior as the MPRP officials and administrators. Citizens knew that the new party was not living up to their expectations of a democratic government. "I consider democracy as governance of people with equal rights. Today people in power, who should represent the people, embezzle state property and ruin the people's trust. This is in violation of democracy," says a woman pensioner with a primary school education (Khovd 1998 Ns033). A skeptical university student (Ulaanbaatar 1998 Mh043) applies the Mongolian equivalent of our expression, 'like father, like son' to government officials: "As it is said in the Mongolian proverb, if the mare-mother is dappled, then her foal-baby will be at least foot-dappled.[2] I

Table 6.1 Mentions of the main attributes of a democratic government, 1998 and 2003[a]

	1998 Total = 867		2003 Total = 416		Significant difference between years
	N	%	N	%	χ^2
Not corrupt or open to bribes	63	7.3	68	16.3	***
Adheres to rule of law	29	3.3	81	19.5	***
Transparent	24	2.8	97	23.3	***

In a two-tailed chi-square (χ^2) test with 1 df, $*p \leq .05$, $**p \leq .01$ and $***p \leq .001$.
[a]By number, percent and Pearson's chi-square test.

pray that the few upright people will not be absorbed into dishonesty in to-day's Mongolia." A self-employed young man (Khovd 1998 Bs014) remarks, "People with high positions are corrupted and harm the country." He later adds, "High officials violate human rights."

In 2003, the MPRP had returned to power. Although it had adopted capitalism, the old guard took up party control once again. This caused some, like this pension-age man (Khovd Bj007), to trust the government again: "I prefer to live in a democracy. Everything is clear now, and I think that this parliament is honest."

But others remained upset by corruption. In fact, 68 (16.3 percent) mentioned corruption or bribery (Table 6.1). This is more than twice as many as 1998. A young farmer (Khovd 2003 Ns066) says, "Human rights are re-spected and well observed in a democratic society. Regrettably, some senior government officials, apparently unable to get rid of their former [socialist] mentality, exert pressure and impose their opinions on ordinary people."

People are irate about corruption because they know its consequences. A 27-year-old (Ulaanbaatar 1998 Ch074) spells them out: "Because our leaders are working illegally, democracy isn't performing in its real meaning." Additional quotations suggest that people believe justice, equality and even democracy are hurt when bribery and corruption take place:

People who have low salaries—especially the people who work for gov-ernment organizations—give and get bribes to make their life better. People are covering up for each other and hiding the truth. Because of that, the possibility to live justly is decreasing. If you should tell the truth, you are going to lose your job and your life. (Ulaanbaatar Ay046)

Democracy does not justify abuse of power. There were many individu-als who abused their power for making money when the Democratic

Coalition was in power. The illegal actions of some people must not be justified by democracy and freedom. For example, some government officials abuse their power by giving permits to build private buildings in the children's playgrounds [within the courtyards of apartment complexes in Ulaanbaatar]. (Ulaanbaatar 2003 Bu053)

People are aware that corruption is part of the culture. In Mongolia, as elsewhere, helping one's family and friends is what a good person does. Helping others is the glue of social networking and cooperation.

One way to control corruption and bribery is for a democratic government to practice rule of law. Rule of law means that everyone—citizen and government official alike—is subject to the law and everyone is equally protected by the law. Then everyone knows the rules and there are no surprises because citizens are protected from the whims of the ruling elite (Diamond (1996:24), including corruption.

Research participants want the government to follow rule of law (29 [3.3 percent] in 1998 and 81 [19.5 percent] in 2003). Again, the numbers suggest that more people desire rule of law in 2003 than in 1998. A girl who finished high school but did not continue on to university (Khovd 2003 Bj063) says, "In a democratic society, the national government has to see that laws are observed by every citizen of the country. In the previous regime, everything was decided in an autocratic way, whereas nowadays the government organizations have to make decisions in full compliance with the relevant provisions of the laws."

Five years earlier, a young high school graduate (Ulaanbaatar 1998 Os021) remarks, "Government should observe the law, that is, the laws must be implemented since they are made for the people's well-being. I don't know how many laws are implemented or observed; I guess 10 out of 100. We must educate people about the law and make them understand the importance of observing the laws. People don't even know which laws exist."

Our research participants focus on two different groups of people who seem exempt from rule of law. The first are government officials. A young Kazakh herder (Khovd 2003 Ns039) says that rule of law "is the principle where the government solves issues not by the interests of officials but according to the law."

In the summer of 2003 Member of Parliament and Vice President of the Democratic Party Gundalai was arrested after boarding a plane for Korea. This action was illegal because (a) members of parliament are immune from prosecution and (b) Gundalai, his wife and four-year-old daughter had already passed through several checkpoints and, according to international law, were in international territory. The Mongolian government does not have the authority to operate in international space. Why was Gundalai arrested? He had protested MPRP parliamentary actions and accused Nyamdorj, the Minister of Justice and MPRP member, of passing state secrets to the Russian Federation's KGB. So he was arrested for defamation of character of a public official. Once Gundalai was released, he drove to the headquarters of the Democratic Party in Sukhbaatar Square and tried to give a press interview. The police immediately rearrested him. The newspaper photos show him in a chokehold that prevented him from speaking. They took him to prison. The next day a large crowd formed in the square to protest Gundalai's unlawful arrest. He was released a few hours later, having spent about 25 hours in prison. This incident shows the MPRP bending the implementation of the law to the benefit of itself, which could not happen if rule of law were firmly in place (July 27, 2003, fieldnotes).

Burmaa Radnaa (September 15, 2003, interview) considered the incident "a shame. As a citizen, I'm afraid that the police force can do whatever it wants. If they do this to a parliament member, what will they do to people like me who criticize the government? I feel that my activities are dangerous [for me]. I feel it inside."

While Burmaa sees the Gundalai incident as an example of broken law and order, a young Kazakh in business (Khovd 2003 Ns075) sees it as proof that even officials must honor the law: "The law enforcement institutions have started to enforce the laws. The recent arrest of Member of Parliament Gundalai proves the commitment and determination of the state to bring criminals to justice. It clearly demonstrated that everyone, including senior state officials, is equal before the law."

The second group seemingly exempt from rule of law is the wealthy. In 1998, an inhabitant of Khovd (Bd021) expresses his concern when he says, "In a democratic society, any issue should not be settled arbitrarily or according to someone's wealth. People should be dealt with in accordance with the laws." A Khovd pensioner (2003 Bj009) sees the situation in class terms: "Even though a number of laws have been passed, no one knows them. The laws don't regulate the rich. The laws serve the poor unfairly."

Katherine Verdery (1996:223) notes the same phenomenon in Romania, adding that one consequence is distrust of government:

> We see, then, encounters that discourage people from perceiving the state as lawful, as well as behavior by which they assert themselves

against the state. Both of these indicate that a legitimating cultural relationship through "law-governed state" is not very robust in parts of rural Romania. Under these circumstances, the fact that privatization—which has its own legitimating effect, independent of the legal encounters that sometimes accompany it—is proceeding so slowly further shapes rural people's dispositions toward the state as either resigned or defiant.

A third way to limit corruption is to have transparent government. The people who mention transparency (24 [2.8 percent] in 1998 and 97 [23.3 percent] in 2003) use the Mongolian term *il tod* or the Russian term glasnost'. Either way, the term has come to mean that only an open, transparent government can be held accountable to the people because then they can see what the government is doing. One government worker (Ulaanbaatar 2003 Bu011) defines transparency, saying "The election campaigns are organized transparently and openly. The sessions of parliament are broadcast by television and reviewed by the press." Her age mate in Khovd (2003 Bj011) explains, "Government activities are open to the public. I have read that during the US presidential election, candidates were written about openly in the newspapers. For our country the same thing is happening."

Burmaa Radnaa contradicts the optimism of these young women (September 15, 2003, interview). When I asked her how she would characterize Mongolia's MPRP government, she replied,

This [MPRP] government says to the public and foreigners that they are for democracy and civil society, but in real life it is not so. They work the way they did under socialism—they don't want the public to have access to information; they control national TV and radio; they don't give civil society a voice or the opposition parties either. There is very high corruption—and no regulations [to curb corruption]. This government became more closed than the previous government.... The law on land privatization was passed a year ago. The draft law was introduced to Parliament only one week before the plenary session; there was no public discussion, no hearings on it. The opposition was against it, but the government didn't care about their opposition.

The same procedure was used regarding the amendments to the Constitution [which allowed parliament members to be cabinet members also]. These passed in 2000 under this [MPRP-controlled] parliament.

The day before the plenary session, they [the government] published the draft amendments in the newspaper, but they passed them [into law] in the plenary session. I started to write some recommendations about the amendments, but they [the MPRP] didn't care about discussing the issue.

The US Embassy gave [financial] support for the Prime Minister to have an open government website—to post draft laws and conduct on-line discussions of the proposed laws. But the Prime Minister posted only a few draft laws, ones that are general and not important. The important laws (anti-corruption, ethics, and land privatization) were not put on the website.

I'm a member of the National Council on Anti-corruption. I've asked several times for the draft law but they won't give it to me. I'm also a member of the General Election Committee, but they won't give me the draft law. Yet they say they are happy for the public to have the draft laws and official information.

The local-level governments are not transparent either. They are becoming more and more closed. All the *khurals* [parliaments from the local level to the national government] don't have regulations about the voting system; they don't show the agenda to the public. We [Women for Social Progress] did a survey in 2001 showing that the officials don't answer the questions we asked. Usually the local governors are MPRP party heads and the assemblymen are staff to the governor. How can the assemblymen monitor the governor if they are his staff?

I saw that the Thailand Constitution says if any issue concerns a [is taken up in] committee, there should be a public hearing on the issue. But we don't have this idea of public discussion in Mongolia.

While I was interviewing Burmaa, Bumaa was interviewing a Buriat university student (Ulaanbaatar 2003 Bu058) who backed up Burmaa:

Information has been open since 1990. Mongolia is a democratic country, but it cannot be considered to have become a real democratic country because of corruption and single-party rule. Following the 2000 election, only one political party has been dominating parliament. In the 1990s, a multiparty system was established, but other political parties are not strong enough to adequately oppose the MPRP.

Table 6.1 suggests significant change over time. There also seem to be some significant differences within years by demographic subcategories. In Table 6.2, we see significant variability in 1998 within five demographic categories for the column Not corrupt. Oddly enough, the difference between Ulaanbaatar and Khovd (Location) is not significant here. I think the whole country is dealing with bribery and corruption. The herders, rural dwellers and those with the least education—all of which categories overlap in personnel—mention corruption more often than others. They must be dealing with corruption more than the urban people, many of whom are government workers. In contrast, the only category starred in the Not corrupt column in 2003 is Location. Perhaps people's perceptions vary depending on whether one lives inside or outside the capital, Ulaanbaatar. Those close to the seat of government and with access to more news coverage than other parts of the country see things differently. They also have a greater stake in the government than others, for many of them work for the government, NGOs or political parties.

People seem to be in tune with one another on government transparency. The media covered *il tod* (glasnost') well, so people were familiar with it. By 2003, people's ideas varied strongly according to their location and weakly for two other categories. Thus, even people's ideas about government's role in assuring rights, justice and equality vary somewhat in both years.

Before leaving this section, I must admit that I am always struck by the tone that these references to government take. By using the phrases, 'we were

Table 6.2 Significant differences within demographic categories in three attributes of a democratic government, 1998 and 2003[a]

	1998			2003		
	Not corrupt	Rule of law	Transparent	Not corrupt	Rule of law	Transparent
Location		*		*	***	***
Residence	***					
Gender						
Age group	*					*
Education	**					
Occupation	***					
Ethnic identity	*				*	

In a two-tailed chi-square test, *p≤.05, **p≤.01, and ***p≤.001. Location, residence and gender=1 df; age group, education and ethnicity=3 df; occupation=5 df for 1998 and 6 df for 2003.
[a]See Table A.10 in Appendix for details.

given complete freedom' (*erkh choloo buren olgoson*), the people sound like passive recipients of their rights rather than active members of a democracy. They appear to see themselves not as the people who demonstrated against the MPRP's single-party control many times during the socialist period but as children who receive gifts from their parents. Perhaps it is a holdover from the cultural concept of big brother that was manipulated by the Russians during socialism. There is a traditional Mongolian idea of older brother/ younger brother (or sister). This concept means that in Mongolian tradition and practice, a big brother is responsible for the welfare of his siblings, while younger siblings owe their older brother respect. I recall a 1998 researcher whose mother-in-law told her husband, the oldest brother, that he was responsible for providing college tuition for his nephews and nieces. By 2003, the obligation had been reduced—or the families interpreted the obligation differently. This time, Bumaa told me that her husband's oldest brother gave them US$100 a year to help in her son's studies (August 5, 2003, fieldnotes).

A DEMOCRATIC GOVERNMENT SHOULD GUARANTEE CITIZENS THEIR RIGHTS AND FREEDOMS, JUSTICE AND EQUALITY

Having explained our participants' expectation that democratic government should be honest and transparent and follow the rule of law, I move on to what people think government should be doing for its citizens (Table 6.3). These include protecting their rights and freedoms and promoting justice. We would expect that people who value political and economic freedom as much as the Mongolians interviewed would also say that a democratic government has the responsibility to protect citizens' rights and freedoms. And they do. Their comments are a variation of the central tenet of liberal democracy—that is, a democratic government must not prevent citizens from exercising their rights and freedoms (Rousseau 1755; Diamond 1996:23).

The numbers and percentages in Table 6.3 are much higher than those in Table 6.1. Still, the jump from 1998 to 2003 remains statistically significant in all but one case (access to education), showing people's growing desire for the Mongolian government to maintain democracy.

I briefly described the two privatization laws and their implementation in Chapter 5. The second one, the Law on Allocation of Land to Mongolian Citizens for Ownership, was adopted in 2002 (to take effect on May 1, 2003) when the MPRP controlled parliament. It made urban plots and agricultural fields eligible for privatization. While further land privatization sounded lovely,

Table 6.3 Mentions of a democratic government's major responsibilities toward citizens, 1998 and 2003[a]

	1998 Total = 867		2003 Total = 416		Significant difference between years
	N	%	N	%	χ^2
Guarantees rights and freedoms	205	23.6	166	39.9	***
Is just (fair)	160	18.5	103	24.8	**
Promotes equality	89	10.3	241	57.9	***

In a two-tailed chi-square (χ^2) test with 1 df, $*p \leq .05$, $**p \leq .01$ and $***p \leq .001$.
[a]By number, percent and Pearson's chi-square test.

some citizens read the draft law and became suspicious. By 2002 they had had enough experience to know that the chances of fair and equal distribution of state property would not take place. A 37-year-old woman in business (Ulaanbaatar 2003 Ay026) aptly summarizes the 1992 privatization experience:

When democracy took place in Mongolia, the government instituted privatization. But the privatization process did not go the right way. State property was divided among the entire Mongolian population, given as shares under the name 'blue ticket.' But afterwards a few groups of people who had economic knowledge bought others' shares at very cheap prices. Because of this, some people became rich and others became poor, lacking property and shares.

With knowledge of this background, people formed "The Fair Land Privatization Movement." Their goal was to obtain fair distribution of land. This new group, which was supported by the Mongolian Democratic Union (the party in opposition to the MPRP), quickly attracted thousands of members in 20 branches all over the country. It tried to register as an NGO and obtain a permit for a peaceful demonstration in Ulaanbaatar's Freedom Square in early October. Neither request was honored (Liberty Center 2002a). Nevertheless, the leadership planned a demonstration for November 13. It was to be led by 100 tractors. The tractors started arriving in Ulaanbaatar the week before the planned demonstration, but the police blocked all but 32 from entering the square. Thousands of people milled around the headquarters of the Democratic Union on the square. According to the email accounts of Liberty Center (2002b) and the Konrad Adenauer Foundation (Undarya email to Konrad Adenauer Foundation's listserv, 2002), police entered the Democratic Union's headquarters and arrested 49 people. Thus, police action (on order from the authorities) prevented citizens from holding a peaceable demonstration, which was contrary to the 1992 Constitution.

Although the leaders of the movement were angry about the treatment of the protesters, they were even more upset by the lack of media coverage. Only two radio stations broadcast news about the arrests (Liberty Center 2002b). The national TV station—under the control of the MPRP—broadcast the incident from the government's perspective only. The editor-in-chief of one newspaper, *Udriin Sonin,* said that the paper's journalists had been arrested and therefore could not publish the news. He added, "When I turned on your FM wave I realized that it was time not to believe communists. I realized that it was time to stand for democracy, I will attend any demonstration to stand for it." The movement leaders feared that Mongolians had been exposed to a biased view of the event and called for another demonstration on November 19 to save Mongolian democracy (ibid.).

The next morning, 60 tractor operators walked to the center of the city with their slogans and pictures of tractors in their hands and organized a press conference and expressed their thanks for all who supported them and criticized the National TV for its outrageous lie. Tractor operators also informed that they invited Members of Parliament, especially those who were elected from their home provinces to an open meeting and dispute on the Land Privatization law.

"It is a question of whether our future to be forever poor or not. The law on land privatization will allow to own all 800.000 hectares of farm land for only around 300 individuals who run bigger farming business or who have enough money to buy those lands on an auction [will allow only around 300 individuals who run bigger farming businesses or who have enough money to own 800,000 hectares of farm land]. Because of this we wanted to convince our MPs that this law has become unfair and that they must to change this law. We tried to hand our letter via the Division of Parliamentary Public Relation but nobody received our letter. So we sent this letter via regular post just before this press conference" said a tractor operator. (ibid.)

A few months later, Mr. Saintogtoh, a poor man and head of a family of 10, appealed to the Mongolian Human Rights Commission because local police and the city construction department had seized his family ger and the land around it. He had occupied land near the center of Ulaanbaatar for years, he said, and had applied to register his claim to this land several times. That way he would own it when the Land Law came into effect. It seems that

23 other families had been able to register their land in the same district. "I did not have any failure in my registration or documentation or something else which would disqualify my application for land permission. I built up my dwelling according to the written permission of city architectural and planning authorities. Since September 2000, I have been constantly apply-ing for getting the final permission from the district governor's office," he wrote in his appeal. The Mongolian Human Rights Commission sided with Mr. Saintogtoh. It lodged a formal protest to the government, demanding that officials give him back the land and make restitution payments as well.

Liberty Center (2003a) believed that the land had been taken because it was very close to the city center and therefore very valuable. "'Land rob-bing has begun openly and is expected to continue widely against poor and helpless families and people,' warns Mr. Bat-Uul, the leader of the Fair Land Privatization Movement, while advocating importance of immediate and serious watch on the land privatization."[3]

Whether people think the Mongolian government is doing a good job or not, they mostly use modal sentences ('should,' 'ought to' or 'must'), emphasizing government's moral obligation to its citizens. As you read the quotations, please note that a few do not mention the government overtly. But when people say that democracy 'provides,' 'guarantees' or 'protects' rights and freedoms, they mean that the government enforces these rights.

People who say that the Mongolian government is doing a good job believe that it is protecting citizens' rights and freedoms. They frequently compare the current constitution with the socialist years. A 55-plus-year-old man who describes himself as unemployed and is of pensioner age says, "In former times we had no freedom; we were under the control of any of the ruling party's organizations [from the local to national level, in schools and unions and so on]. Now we have freedom." A 40-year-old businessman in Ulaanbaatar (2003 Bu013) says, "The state recognizes ownership of pri-vate property in a democratic society. Every citizen has the right to the fair acquisition and possession of private property."

A few others say that the government is not doing a good job. A Kazakh businessman with a primary school education (Khovd 2003 Ns050) says, "Hu-man rights are abused depending on which party holds power. For example, the MPRP fires government officials who support the Democratic Party." And a businesswoman (Ulaanbaatar 2003 Bu023) suggests other abuses:

> Human rights are fully honored in a democratic society. Unfortunately, violation of human rights is a common phenomenon in Mongolia. For

example, some state organizations and officials collect taxes from citizens who have already been exempted [from paying taxes] by the law. Although any citizen of the country has the right to reside in any part of the country, the local authorities that issue land permissions violate that right. Also, rural migrants have to pay special fees in order to settle in the capital. Owners of large and medium trade companies abuse our human rights by importing low-quality food products. The imported food products do not meet national sanitary standards and harm our health. The law enforcement institutions violate human rights by apprehending citizens without any justification and with authorization from competent government bodies.

After government protection of rights and freedoms, people say that a democratic government should promote justice (160 [18.5 percent] in 1998; 103 [24.8 percent] in 2003) and equality (89 [10.3 percent] in 1998; 241 [57.9 percent] in 2003) (see Table 6.3). When they do, two themes intertwine, although they are often hard to separate. The first is that the government should promote just, fair treatment of citizens. The second is that the government should assure the equal treatment of all people. One of these does not make sense without the other.

What is justice? In 2003 I had the opportunity to interview Baabar, the scientist, political activist and government official (Member of Parliament and Minister of Finance) who had written the definitive history of twentieth-century Mongolia (Baabar 1999). He told me that all Mongolian political parties were talking about justice then. But although it was 13 years after the Democratic Revolution, Mongolians were still using the socialist understanding of justice—that is, that the distribution of wealth must be equal for people to be equal. All the political parties equated democracy with economic equality and believed that the government is responsible for all things. Yet Baabar said that world history shows that these goals are impossible. Lately, he added, the Democratic Party members agreed that justice is economic freedom, not economic equality. "Without economic freedom, freedom does not exist," he said (July 16, 2003, interview).

No matter how it is defined, incidents show that justice is not always practiced in Mongolia. Again, the 2002 land law provides an example of injustice. That year, the mayor ('governor') of Ulaanbaatar, M. Enkhbold, signed an order evicting five poor families living in gers in the same district as Mr. Saintogtoh, above. The original settlers were rural men who had come to Ulaanbaatar in 1965. At the time of eviction, their families consisted of pensioners, children under 16, students and unemployed adults, some disabled. The average income per family was US$25 per month. They all had licenses to stay, but when they reapplied to the district office to assure the legality of their licenses after the land law went into effect, the authorities told them they would have to leave. It seems that a coalition of small businesses wanted the land. The five families were given no restitution and no explanation for the mayor's decision (Liberty Center 2003c).

Reflecting on similar incidents in the Khovd region, a 40-to-54-year-old Oirad woman (Khovd 1998 Bd007) says that democracy depends on fair officials. "If the people who have power are unfair and ruin people's trust; that will limit democracy." Others agree:

The constitution guaranteed human rights, liberty and justice, but actually not everyone can express his thoughts. Some principles of justice have been lost and limited in real life. The existing rulers control governance by force and by having a monopoly over money. The law isn't applied to wealthy and important people. Democracy changed into only a slogan [became empty words]. It is a great pity. (Ulaanbaatar 1998 Mh026)

Justice, the main tendency of democracy, is not being realized in Mongolia. Laws and rights mostly serve for people who work in the government, not for ordinary citizens. The latter suffer in some cases. In my opinion, if the government's policy is just, then justice would be for everyone. (Ulaanbaatar 2003 Na016)

Justice isn't functioning in Mongolia. In particular, the law isn't working for the Kazakh people. It is unfortunate. (Khovd 2003 Ns051)

The rule of justice should be actively propagated and advocated through the mass media. In reality, we observe the rule of absolute injustice reigning in the society, especially in the local government administration offices. (Khovd 2003 Ns068)

Respondents also say that a democratic government should maintain fair laws and courts. According to a young businessman (Ulaanbaatar 1998 Ch006), "Judges should be very responsible. They have to determine the real perpetrators of the crime in order to judge them honestly." One university-educated pensioner (Ulaanbaatar 1998 Os026) considers merit as a justice issue. If people earn their jobs through merit rather than their connections, that is clearly an indicator of justice. He says, "During socialist times anyone who was a member of the MPRP was nominated for a higher position regardless of his or her qualifications. In a democratic country, one must deserve to get the position based on his or her achievement."

Another aspect of justice is equality, and people expect a democratic government to treat citizens equally. A young woman in Khovd (1998 Ns019) says it best: "Equality in everything is justice. Without justice we can't develop true democracy." When talking about equality, our research participants mean that the state should guarantee everyone's right to own property, practice any religion, and receive equal treatment in the courts and government offices. Some believe that Mongolia has achieved equality. A 20-year-old working in the health professions (Ulaanbaatar 1998 Ch017) says, "All citizens have equal rights; the general and the soldier really live the same." An older woman (Ulaanbaatar 1998 Mh041) adds,

> Everyone has equal rights with everyone else. Establishing equality does not mean that all people are the same or that differences between people are eliminated. Equality means elimination of the roots of social segregation—discrimination. Therefore, regardless of wealth, ethnicity, social background, or belief, people should be protected by law and have equal rights to get educated, obtain property, and take positions in the society. The notions of freedom and human rights are [actually] based on the notion of equal rights.

Although the people just quoted seem positive about equality in Mongolia, others are negative. One young man (Ulaanbaatar 1998 Os041) says, "Even though we are guaranteed equal rights by the constitution, not everyone is a person before the law. The [law-and-order] laws aren't applied to the people who have power and money." A young herder (Khovd 2003 Ns069) sees ethnic discrimination: "In reality, it seems that I am not treated properly at the local administration office or at a local clinic hospital because of my Kazakh nationality and basic knowledge of Mongolian." A retirement-age Kazakh herder (Khovd 2003 Ns076) says, "Justice is not fully implemented in our society. In my view, justice means regulation of all social issues on the basis of equality and according to the laws." A 46-year-old university-trained government worker (Ulaanbaatar 2003 Na019) states, "In Mongolia there is discrimination on the basis of belonging to a different political party, clothes and the difference between rich and poor."

Table 6.4 Significant differences within demographic categories concerning a democratic government's major responsibilities toward citizens, 1998 and 2003[a]

	1998			2003		
	Rights and freedoms	Justice (fairness)	Equality	Rights and freedoms	Justice (fairness)	Equality
Location	*	**	***	***	***	
Residence	**	***	***			
Gender						
Age group		*				***
Education	***	***	***	***	*	
Occupation		***	***			
Ethnic identity		*			*	***

In a two-tailed chi-square test, *p≤.05, **p≤.01, and ***p≤.001. Location, residence and gender = 1 df; age group, education and ethnicity = 3 df; occupation = 5 df for 1998 and 6 df for 2003.
[a] See Table A.11 in Appendix for details.

Anger stemming from inequality is not limited to Mongolians. Bruce Grant interviewed Natalia Borisovna Ivanova, a literary critic in Moscow. She expressed disgust at the special access to privileges granted members of the socialist Union of Writers even though she had received them herself. "The problem with the old Writer's Union," she said, "is that it was entirely in the service of the state. The new union must be devoid of money, entirely devoid of privileges" (Grant 1993:28–29).

Table 6.4 illustrates how people in different demographic categories perceive a democratic government's major responsibilities to its citizens. In both years, people vary by location more than the other demographic categories. Variability in education is second. The split between urbanites and rural dwellers is significant in 1998 but not 2003. Note that once again, there is no significant difference between men and women.

When mentioning government responsibility for justice, we see that variability exists in the same categories as 'rights and freedoms' with two exceptions. This is because the percent of people who mention justice rises with education level and varies by age group. The age groups that are most active in the job market have the highest percentage of mentions.

DEMOCRATIC GOVERNMENT SHOULD HELP CITIZENS SUCCESSFULLY TRANSITION TO THE MARKET ECONOMY

My feeling that people perceive government as a patron persists when I consider their desire for government help as the country transitions to a market economy. Moving from the socialist command economy to a global market economy was difficult, especially under shock therapy conditions. Imagine spending half your life working for the government and knowing you have a job and pension security and then finding out that you are on your own. Furthermore, because of the cultural concept of big brother's responsibility for one's younger siblings, your mother keeps telling you that as the oldest son, you are now responsible not only for your wife and children but also for your younger siblings' families, including paying for (or at least contributing to) their schooling and university education. That is what happened in Mongolia and other newly democratic states. What would you need from your government to succeed in the new economy? Law and order so that goods and produce you prepare for the market are not stolen. Increased access to education programs so that you can build the skills valued in the global market. You might also want the government to continue providing access to healthcare and maintaining clean air and water so that you have a fighting chance to remain healthy and keep working.

But what if you fail? Or what if your sister fails and your mother keeps nagging you to take care of her and her family? Well, then you want government support for her so that you can concentrate on taking care of your own family. And what if your parents decide they can't make the transition and want to retire? Surely you would want the government to give them a pension so that they can live—with little help from you. These are the supports the Mongolians want, too.

Crime—especially theft of livestock—hurts people's chances of succeeding in the market economy; they can never be sure that their property or their lives are safe. It's that simple. In 1998, 10,712 crimes were committed in Ulaanbaatar, and 518 were committed in Khovd (National Statistics Office 1999:193). These figures contrast with the 1990 figures, when Ulaanbaatar's crime rate was 2,884 and Khovd's was 160 (National Statistics Office 1999:193).

Whenever I went to Mongolia for fieldwork, I would rent an apartment in Ulaanbaatar. From 1996 to 2003, friends would help me find one near the center of the city. Usually one of their friends was going abroad or into the countryside and wanted to make some extra money by renting their place. Every apartment I looked at had a double door. One was usually made of wood; the other was often steel. Both the inner and outer doors had multiple locks and keys. Each lock had a separate pattern: I had to turn one key four times, another one twice. When I asked my friends why there were two doors and so many locks, they said that apartments had only one door and one lock during socialism. But with the Democratic Revolution and the market economy, crime started rising, so people added an extra door and several locks to keep them safe.

One night this safety feature backfired on me. I had been to dinner with my British friend, Brian Hackman. When we finished, it was still light outside, so I told him not to walk me up to my apartment because he had a long walk back to his hotel. I climbed to my second-floor apartment and took out the keychain with three keys and a rubber Minnie Mouse. I don't know what made me look up, but sitting on the stairs above me were two men who were clearly drunk. They might have done nothing, but I was a foreigner and easy prey. I figured if I had stood there and opened all the locks, they could easily rush at me and get into the apartment. They might have done absolutely nothing, but I was unwilling to take the chance. Many ex-pats I had met warned me of crimes against foreigners, who were assumed to have lots of money compared with the Mongolians. So I went back down the stairs onto the main thoroughfare. Just then, two very tall blonde Danish young men were walking by. I stopped them and asked them to help me get to my apartment and they quickly obliged. The drunks were no longer in the stairwell.

Crime and fear of crime was not a Mongolian problem but a postsocialist one (Creed 1999:228–29, 237; Humphrey 2002:29). Humphrey (ibid.:100) writes,

> In Russia, nonstate enforcers of rules (such as rackets and mafias) have to a considerable extent displaced the state in the process of postcommunist transformation because they have been doing a better job than the state in reducing the transaction costs of exchange and production.

Under such circumstances, it is no wonder that several of our interviewees called for a 'dictatorship' or a strong government, as one Ulaanbaatar pensioner (1998 Ch043) does: "Mongolia needs a dictator. In the former society, if someone missed the weekly staff political lecture at work even once, there was punishment for that. Now everywhere in the society disorder and anarchy are growing." A young Kazakh woman with a university degree (Khovd 1998 Ns013) says, "In the socialist system there was dictatorship of one person and people's every action was controlled. Due to the influence of different foreign and domestic ideologies, chaos has settled into this free society."

In 1998, 45 (5.2 percent) mentioned that government should maintain law and order, that is, prevent crime (see Table 6.5). By 2003, people were

Table 6.5 Government attributes related to support of citizens' transition to the market economy, 1998 and 2003[a]

	1998 Total=867		2003 Total=416		Significant difference between years
	N	%	N	%	χ^2
Maintains law and order	45	5.2	45	10.8	***
Provides access to education	82	9.5	33	7.9	
Provides healthy environment (physical and medical)	39	4.5	15	3.6	
Provides social safety net	32	3.7	28	6.7	*
Total transition to market economy	153	17.6	98	23.6	*

In a two-tailed chi-square (χ^2) test with 1 df, *p≤.05, **p≤.01 and ***p≤.001.
[a]By number, percent and Pearson's chi-square test.

still worried about crime (45, or 10.8 percent) even though the crime rate was starting to drop (9,940 in Ulaanbaatar and 335 in Khovd) (National Statistics Office 2004:279).

A few people also want the government to keep Mongolia from slipping into anarchy. A 27-plus-year-old businessman (Khovd 1998 Bj045) discusses chaos, or anarchy, saying, "At first I supported all processes of democratization. But now I can't distinguish between democracy and anarchism. About true democracy, I can only say that I've read about it in books but never seen it." Five years later, an older businessman from Chandmani Sum (Khovd 2003 Ns053) observes, "In our sum, anarchy is taking place. In particular, the chairman of the people's representative is a Democratic Party member; the mayor is MPRP, and they are in conflict with each other. So the public administration is not working. And the chairman frequently beats the mayor." A middle-aged herder woman (Khovd 2003 Ns064) grumbles, "The theft of livestock has become an everyday phenomenon in rural areas. The government does not take any measures to enforce the laws."

Early in Russia's Democratic Revolution, the intelligentsia also fretted about chaos. Aleksandr Andreevich Prokhanov, a novelist and literary critic, asked Grant (1993:34) the rhetorical question,

Can you tell me, does our chaos fit in to the popular idea of the new world order, to new world harmony? We are in complete chaotic pandemonium and there is no going back. What's more, this chaos has spread to Eastern Europe, has destroyed what were carefully implemented economic ties ... in a word, Russian chaos. In response to the

American variety, we respond with chaos. Whereas before we might have answered with submarines, SS20s and the like, today we answer with chaos.

Aside from expecting the government to maintain law and order, interviewees say the government should increase access to education and higher education (82 [9.5 percent] in 1998; 33 [7.9 percent] in 2003). They associate education with economic success and therefore want increased access. When people say there is broader access to higher education now, they mean either that they have the right to the kind of education they want or the newly created private higher education institutions are expanding access to higher education or that education should be free, as it was in socialist times. Interestingly enough, it is a young Khalkh woman with a primary school education (Ulaanbaatar 1998 Ch033) who says, "Everyone has to be provided with the opportunity to study. School should be free in a democracy." She is bolstered by another young woman who has a university degree (Ulaanbaatar 1998 Tj035): "Basic human rights are proclaimed by the constitution, including the right to have an education. The state must provide basic necessities for an individual to obtain an education and develop himself."

Despite broader access, people also say that the government is responsible for a decline in the quality of education. Another older woman who completed primary school (Khovd 1998 Bs012) says, "Education has worsened. It is because of poor [government] provisions for students. For example, now we don't have a dormitory here. Students drop out of school.... We also lack teachers here in the countryside." The numbers support her position. In 1989, there were 22.5 students per teacher in the primary and secondary schools. By 1998, the number was 32.8 per teacher (National Statistics Office 1999:171). By 2003, the proportion had dropped again, to 25.8 to 1 (National Statistics Office 2004:249). In the universities, teachers who had taught Russian for years were given one year of preparation to become teachers of English. How could they possibly accomplish such a rapid transition? And yet they did. But the initial quality of teaching a different subject from the one people were trained in was not high.

A few wanted the state to pay for everyone to go to school. The socialist government paid for students' room and board, books and instruction, but the democratic government required students to pay. This was especially hard on pastoral nomads who had to pay room and board for their children in primary and secondary schools, usually in the sum centers. A 40-to-55-year-old businessman with a baccalaureate (Ulaanbaatar 1998 Ch001) says, "Citizens must have the right to education. The government must help by giving people loans for education. Then people could afford to study." Five years later, the situation was still not resolved. A herder in his 60s (Ulaanbaatar 2003 Bu047) says, "The herders are not able to send their children to secondary schools as they can't afford stationery and hostel fees. The only source of income of the herders is selling livestock products such as meat, dairy products, wool, sheepskin and hides. A lack of financial resources deprives their children of an opportunity to study at higher educational institutions. Most of them face unemployment after graduating from secondary schools. Under socialism, our children were able to study at universities and colleges as long as they passed the entry examinations."

The situation was also stressful on the higher education institutions. In 1994, the rector of the Agricultural Technical College spoke with a group of us. He said that the school was developed as a vocational-technical school to prepare professional agricultural workers under the socialist system. In those days, the government provided everything: clothing, toothbrushes, notebooks and so on. And the administrators had to figure out how to spend all the money they received. Now government money covers only 25 percent of expenses, and the administrators have to think about how to raise money. One way was to save it. That would explain why we had to walk down dark corridors, being careful not to tip up floor boards on the way to his office. The rector was also thinking of closing the college in the coldest winter months to save the cost of heating the buildings, his biggest expense.

The technical college received income from tuition fees for the mechanics program but not the agricultural program. It had 600 hectares (1482.6 acres) of land on which the school raised wheat, vegetables and livestock (sheep, cows and horses). It made cheese, yogurt and mare's milk. It sold these products in Ulaanbaatar, which was not far. The income was spent on improving conditions for students and faculty. But in 1994, the place was an absolute shambles and had a significant budget deficit. The rector said that everyone is frustrated, and he looked haggard (June 12, 1994, fieldnotes).

Quotations from the interviews confirm the problem from the perspective of students, parents and caring kin. A 20-year-old woman (Khovd 1998 Bj020) tells a researcher, "Tuition is charged. It burdens people that all the universities charge money for tuition. What should families with many children do?" At the same time, a young fellow with a baccalaureate but no employment (Ulaanbaatar 1998 Os036) says,

A democratic government must take charge of education and health care because of the high unemployment rate. The government ignores the higher education system. The government must provide financial support for technical schools such as carpentry, plumbing, nursing and seamstress work [community colleges in the United States]. It's understandable why youths are unemployed: they don't have any skills. The government must finance the technical schools. Young kids need to have skills to have a career. Primary school kids must have equal conditions in terms of facilities, quality of teachers, etc.

Having learned of people's expectation that the government provide education options for students, I was surprised to find that so few people expected the government to provide healthcare anymore. In both years, less than half the number of people who wanted access to education wanted the government to provide a healthy environment or healthcare. After all, they had enjoyed free healthcare under the socialist government, even though many resented it. Brian Hackman was in Mongolia to help determine the causes of skyrocketing maternal mortality since 1990.[4] The maternal mortality rate climbed to 241 deaths per 100,000 by 1993. That year the United Nations Population Fund (UNFPA) and United Nations Children's Fund (UNICEF) started staffing the waiting homes again. The maternal mortality rate started to fall in the late 1990s and continued to do so during the first years of the millennium. By 1998, it was down to 163 per 100,000, and in 2003 the rate was 109.5 (Yadamsuren, Merialdi, Davaadorj et al. 2010:196). But the rate was still high. Brian interviewed doctors and staff in Ulaanbaatar and several provincial hospitals. He shared his experiences with me. Under socialism, rural women had to stay at 'maternal waiting homes' starting in the sixth month of their pregnancy. There they were cared for and watched. Of course Mongolian women hated being dictated to and confined, so as soon as democracy came, they stopped going to these homes. As a result, the death rate for pregnant women and nursing mothers rose.

Perhaps the desire for self-determination explains why so few people even thought of healthcare when we asked for characteristics of democracy. This woman, also quoted earlier (Khovd 1998 Bs012), is negative about democracy on the whole. She says, "The vulnerable parts of the population can't get medical treatment because hospitals now charge for treatment." Less negative is a university student (Ulaanbaatar 1998 Tj047) who says, "If people are healthy, the country could develop. A democratic country takes care of the people's health." Finally, a university-educated government worker (Khovd 2003Bd026) says, "The government should work for the people. To assure the right to be healthy, to have education and good living conditions, the government must help."

Less than a handful in 1998 consider government support for environ-mental protection necessary. One herder near Tuv Aimag Center (Ulaan-baatar 1998 En047) tells Enkhtuya, "Environmental problems are lagging behind. The grazed land is devastated because of many messy roads and fires. The state should take care of it."

I met several foreigners who were working on environmental issues. One of them was Sabine Schmidt, a specialist in earth science. She was working for GTZ (pronounced G-T-Zed), meaning German Society for Technical Coop-eration.[5] She frequently went to the Gobi to interest herder communities in thinking about ecological conservation. She said this has to be a bottom-up, long-term project, as top-down projects have no sustainability. It is true that we did not interview in the Gobi, but it is also true that very few people mentioned the environment or the government's role in protecting the environment.

People's last expectation of government is that it should provide sup-port for those who could not survive in the transition to a market economy, namely, the old and the poor. A few (32, or 3.7 percent) in 1998 expressed concern fellow citizens were falling into endless poverty. The 2003 interviews show a much higher percentage of the sampled population (98, or 23.6 per-cent) disturbed by this. This change is just significant, having only one star in Table 6.5. People's feelings are summed up by two pensioners. The first (Ulaanbaatar 1998 Os052) confesses, "Personally, my life has worsened. My 10 children are all jobless. If socialism was in existence, I'm sure all my chil-dren would be employed. So I say this from my own experience." The second is a 75-year-old woman living in Bayandelger Sum Center (Ulaanbaatar 2003 Bu038). She says, "Although everyone has all kinds of freedom now, people's living standards have significantly plummeted. The current social security system is not effective. For example, I receive a monthly pension of 22,000 togrogs, and the pension is not enough to meet my basic needs. Luckily, revenues derived from our livestock supplement our family budget." And a herder (Khovd 1998 Ns056) adds, "The government that doesn't carry out a welfare policy must resign under pressure from the people. This is the main feature of such a society."

Other respondents speak in generalities. For example, a young woman in education (Ulaanbaatar 1998 Mh025) says, "We should never forget to take care of the poor or people of the lower [economic] level. The state and govern-ment should take care of them." A young man in business (Ulaanbaatar 1998 Tj061) states, "The government must take some actions to create new jobs for people. Also government should have social welfare programs such as pensions, healthcare and aid for people who live below the average [income]."

In 2003, people are still complaining that the democratic government does not help the poor. One young herder (Ulaanbaatar 2003 Bu044) wants democracy for its economic freedom and opportunities, yet he still wants a safety net for others:

I wish that the state always supported and helped the poor. The first action to take is to create employment opportunities for the poor. If poor people don't want to work and improve their living conditions, it is their choice. I don't know what measures the government is taking for reducing poverty. We herders are able to support our families on our own. Likewise, people with no livestock can earn a living by working. However, there are no employment opportunities for inhabitants of the sum centers. I think they will become impoverished first.

Some interviewees want the government to take care of pensioners better. One of these (Khovd 2003 Bj062) is a pensioner himself. Using the socialist term 'humane,' he says, "The society is becoming less and less humane. The government does not care for the poor and elderly anymore. The pensions paid to the elderly are barely enough to fill empty stomachs." And a young woman (Ulaanbaatar 2003 Na066) complains about lack of government support for women: "Under socialism my mother got a pension while she was giving birth and raising a baby. But now in the same case I received only a little money. So now people do not want to have many children."

All of the issues that comprise government's obligation to help citizens cope with the market economy add up to 153 (17.6 percent) in 1998 and 98 (23.6 percent) in 2003. While the numbers are still lower than rights and freedoms, they are substantial in an open-ended survey and suggest serious concern on the part of our research participants. Still, respondents show some significant variability, but not much.

The 1998 interviewees do not seem to vary greatly when discussing government enforcement of law and order and government's role in setting policy, which includes economic development policy. However, there is significant variability between those who mention government's duty to provide access to education and a social safety net and those who do not. In both subdomains, people vary by location and occupation. For the Government should provide access to education category, people also vary by gender (twice as many women as men mention this) and education attained. This reflects the fact that more higher education students were women than men in the transition years. For the social safety net, people vary by age, occupation

Table 6.6 Significant differences within demographic categories regarding government support of citizens' transition to the market economy, 1998 and 2003[a]

	1998			2003		
	Law and order	Access to education	Social safety net	Law and order	Access to education	Social safety net
Location		***	***			
Residence						
Gender		*				
Age group				***		*
Education		*	*			
Occupation	***	***	*			
Ethnic identity						

In a two-tailed chi-square test, *p≤.05, **p≤.01, and ***p≤.001. Location, residence and gender=1 df; age group, education and ethnicity=3 df; occupation=5 df for 1998 and 6 df for 2003.
[a]See Table A.12 in Appendix for details.

and ethnic identity. Age and occupation overlap when you see that it is the older people (the ones who qualify for a pension) who mention the social safety net the most. Finally, the demographic category with significant variability in all four subdomains is occupation.

In 2003, there is little or no variability in the subdomains. Looking across the rows with stars in Table 6.6, the age group category indicates variability in the Enforces law and order and Provides a social safety net categories. Again, the older people seem most concerned about these issues. They had lived the longest under a socialist system that vigorously enforced law and order and provided a social safety net to practically all people. They were having a difficult time adjusting to the new idea that each person should take care of himself. And the interviews expressed their concern for their children's welfare.

UNDERLYING VALUES THAT SURFACE WHEN TALKING ABOUT GOVERNMENT RESPONSIBILITIES

I have found some of the same underlying values when people talk about government responsibilities that appear in most of the preceding chapters: personal dignity, justice and equality. There is also reference to national dignity, which appears only in the chapter on human rights (Chapter 3), and economic survival, which is also in the chapter on economic rights and freedom (Chapter 5). The deeply held values that people associate with government responsibility are recognizable in the earlier anecdotes and quotations. Here I provide a few quotations so that you may see for yourself people's association of some values with government responsibilities.

The first value, personal dignity, is frequently discussed with freedom from government control and government respect for citizens' rights and freedoms (151 [17.4 percent] in 1998; 92 [22.1 percent] in 2003) (see Table 6.7). For example, a young government worker (Ulaanbaatar 2003 Bu005) says, "The state must respect the dignity of every citizen." Prior to 2003, a recent high school graduate who is Christian (Ulaanbaatar 1998 Mh043) says,

The term "humane democratic society" (*khunii toloo niigem*) was used during socialism and communism. The term may make you think how generous and great communist governance was. However, Mongolians like to make great promises and never fulfill them. Mongolia's new democratic society was supposed to protect the rights of people, but there is no law passed to protect women's rights. Still, I wouldn't say democracy is moving incorrectly. It is because all social formations [structures] are the same. In any society, both good and bad will progress. If the good things prevail more than the bad things, the society will advance. Reversibly, the prevalence of bad things will lead to the end [of democracy].

Next is the desire for justice, or fairness. People want to be treated fairly—the same as everyone else—especially when applying for plots of land or coming to court. Yet they know that their expectation of justice is not being met.

A just state is one that serves the people and is for the people. (Khovd 2003 Bd046)

Table 6.7 Mentions of deeply held values associated with a democratic government's responsibilities toward citizens, 1998 and 2003[a]

	1998 Total=867		2003 Total=416		Significant difference between years
	N	%	N	%	χ^2
Personal dignity	151	17.4	92	22.1	*
Justice (fairness)	164	18.9	122	29.3	***
Equality	88	10.1	212	51.0	***
National dignity	89	10.3	38	9.1	
Economic survival/success	36	4.2	54	13.0	***

In a two-tailed chi-square (χ^2) test with 1 df, *p≤.05, **p≤.01 and ***p≤.001.
[a]By number, percent and Pearson's chi-square test.

Justice, pluralism and respect for laws—all these are important to prevent corruption. They are also important for free-thinking and creating as well as for strengthening relations between the state and the people. Therefore they are fundamental features of democracy. (Khovd 1998 Ns018)

Justice is not being realized in Mongolia even though it is the main tendency of democracy. Laws and rights mostly serve people who work in government (parliament, the ministries), not for ordinary citizens. The latter suffer in some cases. In my opinion, if the government's policy is just, then justice would be for everyone. (Ulaanbaatar 2003 Na016)

Part of justice is the desire for equal treatment by the state. Table 6.7 shows that more people mention justice than equality in 1998 (164 [18.9 percent] and 88 [10.1 percent], respectively) but that a far greater portion do so in 2003 (122 [29.3 percent] versus 212 [51.0 percent]). A Christian student (Ulaanbaatar 1998 Ch053) makes the connection between government, the people and equality in 1998, when she says, "People elect the state and control it. The laws should serve equally for all." A woman in her 40s (Khovd 2003 Bd005) says, "The state serves all the people equally. The state protects the interests of the people and operates within the confines of their interests."

Aside from rights and justice, people also mention a government's responsibility to uphold national dignity, also associated with human rights (see Chapter 3). If the propagation of justice, equality and so on builds Mongolia's dignity in the eyes of the world, then the deep-seated need for national dignity is met through government support of citizens' rights and other government actions. While most of our research participants do not speak directly of this association, they refer to constitutional support or government protection of rights and needs such as education access or welfare. Table 6.7 shows that there is no significant difference between people in 1998 and 2003 (89 [10.3 percent] in 1998 and 38 [9.1 percent] in 2003). A herder (Khovd 1998 Gn061) believes that the very mention of human rights in the Mongolian Constitution is a basic condition for democratic society, saying, "Human rights were stated in the constitution. Those rights should exist in any democratic society." And a young student (Khovd 1998 Ns005) contrasts the current government actions with socialism when she says, "In the previous society, people had some rights but they couldn't enjoy them truly in life. Now the laws protect human rights. Man is in the center of policies in the society. That is one of the main features of democracy." Along similar lines, a university graduate working as a manager for the government (Khovd 1998 Ns019) talks about government and democracy, saying, "If a competent government respects human rights and justice and citizens consciously understand their duties, the fertile soil for development of democracy will be established in the country." A high-school graduate (Ulaanbaatar 1998 En033) directly relates the Mongolian government's democratization to international respect: "Democratic countries respect human rights. Our country is developing the democratic way. We already had proved human rights by law."

The last deeply held value connected with government responsibility is for economic success or at least survival in the global market (36 [13.0 percent] in 1998 and 54 [13.0 percent] 2003). Even though the numbers are low, the higher rate of people mentioning this in 2003 is significantly different from 1998. Here, people such as this young man just starting out in business (Ulaanbaatar 1998 Os041) talk about government support for all citizens: "One of the key aims of democratic government is to promote a better life for its citizens." But most of the comments focus on government support to help individuals reach their own goals. A young woman working in education (Khovd 1998 Gn005) says, "Not only should people themselves care about improving their lives but also the government and society should take care of that." And a young government employee (Khovd 2003 Bd051) remarks, "The state supports small businesses. We hope that small business will reduce unemployment." Perhaps it is not surprising that all of these remarks come from people in their 20s who have a high school or university education, for they are most concerned with their futures and have the knowledge to understand the government's role in their futures.

Table 6.8 shows the association between people's ideas on government responsibility and the underlying values that I could extract from the interviews. As we found in other chapters, there is greater variability in 1998 than 2003, suggesting that the population is becoming more homogeneous in its thinking. Personal dignity suggests little variability in that year. However, the 2003 columns suggest there is some variability in 'justice' and 'equality.'

Based on my readings and ethnographic observation, I observed that Mongolians on the whole were becoming more comfortable with living in a democracy and market economy. Their common experience of dealing with a bureaucracy that exhibited significant corruption would make more people from different walks of life concerned about achieving justice (fairness) and equality. Knowledge that they really did have only their extended networks of kin, friends and workmates to rely on would make them think more about

Table 6.8 Significant differences within demographic categories regarding people's underlying values when discussing government responsibilities, 1998 and 2003[a]

	1998			2003		
	Personal dignity	Justice (fairness)	Equality	Personal dignity	Justice (fairness)	Equality
Location		**	***	*	***	
Residence	*	**	*			
Gender						
Age group		*				***
Education	***	***			*	
Occupation	*	***	**			
Ethnic identity		**	*		**	**

In a two-tailed chi-square test, *p≤.05, **p≤.01, and ***p≤.001. Location, residence and gender = 1 df; age group, education and ethnicity = 3 df; occupation = 5 df for 1998 and 6 df for 2003.
[a] See Table A.13 in Appendix for details.

economic survival or success. And personal dignity, always a consideration among Mongolians, may be connected with their growing self-reliance as well as their desire for human rights.

CONCLUSION

One spring day in 1996, Erdenetsetseg (one of the English teachers who translated the 1996 interviews) had given me her free-list translations, so I went home and looked them over. They looked rather good. If I had to summarize what they said, I would say that the higher education administrators interviewed generally wished that the post-communist transition period have less crime and more social order. At the same time, they hoped the government will sustain a truly democratic society with human rights, free elections, government responsibility and economic opportunity. Instead, they were experiencing societal turmoil—partly (or largely) because the government did not know how to write laws that fit a market economy (May 8, 1996, fieldnotes).

In 1998, the people interviewed seemed shocked by revelations of government corruption. By 2003, they were peeved. That is because in all my research experience, people expressed the desire to trust their new democratic government as one that is 'of, by and for the people.' They wanted a government that would be honest and treat them fairly. But they quickly realized the huge gap between their ideal and the reality.

Are their ideals really the responsibility of a democratic government? Many believe that it is the reality in older democracies. Certainly the government responsibility to uphold citizens' rights and freedoms is found in many if not most democratic constitutions. But that doesn't mean that these sections in democratic constitutions are always upheld. Note, for example, a recent US Supreme Court case regarding the requirement that police have a warrant before entering a home (Darin Ryburn, et al. v. George R. Huff, et al.) While our Bill of Rights protects us from search and seizure (Fourth Amendment), this new ruling limits that right.

Still, we know that the achievement of democracy ultimately rests on the honesty and fairness of government. These remain the ideal, as Freedom House and Transparency International's standards are based on the evaluation of a government rather than on citizens' behavior or ideals.

In addition to wanting almost-universal standards for democratic government, a small group of Mongolians also want their government to help them succeed in the market economy. Mongolians seem unable to separate democracy from capitalism, as I myself could not do for many years. So perhaps the question of the book should not be whether the desire for democracy is universal, but whether the desire for *capitalist* democracy is universal. And just as Mongolian research participants expect education rather than health-care from their government, so Americans expect government-sponsored K–12 education but not government-sponsored healthcare for those who are working. The Mongolians seem to be close to the Americans on this issue.

CHAPTER SEVEN

Citizens' Rights or Civic Duty: Citizens' Relationship to Democratic Governance

When I first read the 1992 Mongolian Constitution, I assumed that it would include a section on citizens' duty to maintain democracy. For example, citizens should elect representatives, stand for election and participate in policy decisions by demonstrating and publishing their opinions and so on. At least some citizens should act as watchdogs to keep the government honest, transparent and oriented toward the people. But active citizen participation in governance is not in the constitution. The relevant article (Mongolia 1992: Article 17) reads as follows:

(1) Citizens of Mongolia, while upholding justice and humanism, shall fulfill in good faith the following basic duties:
    1) to respect and abide by the Constitution and other laws;
    2) to respect dignity, reputation, rights, and legitimate interests of others;
    3) to pay taxes levied by law;
    4) to defend the motherland and serve in the army according to law.
(2) It is a sacred duty for every citizen to work, protect his or her health, bring up and educate his or her children and to protect nature and the environment.

Just for fun, I checked the US Constitution. I couldn't find references to citizens' responsibilities there either. However, the Constitution Society (2011) notes that our constitution assumes or implies a few duties: (a) vote in elections, (b) serve on juries and (c) serve in the military in times of war, (d) do not commit treason and (e) obey the law. All these are in Article 17. In both countries, it seems, citizens have little responsibility toward governance but the government has responsibility toward its citizens.

In this chapter, I distinguish between citizens' rights and duties (as our research participants interpret them) regarding elections and participation in governance, civil society and access to information. Rights and duties are traced according to the sentence structures people use: modal ('should,' 'ought to' or 'must'), declarative (for example, 'people now vote'), or assertion of rights (for example, 'people have the right to vote'). You will see a significant shift in thinking between 1998 and 2003 in these categories. However, the three values underlying the discourse of citizenship—the desires for personal dignity, justice (fairness) and equality do not change.

Table 7.1 shows that there is statistically significant change in almost all subdomains between the two years. The data regarding active citizenship are divided into years and then into three parts: elections, other civic activities (discussed in the following section) and the rights versus duties of citizens. The stars in the last column allow us to see the increased number of mentions of subdomains from 1998 to 2003. The rows enable comparison of those who talk about duty and those who talk about rights. For example, in 1998, 37 (4.3 percent) mention that participation in elections is a duty while 178 (20.5 percent) perceive it as a right. People who say citizens have rights are always more numerous than people who say citizens have a duty to take action. The last row shows that passive citizenship (respecting the laws) is seen only as a duty, not a right. As such, it does not vary significantly from 1998 to 2003.

I include Table 7.1 to point out that there is a gap between considering participation in governance as a right or a duty. This suggests a change in thinking from one year of the study to the next. Therefore, we cannot say that thoughts about citizen participation in governance are universal within Mongolia.

PARTICIPATION IN ELECTIONS AND OTHER CIVIC ACTIVITIES: DUTY OR RIGHT?

The first form of active citizen participation is participating in elections. Mongolians vote for everyone from the president and national parliamentary representatives to their local administrators. In the quotations about voting that follow, few people consider voting a duty. This is interesting because during the socialist years, voting was imperative. The MPRP had already selected the 'representatives,' and the only value to the elections was to show the world what a high percentage of people had voted that day. One day in 1996, I supped on ramen noodles in the technological university's student cafeteria with Vincent Costa. At the time, Vince was a graduate student at the University of Pittsburgh, researching teacher education in the context of political and economic change. The teachers he met said that they thought they were already practicing democracy during socialism partly because everyone voted (May 2, 1996, fieldnotes; see also Sabloff 2001:115). I for one was quite impressed when I learned that ballot boxes were brought to

Table 7.1 Mentions of citizens' participation in governance, 1998 and 2003[a]

	1998 Total=867		2003 Total=416		Significant difference between years χ^2
	N	%	N	%	
Citizens actively participate in governance					
I. Elections					
Citizens elect officials	37	4.3	80	19.2	***
Citizens have a right to elect officials and stand for election	178	20.5	182	43.8	***
TOTAL concerning elections	**195**	**22.5**	**197**	**47.4**	***
II. Other activities					
Participate in civil society	0	.0	4	1.0	**
Citizens need information to perform their duties	8	.9	1	.2	
Citizens have a right to information	24	2.8	46	11.1	***
III. Politically active citizens: right versus duty					
Citizens are (or should be) politically active	77	8.9	102	24.5	***
Citizens have a right to participate in governance	161	18.6	184	44.2	***
Active versus passive participation in governance					
Passive (respect/obey the laws)	69	8.0	24	5.8	
Active (elect, civil society; right and duty)	217	25.0	213	51.2	***

In a two-tailed chi-square (χ^2) test with 1 df, *p≤.05, **p≤.01 and ***p≤.001.
[a]By number, percent and Pearson's chi-square test.

Figure 7.1 A young couple coming to cast their ballots for president, Erdene Sum. (Paula L.W. Sabloff, 2000).

the homes of the sick so that they and their caregivers could vote, a practice begun during socialism but continued into the democratic years.

If voting was nothing more than a duty, why vote? To fulfill one's duty, of course. Also, the socialist government organized sporting contests to entice people to the election polls. People would get dressed up, as it was a festive event (July 27, 1998, fieldnotes).

In May 2001, Bumaa took me to Erdene Sum Center to observe the presidential election. There I could see some holdovers from socialist elections. People came to vote dressed in their silk deels. Most dramatic was the entrance of a young man and woman who galloped up to the building, hopped down from their wooden saddles, threw the reins of their mounts over the horse-line (a rope about five feet off the ground attached to two poles; it looked like a clothes line to me) and marched in to vote (Figure 7.1). They were both in silk deels. Their boots were newly polished, and the woman's hair was carefully arranged. The hall in which people voted held two voting boxes painted orange and designed with the Mongolian state emblem. All of this appeared to be a socialist holdover to me.

What was new was the long table where members of several political parties, all looking rather stern, checked the voters' names off a list and handed them a ballot. In other words, elections were now carefully monitored by several people (Figure 7.2).

Voting in elections is an *active step* on the part of citizens. Citizens have to consciously and physically register in their districts and go to the polls on election day, which is a Sunday. In 1998, a total of 195 (22.5 percent) say that active citizen participation means voting for representatives. In 2003, 197 (47.4 percent) agree. The constitution considers voting a duty and so do some research participants: 77 (8.9 percent) in 1998 and 102 (24.5 percent) in 2003. These participants signal their feelings by using modal or declarative sentences. A pension-age herder in Tuv Aimag (Ulaanbaatar 1998 En046) says, "Everyone has to participate in the election and vote for the candidates of their choice. Among the parties, only the MPRP can lead and manage the country, I think."

At the opposite end of the demographic spectrum, a 20-something university-educated woman (Ulaanbaatar 1998 Uy008) says, "Every adult has to participate in the election in a democratic society. But people should choose the persons they vote for themselves." These examples are from the 1998 interviews; I could not find any modal sentences among the 2003 interviews.

There are, however, examples of declarative sentences in both years of the study. A woman in business (Ulaanbaatar 1998 Mh054) says, "Mongolia had its first democratic election on July 21, 1990. Citizens exercise their governing power by participating in direct elections. Since the outcome will influence one's life directly, voting is the highest responsibility of a citizen." And a recent high school graduate (Khovd 2003 Bd058) adds, "Citizens establish the government. A democratic government is established through free elections." Finally, a university student (Ulaanbaatar 2003 Bu042) says, "The nature of parliamentary democracy is that it enables opinions, ideas and the wishes of ordinary people to be reflected in the laws and policies. The parliament initiates and passes the laws. All citizens who qualify for elections participate in elections. Many different political parties also take part in elections."

Not everyone who uses declarative sentences is positive about citizen participation in democracy. There are those who still feel that elections are not truly democratic. A university-trained young woman (Ulaanbaatar 1998 Tj067) represents this viewpoint, saying, "People select representatives to various governing bodies from political parties' candidates. Because the political parties select the candidates, people vote for candidates based on

(a)

(b)

Figure 7.2 (a) Showing their citizenship booklets in order to vote, and (b) voting, Erdene Sum. (Paula L.W. Sabloff, 2000)

the background that sounds better than others. But the public can't select the individuals who are the right candidates."

More people see voting as a right than a duty. In 1998, 161 (18.6 percent) talk about participating in elections as a right. In 2003, the number is 184 (44.2 percent). And perhaps this is as it should be. It would not be democracy if people were forced to be politically active; it would be socialism as Mongolians experienced it (Bawden 1989:419). A strong assertion-of-rights statement comes from a young woman with a technical degree who is working in the private sector (Khovd 2003 Bj061). She says, "During the old regime, candidates were nominated for elections by the party leadership. Local party officials had the candidate 'elected' by the voters. Now, we have a completely different situation. The right to vote in or run for elections became one of the basic rights of every citizen of the country." Taking advantage of her education, this young woman (Ulaanbaatar 2003 Na066) explains her process of thinking before voting: "Since democracy took place in my country I have been taking part in elections. I study the biographies of three or four candidates and choose according to my opinion. Anyone who has skills, education and desire can be elected."

One consequence of this viewpoint is the addition of the idea that ordinary citizens can run for office. The phrase *songogh songodog erkh* means the right to choose and be chosen, or elect and be elected (people translated it both ways). This phrase was peppered throughout the interviews in 1998 and 2003, in Ulaanbaatar and Khovd. The use of the term by a decent number of interviewees (38 [4.4 percent] in 1998 and 39 [9.4 percent] in 2003) suggests that it is a stock phrase used to express electoral rights. A Kazakh Muslim farmer (Khovd 1998 Ns050) uses the phrase, explaining it thus: "The right to choose and be chosen. At elections [during socialism] people were forced to vote for one party, for candidates from this party. Today as a result of democracy the electoral system has changed fundamentally. To elect and be elected became a human rights issue." Coming from the opposite side of the demographic spectrum, an urban pensioner with a technical college education (Ulaanbaatar 1998 Mh024) says, "The right to choose and be chosen. People vote for the candidates who understand democratic ideas and know how to develop the country. Herders, doctors, farmers all have the right to be elected." And an optimistic youth (Khovd 2003 Bd060) observes, "If you want, you may nominate yourself as a candidate."

Although a focus on rights rather than duties makes sense in the Mongolian context, there is a problem. It is rare for our interviewees to connect citizen action with a sense of responsibility to sustain democracy. People often mention the right to a free press or access to information, but they do not say that these rights help them keep government officials accountable. Indeed, some say that the only thing people have to do to be good citizens is respect the government and obey the laws.[1] In reading through the transcripts, I had the feeling that many want officials to do their work honestly and fairly without citizen intervention. They just want to be left alone. Their sole focus is to put their lives together as they face the challenges of transitioning from socialism to capitalism.

My evaluation may be a little harsh. Mongolians cannot be the only people who feel this way. If we use the percentage of voting-age people who actually vote as an indicator of political involvement, we see that the percent of US citizens who voted in presidential elections was 49.1 in 1996 and 51.3 in 2000, which was about the time of this research (Infoplease 2011). In the 1997 Mongolian presidential election, 70 percent voted; 67.9 percent voted in the 2001 election, which is a much higher participation rate than the US voting rate (International Idea Institute for Democracy and Electoral Assistance 2011). For congressional elections, 36.4 percent of US citizens voted in 1998 and 37.0 percent in 2002. In contrast, 73.6 percent of Mongolians voted in the 1996 parliamentary elections and 71.0 percent did in the 2000 elections. So in both presidential and parliamentary elections, Mongolians are still more engaged than Americans.[2]

The fact is that Mongolians actively maintain democratic governance, something most other Central Asian countries have not achieved (Landman et al. 2006). How have they managed this? It seems that whenever democracy is threatened, enough people become so agitated that they hold demonstrations. In 1994, I noticed a few tents set up on the platform of the National Museum of Mongolian History, which is directly across the street from parliament. The tents were in full view of government officials and people passing by. In fact, this was one of the busiest traffic corners in Ulaanbaatar. When I asked what they were for, R. Gonchigdorj, a Member of Parliament and former Vice President of the Small Parliament (Baga Khural) that wrote the 1992 Constitution, replied they were for the hunger strikers. The Democratic Union, a new NGO, had tried to get parliament to allow a free press, establish a new election system that would allow minority parties to gain parliamentary seats and improve welfare and health programs for the poor. When the MPRP-controlled parliament refused, 30 members of the Democratic Union started a hunger strike. As the MPRP still refused, some went on a full hunger strike, meaning they even refused water. A hunger strike had proved effective during the Democratic Revolution, so people thought it would work again. But it did not. Still, demonstrations, hunger strikes and other forms of protest helped maintain democracy.

Some people consider these activities a duty, again using the modal sentence structure. One university student (Ulaanbaatar 1998 Tj023) says, "The public must be able to control the government's actions. As the people have chosen the government, so they also have the right to make it resign." She continues, "There must be a mechanism to stop any negative actions. This means that even leaders must resign if they act incorrectly. The right to make a decision in this case must belong to the people."

Others use declarative sentences to describe active citizen participation. For example, another woman (Khovd 2003 Bd005) tells us that democracy means that "people participate in state leadership. People can participate through elections and by giving their views to their representatives." A compatriot working for an NGO (Khovd 2003 Bj063) expands on her statement, saying, "People co-rule the country. In a democratic society, everyone takes part in ruling the country. In other words, parliament is made up of MPs elected by the people. The people's co-rule is exercised if MPs heed and accomplish the requests of the electorate."

Still others talk in terms of rights as the following quotations illustrate:

Government power is in the people's hands. People have the right to participate or have representation in the process of state-level democracy. (Ulaanbaatar 1998 Ch031)

People have the right to voluntarily join political parties. (Ulaanbaatar 1998 Os056)

People now have the right to speak up or engage in political activities that support or oppose the law. (Khovd 2003 Bd003)

A citizen has the right to measure and evaluate the government's activities and other members of the society against his/her personal criteria. The evaluations, reflections and attitudes of the person can be freely expressed through the mass media. (Ulaanbaatar 2003 Bu012)

While the quotations for 1998 and 2003 look similar, Table 7.2 suggests that the right or duty to participate in elections and even run for office varies most often with people's education level. Table 7.2 in the Appendix shows a difference between those who have completed high school, vocational school

Table 7.2 Significant differences within demographic categories concerning participation in elections, 1998 and 2003ª

	1998			2003		
	Vote (duty)	Vote (right)	TOTAL	Vote (duty)	Vote (right)	TOTAL
Location	***				*	**
Residence		***	***			
Gender						
Age group						
Education	*	***	***	**	***	***
Occupation	*	***	***			*
Ethnic identity	**					

In a two-tailed chi-square test, $*p \leq .05$, $**p \leq .01$, and $***p \leq .001$. Location, residence and gender = 1 df; age group, education and ethnicity = 3 df; occupation = 5 df for 1998 and 6 df for 2003.
ªSee Table A.14 in Appendix for details.

or university are more likely to mention participation in elections than those who did not. This dovetails with residence (rural versus urban) and therefore probably reflects the greater physical and emotional distance of rural dwellers from political activity than urban dwellers.

Table 7.1 covers the next sections of this chapter as well as elections. It suggests that there is a gap between rights and duties. This, in turn, implies a lack of uniform thinking among our research participants. Therefore, we cannot say that people's thoughts about citizens' participation in governance within Mongolia are universal.

CIVIL SOCIETY

Another dimension to active citizenship is participation in civil society. Citizens in democracies often gather to discuss or act on political issues separate from the government. Operating between the family and government levels of organization, they are perennially in a state of tension with the government (Keane 1998:6). They also unite people across the usual boundaries of politics, religion, ethnicity and class. American examples are volunteer church groups, professional organizations such as the American Medical Association (AMA), environmental action groups (Natural Resources Defense Council, Sierra Club) and political action groups such as the Tea Party or Occupy Wall Street. These organizations argue their particular cause to the government, lobbying for citizens' interests. UNDP and USAID, among others, believe that democracy cannot be sustained without civil society. At least, that is what Doug Gardner, UNDP's Resident Representative and the UN Resident Coordinator, said to me in 1998 (June 30, 1998, fieldnotes; see also

Chapter 2). During Soviet times, civil society was blocked in Romania and Russia even though some people wanted to engage in civil society (Verdery 2002; Petro 1995:1–2). Once the Soviet system imploded, civil society in the form of NGOs sprang up. Hemment (2007) provides an excellent account of several Russian women who learned how to operate and fund women-centered NGOs. But how do you get people to volunteer when they do not have the concept of the NGO in their background? Kalb (2002:319) and Mandel (2002) write that civil society did develop, but it never reached the industrial or agricultural workers.

In Mongolia, several forms of civil society sprang up. Local NGOs formed, following the pattern of other postsocialist nations. That is, the urban intelligentsia formed NGOs. Volunteers came from two sources. The first was educated women who found themselves left out of government. Several women told me that with the advent of democracy, parliamentary representation was reduced from 370 female delegates to 76. At that point, women lost their seats and their voice in government. As most were already working for women's rights in one form or another, forming or staffing an NGO made sense. They gained employment and a voice on an issue they cared about. In addition, those working for international agencies were also making three to five times the salaries of university faculty.

Other people were stimulated by the 1989–90 Democratic Revolution. One of these was Burmaa Radnaa, who had obtained a degree in electrical engineering in Bulgaria before the Democratic Revolution but joined the revolutionaries at the beginning of the democratic movement (September 15, 2003, interview). She explains,

At that time, I thought democracy should be a multiparty system because we had only one political party. We had only three public organizations under the MPRP: the Women's Federation, the Youth Organization, and the Trade Union. At first, I was one of the founding members of the Social Democratic Women's Movement established by the party. I thought all public organizations should be under the party. But later when I had a chance to learn about other countries, I found that there are NGOs—politically active organizations that are independent of a party or government. I told the party that I wanted to establish an NGO, Women for Social Progress, which would be independent of the Democratic Party. But some women party members didn't like the idea and so they established a separate movement within the party. I went ahead and formed an independent organization. I had no funding then. I worked out of a very small room—a cloak room, actually.

Her counterpart is Zanaa Jurmed, head of CEDAW-Watch. I asked her why she had volunteered to head the Mongolian branch of this organization. She said she had been a teacher of Russian, but she was always involved in politics. She had helped the hunger strikers in 1990 because she was angry that the Communist Party did not step aside for democracy. She, like many other young people, felt that the old communist leaders could not lead her country to a democratic way of life. How can old men steeped in Marxist-Leninist doctrine lead a democratic country, she asked (August 11, 1999, fieldnotes). She wanted to keep being politically active and so she volunteered to lead CEDAW-Watch.

A few organizations formed NGOs from necessity and with outside stimulation but no monetary support. In 1994, Sukhbaatar, president of the College of Commerce and Business, had established a Business Council whose members—all alumni—were in business. The purpose was for them to offer advice on what the college should be teaching students so that they could succeed in business. Thirty of them pledged 3 million togrogs to help the school (June 13, 1994, fieldnotes). So I learned that civil society organizations are possible in Mongolia.

Branches of international organizations were staffed by Mongolians who could speak English. These include the Rotary Club, Save the Children, USAID and World Vision.

Yet another form of NGO arose, the political action committee (PAC). Many formed around political candidates to push their ideas and collect money for their election or reelection campaign. The political system had been set up so that people who wanted to run for office had to deliver a certain amount of money to their political party. Therefore, fundraising was essential. Amarjargal, the Economics College president I had interviewed in 1996 (see Chapter 3), set up the Amarjargal Foundation in 2001 with the goal of encouraging democracy and supporting his election to parliament. He served as prime minister between 1999 and 2000.

By 2003, more than 7,000 local and international civil society organizations were registered with the Mongolian government. Still, the concept of civil society and volunteering was not readily acceptable to Mongolians. During my research years, I also worked with the National Museum of Mongolian History, preparing an exhibition on Mongolia that would tour the United States. I spent many hours at the National Museum working

Figure 7.3 S. Idshinnorov, Director of the National
Museum of Mongolian History. (Paula L.W. Sabloff, 2000)

with the director, Idshinnorov (Figure 7.3), and the curators, Drs. Bumaa
and Nansalmaa and Mr. Ayush. They had been directed to convert their
museum from a storehouse of artifacts (anything from Paleolithic stone
tools to President Ochirbat's inaugural deel) with limited access to an open,
educational museum where any Mongolians or foreign tourists could learn
about Mongolian history. I spoke with Idshinnorov, who was concerned
about funding. I suggested he set up a volunteer organization of docents
and helpers, but he said that Mongolians don't volunteer. When I argued
that there are so many educated, bright retirees who would probably love
something interesting to do, he still balked.

Burmaa agrees with Idshinnorov. She said in our interview that many
people were thinking about civil society, but

> Our constitution says the local-level [bag] khural is part of civil society
> because its members represent the citizens. They are supposed to monitor
> the government, but in real life they are MPRP members and follow the
> view of the party leaders. In Ulaanbaatar, for example, there are many

new buildings. The public spaces between apartments [that function as] playgrounds are being filled in with buildings. The citizens are against this; they want to see the permissions [that allow people to build these new structures]. The Ulaanbaatar mayor issues the permissions; they [the city government] bring in dogs to patrol the site and people build their buildings. Where are the elected officials representing us to monitor the mayor's decisions? There was never public discussion on this issue—or on individual buildings. Citizens don't have the regulations or the practice [experience] to watch the local government sessions.

Burmaa added that in Thailand where she had visited, committees concerned with public policy issues hold public hearings. "But," she said, "We don't have this idea of public discussion in Mongolia."

Backing up Idshinnorov and Burmaa's point, I found no mention of civil society in the 1998 interviews. In 2003, only four people (1.0 percent) do. One is a Khovd female farmer with a high school education (Khovd 2003 Ns062). She says, "Democratic society must bear the following features: the functioning of fair, open and transparent civil society, free elections and freedom of religion, the press, etc." Two others are Ulaanbaatar university graduates (Bu14 and 15). One man works for the government and the other is in business:

Presidential democracy is the most suitable form of political power for Mongolia. Today, when democratic civil society is in its embryonic phase, our country needs presidential democracy. Numerous political parties tend to stray from their original concepts and incorrectly evaluate the socio-economic situation in the country. Unlike the political parties, presidential democracy will not be swayed from its concepts and principles. (Ulaanbaatar 2003 Bu014)

Citizens in a democracy exercise their rights within the framework of existing laws. The laws regulate the life of every citizen of a democratic country. The legal mechanisms that regulate all relations of the civil society already function in Mongolia. However, every member of the society does not abide by the laws. (Ulaanbaatar 2003 Bu015)

It appears that the concept of civil society is not on people's minds, even though Western advisors tout it as a hallmark of democracy. Even in the educated stratum of the interviewees, few think to mention it or link it to sustaining democracy.

ACCESS TO INFORMATION

People also talk about the need for information, but most do not connect it with citizens' responsibility to maintain democracy. The 1998 media law stipulates that the government cannot control—censor or dictate—what the media broadcast. Yet the Mongolian government continued to control the national press long past ratification of the law.[3] Liberty Center (2003c) tells that the government brought charges of "defamation and libel" against a journalist who was trying to investigate government corruption. This was not the only case in 2003; many people mentioned other cases to me that year.

But the people interviewed did not see access to information as anything more than a right. When I cross-referenced access to information with citizens' duties in the database, I found only nine quotations in 1998 and one in 2003. One is by a government administrator (Ulaanbaatar 1998 Ts040), who says, "I must have access to all necessary information related to the people and organizations serving me [as a citizen]. Then I can make a choice or monitor and assess them. People must be able to track the taxpayers' money: how and for what was this money spent? Of course, private and business-related information shouldn't be open to everyone." Another is by an education professional (Ulaanbaatar 1998 Mh067) who adds the responsibilities of the media to the discussion: "The press and media play a role in the people's control of government. They provide information on people's life and leaders' actions, and they enable people to judge and assess a situation. Through the press and media, the people can stop incorrect [bad] activities."

Notice that information is treated as a duty of the government or the media, but the right of citizens. Therefore, we find several who complain about the inadequacy of information. This suggests that Mongolians still see information as government-controlled. An older man with a high-school education (Khovd 1998 Nd016) blames the media: "We don't know what is going on in the state. Although the mass media are now free, they serve a particular [political] party and refute each other's information. Therefore they cannot provide true information. The state doesn't care much about the people. The people's opinions don't reach the state; therefore, it is useless to say anything."

Information has another meaning to our respondents—namely, practical information such as how to farm or herd livestock. The socialist government used to distribute pamphlets to help people understand farming techniques or home economics. It gave lectures on hygiene. And after World War II soldiers went into the countryside to teach adults and children to read and write. Some interviewees miss these government programs and wish the democratic government would provide them, too. Starting with a woman whose education ended early (Khovd 1998 Bj010), people expect the government to educate them: "I don't know about democracy. I only have three years of primary school education. Because of that I don't understand. Nobody from the bag or sum administration explains to me. I think the old system was better because we had everything available." A middle-aged Kazakh woman (Khovd 1998 Ns014) summed up the problem in 1998: "I don't know [about democracy]. In Khovd the electricity was shut down. There is no radio or TV. The press doesn't reach us. Nobody organizes seminars and lectures about democracy."

I spent quite a lot of time in Khovd in 1998, and the electricity did shut down. Professors at the university were running their computers off of car generators, and apartment dwellers filled their bathtubs with water to supply the family for a few days at a time. Life was hard indeed in Khovd for several years after the Democratic Revolution. And news could not get through without transmitters or deliveries of Ulaanbaatar newspapers on the planes.

The following summer I joined the Decentralization and Democracy Support Project team led by Oyunbileg, National Project Coordinator for the United Nations. Mongolian faculty from the Institute for Management and Development (IAMD) were going to Mandalgov' in the northern part of the Gobi to give workshops on democracy and market economy to the Dundgov' aimag bag governors. It was a pleasure to watch the workshop as everyone was deeply engaged, even though my Mongolian was not good enough to understand all that was going on.

On the second day, I asked some participants what they thought of the workshop. They said it was good because no one else has paid attention to them. Sponsored projects usually focused on the sum level of government, yet the bag governors are the ones who have to explain democracy and market economy to their people. They are responsible for enforcing and teaching basic principles at home. When I suggested that the workshop was also valuable because it encouraged the 40 or so bag governors to network, one man said, yes, there is little communication within and between the bags. They are definitely getting to know one another better. We learned later that the bag governors were attending the sessions during the day and organizing volleyball and drinking parties at night.

I have to point out here that the Mongolian government allowed the program but did not run it. The initiative and execution came from the UNDP. All this is to say that information of both kinds (news and educational) was

Table 7.3 Significant differences within demographic categories concerning civil society and access to information, 1998 and 2003[a]

	1998			2003		
	Civil society	Access to information (duty)	Access to information (right)	Civil society	Access to information (duty)	Access to information (right)
Location			*			
Residence						
Gender					*	
Age group						
Education			*			
Occupation		*				
Ethnic identity						

In a two-tailed chi-square test, *p≤.05, **p≤.01, and ***p≤.001. Location, residence and gender = 1 df; age group, education and ethnicity = 3 df; occupation = 5 df for 1998 and 6 df for 2003. [a] See Table A.15 in Appendix for details.

considered an obligation of the government, as it had been during socialism. And few people connected the dissemination of information with providing citizens the knowledge needed to be informed, active citizens.

Although Table 7.1 suggests some significant difference between 1998 and 2003, Table 7.3 infers little difference between those who discuss civil society or those who consider access to information a right or duty. Some variability within residence and education occurs for the right to access information, echoing Table 7.2. However, the significance is not as strong as it is in Table 7.2, and it is not backed up by the trends found in other columns.

PASSIVE CITIZENSHIP: OBEY THE LAWS

The previous sections describe our Mongolian research participants' attitudes toward participation in governance. Explanations of their ideas about voting, standing for election, holding demonstrations, participating in civil society or (not) using information to hold elected officials accountable to the people are all active ways of engaging in democracy. This last section—one that coincides with the 1992 Constitution's expectations of citizens—is a passive approach to citizenship activities. Simply put, 69 (8.0 percent) people in 1998 and 24 (5.8 percent) in 2003 say that the way to be a good citizen is to obey the laws and respect the authorities. This approach to governance reflects the idea that people want to focus on economic survival and hopefully success. None of my friends had this attitude, for they were mostly government employees and actively involved in politics. Yet the attitude is valid and important to note.

The quotations that follow are in the modal or declarative forms of speech; there is no reference to assertion-of-rights speech. Obeying the law is a duty and not a right. Note that some of the quotations refer to the public and to officials:

People should not only enjoy their legal rights; they should also follow and respect the laws issued by the government. That is their duty as citizens. (Khovd 1998 Gn015)

It would be beneficial if everyone would respect the state like he does his parents. (Khovd 1998 Gn061)

Democracy is not chaos. It is very important that people live and work consciously within the legal framework and respect the laws. But there is little possibility for this because there are many gaps in the law. (Khovd 1998 Ns022)

There is no society without law. In a democratic society, law enforcement is connected to the people's will. Individuals' everyday life and economic situations are protected by the law. In a democratic society, the law regulates people's behavior; everything must be within the law. However, today's Mongolia is addicted to corruption. (Ulaanbaatar 1998 Mh039)

The state is not respected. The reputation of the state organizations has worsened. Work is not advancing because we have lost the Mongolian custom of "honor the state." (Khovd 2003 Bj002)

The party, state, ruling organizations and elders are not respected. No one is responsible for this disorderly situation. Under socialism, anyone who did something wrong was given a monetary fine. Disorder should be regulated by law. (Khovd 2003 Bj006)

People don't respect the law. The common people and those who are supposed to be implementing the law, violate it. Children are not disciplined and are breaking the law. (Khovd 2003 Ns008)

All social processes are regulated by law. There is no form of oppression in a democratic society. Every citizen of the society must observe the

Civil Law. This principle was followed in the time of the Great Mongolia Empire founded by Chinggis Khaan. (Ulaanbaatar 2003 Bu055)

Once again, people's ideas vary by residence and education, this time in the first three columns of Table 7.4. The columns concerning political passivity are blank, suggesting a relatively even distribution of people who only say that people should obey the law. These two columns should be compared with the columns to their immediate left, the totals of people who state that citizens of a democracy are or should be politically active. While there is probably some variability in those who advocate a politically active citizenry, there is no such variability in those who suggest a passive approach to citizenship.

DEEPLY FELT VALUES ASSOCIATED WITH CITIZENS' RIGHTS AND DUTIES

When talking about citizens' activities or responsibilities toward maintaining democratic governance, I sometimes detected people's concern for personal dignity, justice and equality. Whenever informants talk about personal dignity, they connect it with the rights of citizenship rather than with duty. A Kazakh who just graduated from high school (Khovd 2003 Ns072) gets to the essence of personal dignity in democracy: "A society that honors and respects the opinions of its citizens is a real democratic society." A businessman (Ulaanbaatar 1998 Mh021) talks about dignity in a slightly different way, saying, "People respect each other in a democratic society. They can express their thoughts. Every individual is considered an autonomous world [with his own values, views, attitudes and habits]." And a university student (Ulaanbaatar 1998 Tj047) brings in causality by saying, "A democratic country respects human rights highly; therefore, people respect each other and communicate politely." Another young (27–36) person in education (Ulaanbaatar 1998 Mh004) says, "Democracy means to respect minorities' rights. While making decisions based on the majority's opinion, a democratic society is tolerant and listens to a minority's arguments also. Especially, a democratic society respects a minority's right to express its opinions and views." A high-school graduate (Ulaanbaatar 1998 Uy041) associates dignity with citizen action and ethnic minority rights: "All citizens have the right to vote and to be elected without consideration of age, sex, ethnic origin, race or social status."

People also mention justice along with citizen participation in democratic society. In 1999 I met with Chinchuluun, head of the Women Lawyers'

Table 7.4 Significant differences within demographic categories concerning citizens' political activity, 1998 and 2003[a]

	Active versus passive participation in governance							
	1998				2003			
	Politically active (duty)	Politically active (right)	Total politically active	Politically passive	Politically active (duty)	Politically active (right)	Total politically active	Politically passive
Location	*							
Residence	*	**	***					
Gender						*	*	*
Age group				*		*		
Education	***	***	***					
Occupation	*	***	***	***	**	***	***	
Ethnic identity								

In a two-tailed chi-square test, $*\, p \leq .05$, $**\, p \leq .01$, and $***\, p \leq .001$. Location, residence and gender=1 df; age group, education and ethnicity=3 df; occupation=5 df for 1998 and 6 df for 2003.

[a]See Table A.16 in Appendix for details.

Association, a Mongolian NGO that was formed in 1992 and had 38 branches throughout the country by 1999 (August 6, 1999, fieldnotes). Staffed by women, its original purpose was to raise the professional level of women lawyers. About 70 percent of the nation's lawyers were women, and most of them held only a baccalaureate degree. The new association soon broadened its mandate to advocate for the legal rights of women and children, including domestic violence, child abuse, sexuality, and property rights. By 1999, the association was also analyzing bills before parliament and lobbying to get the wording changed so that laws would be friendlier toward women. Sometimes they were successful. Chinchuluun added that the association works closely with the Ministry of Justice. It continues to help write or evaluate bills for the parliament.

Chinchuluun estimated that Mongolia had 800 NGOs operating, and at least half were run and staffed by women. Why, I asked, were women so active? She said that women are always active in social issues, probably because they get hurt the most and suffer from injustice the most.

Aside from women's issues, people associate a desire for justice with civic activity, be it active engagement with the political arena or passive respect for the law. The first quotation from a teacher with a baccalaureate (Khovd 1998 Ns018) relates justice to corruption: "Justice, pluralism and respect for laws are important for preventing corruption. They are also important for free thinking and creating as well as for strengthening relations between the state and the people."

It is always comforting to find that young and old are thinking along the same lines. Here, a retired man with a university degree (Khovd 2003 Bj044) talks about justice in a complementary mode to Ns018 (quoted earlier): "People monitor the country's activities through the representative body so any activities can be decided as just." When a 79-year-old Kazakh talks in a similar manner, we can assume the thinking spans demographic boundaries. This fellow (Ulaanbaatar 2003 Bu056) says, "A society can be considered democratic if the state pursues justice and honors the rights of its citizens. The government should care for its citizens and exert all efforts to improve their living conditions. Unfortunately, the government does not care for us in this country."

The last relevant underlying value is equality. In 1998, a few people seem to link citizens' right to participate in governance with equality. That is, everyone has the right, no matter their gender, ethnicity and so on. But in 2003, people branch out and discuss equality when talking about citizen activities and duties. An education professional (Khovd 1998 Ns018) connects all kinds of equality with governance: "Equal rights means that people have equal rights regardless of their race, nationality, education, wealth or gender. It is important for the involvement of people in state affairs." He is seconded by a 20-something fellow in business (Ulaanbaatar 1998 Os041): "Men and women enjoy their rights in the political and social fields. Without the rights to express opinions, speak, have a free press or organize and participate in demonstrations and assemblies, there is no way to build a democratic government."

Another person, a female pensioner (Khovd 2003 Bj050), focuses on the importance of individuals fighting for the things that are important to them. He says, "Everyone is provided with the possibility to fight activities that they don't like by participating in political life."

A health professional (Ulaanbaatar 1998 Ch016) stresses the side of equality that means lack of discrimination: "Everyone should participate in elections, no matter their ethnic origins or social status. And they should vote for the candidates they like."

Table 7.5, on deeply held values, shows no significant difference between 1998 and 2003. Perhaps the numbers are too low to show significant change. Still, the fact that I could discern a few examples that link citizen activity with underlying values suggests some association between the two, especially for I equality.

What interests me here is all the categories where I could not find any correlation between citizen participation and values within years (Table 7.6). To me, this means that few or no people link their values with citizens' duties. They see little connection between their basic interests and citizenship. This observation holds in Table 7.6, where little difference between demographic categories exists. This probably reflects the very low numbers of people who express particular values and citizen participation in governance.

Table 7.5 Mentions of citizens' duties associated with deeply held values, 1998 and 2003[a]

	1998 Total=867		2003 Total=416		Significant difference between years
	N	%	N	%	χ^2
Personal dignity	11	1.3	4	1.0	
Justice (fairness)	4	.5	6	1.4	
Equality	17	2.0	10	2.4	

In a two-tailed chi-square (χ^2) test with 1 df, *p≤.05, **p≤.01 and ***p≤.001.
[a]By number, percent and Pearson's chi-square test.

Table 7.6 Significant differences within demographic categories regarding the perception of citizens' participation in governance and their deeply held values, 1998 and 2003[a]

	1998			2003		
	Personal dignity	Justice	Equality	Personal dignity	Justice	Equality
Location				*		
Residence						
Gender	*					
Age group						**
Education						
Occupation						
Ethnic identity						

In a two-tailed chi-square test, *p≤.05, **p≤.01, and ***p≤.001. Location, residence and gender=1 df; age group, education and ethnicity=3 df; occupation=5 df for 1998 and 6 df for 2003.
[a]See Table A.17 in Appendix for details.

CONCLUSION

The quotations in this chapter advance the idea that our research participants see themselves as citizens of an independent Mongolia. However, they are more focused on the rights of citizenship than on the activities necessary to sustain democratic governance, that is, to run for office or hold the government accountable to the people. This attitude must pervade other postsocialist nations, for Walter Clemens (2001:74) writes, "Democracy is not something that one 'gets' once and for all in the Constitution. Rather, democracy—like all ingredients of fitness—must be fought for and won on an ongoing basis. If citizens do not engage in this fight, there will be no democracy—and little fitness."

Although Mongolians had hoped to establish a government they could trust when they participated in the Democratic Revolution, the interviews show that many do not trust the government. Still, they seem to think that citizens need not check up on officials; the government will take care of itself. This is a very optimistic attitude, one that our forefathers did not share. It seems as though respondents rarely connect citizenship with their deeply held values. When they do, they emphasize equality, justice and personal dignity, all of which are linked to rights rather than duties of citizenship.

CHAPTER EIGHT

Conclusion: Shared Experiences, Shared Ideas

Mongolian friends and colleagues like to think of their country as unique. My research has led me to believe that Mongolia is indeed special, but not because it has different features from other nations (see Sabloff 2011). Rather, it is a unique combination of environmental, psychological, historical, cultural and sociopolitical patterns found elsewhere, especially in other postsocialist nations. I have tried to show in this monograph that the Mongolians we interviewed have bought into a good part of the Western concept of democracy. They name familiar subdomains of democracy (political rights and freedoms, economic rights and freedoms and government responsibilities toward citizens) as its core features. And they certainly want the freedoms found in the Universal Declaration of Human Rights. However they prioritize the subdomains and attributes of democracy in a way that fits the Mongolian experience, not that of other nations.

I propose that our research participants' ready acceptance of a political ideology different from the one in which they were raised comes from layer upon layer of complex cognitive thought. They resemble a seven-layer cake—only with four layers. These range from universal human emotions to particularistic interpretations of democracy. We will work up through the layers of the cake in order to understand the ingredients used to create their particular view of democracy.

The ingredients for the bottom layer are emotions that are universal or nearly so. Psychologists and anthropologists have determined that there really is something called human nature. It is encapsulated in a small number of universally shared emotions and experiences, as I described in Chapter 1 (Ekman 1999:55; Brown 2000:156) . There are political scientists who connect human emotions to political thought. Citing Gabriel Almond and Lucian Pye, Nicolai Petro (1995:5) proposes that emotions are a critical part of politics, although he does not specify whether people's verbalized feelings are universal or culture-specific (see also Pye 1991; Lakoff 1996, 2008). Timur Kuran (1995:31) proposes new universal emotions when he writes that (all) people derive satisfaction from "individuality, autonomy, dignity, and integrity. I am proposing that we value the freedom to choose; that we derive self-esteem from resisting social pressures ... and that we find satisfaction in speaking our minds, opening up our hearts, acting ourselves." He considers personal dignity, derived from being true to ourselves, to be a truly universal emotion. Later in the book, he explains the connection between these universals and different political systems. When people have to hide their opinions in order to gain acceptance by their group or avoid punishment by a government, he states, they risk their own dignity (ibid.:181–84).

A rather extensive study showing the association of emotions and governance was conducted in 88 countries between 1981 and 2007. The authors (Inglehart, Foa et al. 2008:266) found that people are happier in a democracy because they have more "free choice," that is, "freedom of expression, freedom to travel and free choice in politics."

Underlying the political scientists' analyses is the understanding that people's discussion of 'good governance' reveals their ideas about how a government should treat its citizens and how people should treat each other. In other words, political conversations concern morality and ethics just as much as religious discussions do. Morality and ethics are, of course, derived from universal emotions, among other things. Therefore, we would expect Mongolians to associate democracy (which most of them consider good governance) with some principles about how people should treat each other and be treated by their government. I have presented evidence of this for Mongolian research participants in Chapter 6.

The second layer of the cake consists of the deeply held values that people relate to their ideas of appropriate governance. Table 8.1 covers the most frequently mentioned values that our research participants mention when asked to describe democracy. It shows that the desire for personal dignity is mentioned the most (42.4 percent) in 1998 but that equality tops the list in 2003 (59.6 percent). The other emotions and values with relatively high frequencies are the desire for economic survival/success and justice (fairness). These four remain at the top of the frequency charts in both years; the only difference is that the top two appear in reverse order in the two years of the survey. Other values that the interviewees associate with democracy are national dignity, self-determination and freedom from oppression. The numbers rise significantly from 1998 to 2003 for all values except freedom from oppression. Perhaps our research participants are thinking about the socialist period less frequently as time goes by.

The values in Table 8.1 may be as universal as the universal emotions from which they are derived. More comparative research is needed to determine whether or not this is so. Still, it appears that Mongolians' deeply held values resonate with people in other postsocialist states. To give an

Table 8.1 Deeply held values mentioned by number and percent of interviewees, 1998 and 2003[a]

	1998 Total=867		2003 Total=416		Significant difference between years
	N	%	N	%	χ^2
Personal dignity	**368**	**42.4**	216	51.9	***
Equality	320	36.9	**248**	**59.6**	***
Economic survival/success	264	30.4	227	54.6	***
Justice (fairness)	198	22.8	142	34.1	***
National dignity	102	11.8	51	12.3	
Self-determination	79	9.1	81	19.5	***
Freedom from oppression	42	4.8	14	3.4	

In a two-tailed chi-square (χ^2) test with 1 df, *p≤.05, **p≤.01 and ***p≤.001
[a]By number, percent and Pearson's chi-square test. Most frequently mentioned attributes are in bold for each year.

example, Walter Clemens (2001:229) attributes the values of "individual dignity, self-reliance, and freedom combined with confidence that virtue and hard work should and will be rewarded" to the adoption of democracy in the Baltic States (Latvia, Estonia and Lithuania). He writes that these values are shared with Western democracies. Except for the last item, the same values are found in Mongolia, too.

The main ingredient in the second layer is the desire for personal dignity. Alexander Lukin (2000:183) writes that the Russian democrats' anger toward socialism comes from a desire for personal dignity: "the authoritarian regime, or totalitarianism, in their view, began to distort the personality, depersonalized the human psyche, and transformed human individuals into slaves—slaves not only in terms of their social status, but conscious slaves who were satisfied with their subordinate position and considered it quite normal."

One of the most poignant analyses of personal dignity was written by Djanaeva, a Kyrgyz woman whom I happened to meet on the street in the summer of 2003. She thrust her newly published book (in English) into my hands. "Please read this!" she said. "It is about women's rights in Kyrgyzstan," another postsocialist, independent nation. That night I read the book from cover to cover. Contrary to the previous examples in which people felt they had gained dignity after the democratic revolutions of the last two decades of the twentieth century, Djanaeva (2002:16–18) believes Kyrgyz women gained personal dignity during the Soviet years but lost it after Kyrgyzstan turned away from Soviet socialism. Before socialism, she explains, women had been locked into polygamous marriages, blocked from obtaining education or owning any property. Indeed, they had been treated as property that could be bought or stolen. She describes the socialist years as ones of gender equality in health, employment, education and politics. After socialism, Kyrgyz women did have the opportunity to mobilize NGOs and women's groups, but they lost ground in education, salary and increased unemployment. Along with the introduction of drug trafficking came human trafficking and therefore prostitution (ibid.:18–32).

As in the previous examples, the frequency of mentions of personal dignity is greater than for other deeply held values. This may be seen in Tables 3.5, 4.5, 5.5 and 6.7.

Mongolians also share the value of self-determination with people in other postsocialist nations. By self-determination, they mean national independence from the Soviet Union or personal freedom from state control. Regarding the former, Poland started demonstrating for national self-determination in 1980. Others, including the people we interviewed and citizens of the Baltic States, followed in 1989 (Clemens 2001: 43–46).

Examples of individual self-determination from the postsocialist countries include Alexander Lukin's report on the Russian 'democrats' who associated it with personal freedom (Lukin 2000:196–98). More indirect evidence comes from Caroline Humphrey's major study of Russia (1998:457). She suggests that farmers in Buriatia, Russian Federation, were actually making their own economic decisions when they pooled their resources or moved to urban centers for wage labor (see also Ries 2009:187–88). Self-determination enters the Mongolian database with discussions of human rights (Table 3.5), political freedom (Table 4.5) and economic freedom (Table 5.5).

The desire for justice in the sense of fairness is another value shared among postsocialist people. Mongolian respondents mention justice in conjunction with government responsibility (Table 6.7) and citizens' duties (Table 7.5) but not in relation to human rights or other rights and freedoms. I found the most telling anecdote about another postsocialist country's people. Katherine Verdery (996:222–23) explains Romanians' thwarted desire for justice in her account of the Romanian court system:

> Among the things court spectators learn are that the court does not have power to resolve many of the cases brought before it, particularly against local officials' resistance; that much of the court's work is carried on in arcane, specialist language to which ordinary people do not have access; that they can be tripped up by numerous procedures and

rules; and that the practices of participation in defense of one's rights eat up large amounts of time and money....

I read postural and behavioral signs [of spectators] as suggesting that many parties to a suit had not come there confident of their rights but, rather, as supplicants. The same attitude appeared in the behavior of those coming to legalize inheritances at the state notary. These orientations to law continue those of the socialist period, when the governors perceived the governed as "children to be corrected and educated" rather than as legal subjects with certain rights.

Yet another key value shared by postsocialist people is equality. Mongolians mention equality in relation to government responsibility (Table 6.7) and citizens' duties (Table 7.5), just as they did for justice. In the Bulgarian village where Gerald Creed (1999:236–37) conducted fieldwork, people voiced their desire for economic equality. As the gap between rich and poor expanded in the early postsocialist years, villagers started saying that capitalism, corruption and criminal activity were destroying the economic equality that had been achieved during socialism. In Kyrgyzstan, Russia and other countries including Mongolia, women began mobilizing to promote female candidates for parliament in order to give themselves an equal voice in government (Tripp 2002:392; Hemment 2007:5–8).

The more I read through the Mongolian interviews, the more I became convinced that our research participants believe democracy can help them achieve a lifestyle that lets them practice their deeply held values better than other forms of governance. Political and economic freedoms inherent in democracy align with personal dignity, self-determination and the hope of economic survival or success. Equality, guaranteed in democratic systems, reinforces the values of justice and personal dignity. Because people associate democracy with some universal emotions and values, I consider democracy—once achieved in one form or another—to be a means to achieving certain ends, especially the alignment of personal values with daily life. Lukin (2000:195–217) has come to the same conclusion.

Having reviewed some of the deeply held values found in the second layer of the cake, we proceed to the third layer. It consists of international or regional politico-economic historical trends and the physical environment context in which these trends play out. People living in neighboring countries or who have experienced similar histories may share both. In this case, I am referring to Mongolia's neighbors, especially those that also experienced Soviet-influenced socialism and the end-of-millennium release from it.

Mongolians share with neighboring and distant nations the experiences of feudalism and socialism. Mongolia's history of vassalage to China's Manchu rulers bound its political economy and material culture to China for three centuries. As a result, the few remaining Tibetan Buddhist temples and monasteries are highly reminiscent of Chinese architecture. Men and women still wear deels in the countryside, which are copies of Chinese silk robes.[1] City women dress in them for festive occasions. People in the urban centers and countryside eat wheat noodles, which were developed in China. Sometimes they mix noodles with chopped meat and vegetables; sometimes they stuff noodle dough with mutton or beef to make the national dish, boodz, which resembles wonton.

Following the Manchu Dynasty's demise, Mongolia's 70-year socialist political economy and Soviet satellite status caused people to emulate Russian ways. They added leather belts to their deels, fedoras to their heads and Russian-style black boots to their feet. These styles are still worn today. In fact, several people have told me that the best quality deel has Chinese silk on the outside and Russian cotton lining inside. People started dumping potatoes, turnips and onions into the pot to boil with their traditional mutton, and they learned to grow hothouse tomatoes and cucumbers, another Russian practice.

Shared socialist experience and international trade with the COMECON countries introduced Mongolians to cultural, political and economic trends found in other parts of the Soviet Union. But most of the shared history was repression, misery and revolt. Just as Mongolians were frequently trying to escape or destroy the socialist political economy, so were the Russians. I quote from Nicolai Petro's book, *The Rebirth of Russian Democracy* (1995:119–20) because I did not know these facts and assume that many readers don't either.

When the German Reich invaded Soviet Russia on June 22, 1941, many welcomed it as a liberating army. In less than a month the Germans had captured more than 200,000 prisoners. Entire units crossed over to the Germans. From the very outset of the war, therefore, the German army was in the unusual position of having several hundred thousand enemy volunteers, eventually known as Hilfswillige (Hi-Wis). A leading British authority, Catherine Andreyev, conservatively estimates that at its height there were nearly 1 million former Soviet citizens fighting in the German Wehrmacht, and another 3 million forced laborers.

How does shared history turn into shared ideas about democracy? To begin, people place their concept of good governance in the context of their own past. Quoting Solzhenitsyn and Havel, Kuran (1995:118–27) explains that the Soviet states punished and humiliated dissenters, turning citizens powerless. They were instructed to tattle on each other for even minor offenses. This practice caused them to withhold respect from one another and lose their own dignity. With the breakup of the Soviet Union, people who had been deprived of living their deeply held values wanted to incorporate them in their daily lives.

The spread of uniform government institutions and Communist Party structure as well as the organization of labor across the Soviet Bloc probably stimulated similar reactions among everyday people across national boundaries, too. For example, the Communist Youth League operated in Russia and Mongolia. In Mongolia it was called Revsomol and in Russia it was called Komsomol. But the organization and its mandate were the same: indoctrinate the youth into communism. In the interviews are respondents who talk in terms similar to Iurii Poliakov, a 37-year-old Russian poet, novelist and critic (Grant 1993:42):

The Komsomol … is an astonishing organization when you consider how little people believed in it yet how forcefully they pretended otherwise. You have entire generations of schoolchildren who don't believe in anything, and teachers who don't believe in anything. But the teachers have to give the impression that they believe in something, and the students have to give the impression that they believe the teacher. It's staggering. How are those relations established?

With the disintegration of the Soviet Bloc, many—but not all—of the NIS experienced a transformational process similar to Mongolia's. The political economy transitioned from a planned central economy to a market economy, people changed from working for the state to working in private business and government changed from a totalitarian, one-party system where voting was *pro forma* to multiparty elections. These shared transformations resulted in similar ideas about democracy. People in Mongolia and many other NIS were asking themselves: How will the government treat people—with equality and justice or with corruption and bribery? How should people treat each other—by being honest and concerned or by stealing and criticizing? As in Mongolia, so in Russia. Petro (1995:151) writes that although Russians desire law and order, they also want justice and political freedoms.

An extensive survey of more than 10 thousand Russian citizens in eleven regions of the country conducted in 1993 shows that though nearly half favored a "firm hand" in government, this meant "regulation of the economy and protection of the individual against high-handedness and lawlessness, accompanied by the preservation of political freedoms … [however,] the last thing they have in mind is to wind up in the iron embrace of some homegrown Pinochet who would pave the way to the kingdom of the market through arrests, exile and executions."

The fourth and top layer of the cake consists of the national culture and history that makes a people's prioritization of democratic attributes unique. The pastoral nomadic economy and culture, Tibetan Buddhism, vassalage to the Manchu Dynasty of China followed by subordination to the Soviet Union, the 1989–1990 Democratic Revolution and, finally, the 1992 Constitution were played out in a process unique to Mongolia. While other countries experienced vassalage (China controlled Inner and Outer Mongolia, Tibet and Xinjiang), only Outer Mongolia had true vassal status (see Chapter 2). And Mongolia was similar to but different from the Soviet Union, for it remained a sovereign nation even though it was a satellite of Russia. It shared this status with Cuba. Mongolia was also the only country to go from Chinese to Russian dominance. Mongolia's unique journey through history is found in Chapter 2 and subsequent chapters as well. In sum, although the base of the cake contains ideas about democracy that are shared with all humans or just postsocialist peoples, the top layer is made of Mongolians' own interpretation of democratic subdomains. These are a mixture of shared and unique ideas.

The icing on top of the cake contains people's understanding of the present and their hopes and fears for the future. Concerning the present, some views are shared with people in other postsocialist states. They all want the government to protect them from crime, especially theft, which rose precipitously in the 1990s (Humphrey 2002:100). Some Bulgarians even advocate a return to socialism in order to regain law and order:

An increasing number of villagers expressed support for socialism as a remedy for criminality and the apparent breakdown of authority, perhaps most evident in the problem of theft. Reports of village theft multiplied each summer during the 1990s, becoming grander and more brazen. One woman tried to start a photocopying service in the town hall, but someone stole the machine the day it arrived. After the village livestock have been returned or sold, losers leveled the cooperative building for bricks and other construction materials. (Creed 1999:237)

The tremendous drop in GDP in the postsocialist nations naturally caused people to worry about economic survival/success (see, for example, Hann 2006:71). Djanaeva (2002:25–26) tells us what the stakes really were. Her English is not very good, but then my Kyrgyz in nonexistent so I cannot complain about her writing. Quoting from a government report, she writes that life in the Kyrgyz villages deteriorated so badly that "61,5% [61.5 percent] of villages didn't have drinking water, water tubes [pipes], system of irrigation, 85% didn't have working kindergartens, 78% didn't have washing places, 60% didn't have good roads, 15,3% didn't have working schools, 30,7% didn't have access to healthcare institutions." Between 1993 and 1996, she continues, the percent of people "living below the poverty line increased from 40% to 63%, in rural areas 75% of people lived in poverty." In 2001, the average monthly salary was less than US$15, which caused many to work two or even three jobs. Many educated women went abroad to work as nannies and housekeepers. Some women even sold their babies (ibid.:25–27).

People in other postsocialist countries also talked about the huge drop in income they experienced as socialism broke apart. Nancy Ries (2009:188) found that "between 1990 and 2000 the real value of average cash income was halved, precipitating a profound, even historically unprecedented peacetime decline in the standards of living of the population ... even in 2006 roughly half of the population of the Russian Federation lived on the ruble equivalent of $10 or less in wage income per day, and in that year, 15 percent lived on less than the average subsistence minimum of $4 per day." How did people survive? According to Ries, they grew potatoes and other vegetables in their backyards.

People in the other postsocialist countries also complain about a lack of individual opportunity and regional economic development (Humphrey 1998:444–46, 459; Shubin 2007). In Bulgaria, Creed (1999:227–31) writes, the local industries provided only erratic work and therefore intermittent salaries because they preferred imported goods to those made locally. They were also plagued by inflation and the depletion of cash crops like local wild mushrooms and snails. Some returned to farming in order to feed their families.

Despite extreme privation, postsocialist people share the hope that the future will be better than the past. They are usually referring to political freedoms and economic security. The 67 Russian 'democrats' that Lukin (2000:194–95) interviewed believed that economic prosperity is strongly associated with democracy. Others hoped that democracy would bring an ideal society, one that would consist of "(1) freedom (sometimes interpreted as 'democracy' in the narrow sense); (2) justice; (3) well-being; and (4) spiritual and moral perfection."

Even Djanaeva (2002:11) notes, "People believed in the better future [that democracy would bring] politically and economically. Instead of this bright future now we have corruption, demagogy, poverty, violation of women's rights, appearance of illiteracy, loss in quality of life, deep gaps in economic status of people."

I have discussed the optimism of Mongolians in Chapter 5. It seemed out of proportion with their current condition when I conducted research in 1998 and 2003. I now think that it was related to their knowledge that mineral extraction would soon boom, as it is doing as I write in 2012.

This, then, is the layer-cake model of Mongolians' (and others') ideas about democracy. In order to understand Mongolians' ideas on democracy, one must cut through all of the layers at once and eat them together in one forkful. Just eating the icing, that is, the face value of people's ideas, will not do.

To turn this static model into a processual one, I modify the original model presented in Chapter 1, Figure 1.2. The modified model is seen in Figure 8.1. The only difference between the two is found in the third row, where I have substituted the layers of the cake (now lying on its side) for the more simple temporal categories in Figure 1.2. The five boxes of Figure 8.1 incorporate the three boxes of Figure 2.1 and give greater clarity to the actual cognitive process of deciding what to say about democracy.

To demonstrate the complexity of this model, I use the example of Mongolian herders and farmers. While they share universal emotions and deeply held values with people from all over the world, but especially with people in the former Soviet Bloc, their conceptualization of democracy reflects their experience of living through marketization, democratization, weather changes, political changes and so on. The herders interviewed increasingly championed individual rights, especially economic rights and the right to make their own decisions. Their appreciation of political rights also grew, as did their understanding of the association between democratic government and multiparty elections, a rejection of socialism and the preference for parliamentary, or truly representative, governance over presidential, or administrative, governance. These trends suggest that the Mongolian herders and farmers interviewed were moving toward the principles of democracy written into the 1992 Constitution as well as the advice and desires of the Mongolian intelligentsia and international NGOs.

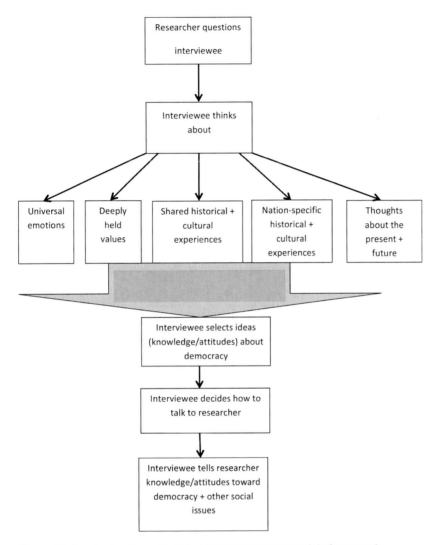

Figure 8.1 A revised anthropological connectionist-theory model of a person's decision-making process concerning what to tell researchers about democracy.

However, herders' and farmers' ideas on democracy were counterbalanced by other trends that suggest they care about their freedoms and an orderly society but not active citizenship. Their continuing indifference toward fulfilling citizens' duties suggests political passivity. They just want to be left alone to figure out how to survive in a capitalist economy.

Several factors, including change in the weather pattern (years of drought and dzud killed millions of livestock), probably influenced this change in attitude. I think the biggest change was that herders and farmers now had to take on all economic risk. Big gains were possible, but so were big losses.

Increasing understanding of how to use markets better and the expansion of markets into the countryside comprise another influence. Many of the herders living around Ulaanbaatar had moved from Bayan Ulgii Aimag to be closer to the Ulaanbaatar market (2003 interviews). People in Khovd complained that they were too far from the Ulaanbaatar market because the lack of Mongolian infrastructure makes transport of goods expensive. Khovd still exported most of its meat and animal parts to Russia, but the domestic market was shifting to Ulaanbaatar as its population expanded to over one-third of the nation. At the same time, Mongolia's animal products became subject to the international market. The price of cashmere was especially sensitive to global fluctuations.

The rural loan system developed with the help of the international banking community. For the first time, herders had access to loans to build their herds and tide them over from one fall (when animals were sold) to the next. This had to influence their thinking.

During this time, the government structure changed as the opposition party gained a foothold in parliament and then lost it again. The constitution did not change; parliament did not change—but how policies were made and enforced was still shifting. To Mongolia's herders and farmers, all these changes meant the attainment of some independence and their freedoms (especially economic freedoms), which they wanted. But they also wanted government support to help them get on their feet. They did not consider participating in governance beyond voting a duty but a right. They still saw the government as doing *to* them rather than *for* them.

The herders and farmers represent a small segment of the interviews (112 [13.1 percent] in 1998 and 64 [15.6 percent] in 2003). They exhibit some different ways of thinking from, say, urban government workers, as the tables in Chapters 3–7 suggest. We would expect this because their experience and history differ somewhat. These ways of thinking, in turn, influence their thought processes, which are modeled in Figure 8.1. It means that people's experience and therefore their ideas vary from one place to the next and even from one person to the next. In deciding how they talk (and think) about democracy, people integrate and prioritize different parts of their culture (their economy, religion, ideas of leadership and so on), their history (from national to personal), their current circumstances (from national to personal) and their goals. Because people in demographic subcategories sometimes share experiences, they also share ideas. But Mongolia is rather a homogeneous population and so we often see that people's ideas do not vary (significantly) by their subcategories.

These data suggest that a preference for democracy may be practically universal in the 21st century, but it probably was not 'universal' throughout time. Certainly people living in pre-state societies did not think of democracy because they did not have complex, state government. Even now, the word democracy may be familiar but its meaning veers away from the more common usage. I have only to look at Schaffer's remarkable work (1997:41–42) on democracy among the Wolof of Senegal. They define *demokaraasi* as "treating people fairly," that is, equally; "sharing responsibility for one another's well being" and reinforcing a sense of community, or interdependence, by coming to consensus. While a glimmer of universal democratic principles may be found in the Wolofs' definition, their ideas barely relate to other people's concerns, as the previous sections illustrate.

Although it would be convenient if everyone defined democracy the same way, people clearly do not. People in the postsocialist countries do not think exactly alike (Dryzek and Templeman Holmes 2002:5; Breslauer 2001), and neither do Mongolians.

IMPLICATIONS OF THE MODEL

The research for this book actually started as a test of Pierre Bourdieu and James Scott's idea that states compartmentalize people in order to regulate them. By putting people in demographic boxes, to use Scott's terminology, states have an easier job administering to them. Scott (1998:2) writes that the state needs to make people "legible, to arrange the population in ways that simplified the classic state functions of taxation, conscription, and prevention of rebellion." Before him, Bourdieu (1990:59–60, 1998:38–46) wrote that the state slots people into demographic categories in order to better 'divide and conquer.' By pitting one group against another, the state maintains control of all groups. Bourdieu adds that the government uses the social sciences, especially sociology (his discipline) to legitimize the demographic division of the population by supporting analyses of the population by demographic subcategories, especially class divisions.

But do people really think 'inside the box?' That is, do people's knowledge and attitudes really vary by demographic category? My research suggests that the answer is 'not always' and 'not consistently.' Our interviewees speak of democracy in terms of five subdomains: human rights, political freedom, economic freedom, responsibilities of the government and duties of citizens. Within all of these subdomains, they mention 50 attributes, some concerning their knowledge about basic democratic principles and others about their attitudes toward democratic practice. If we go back to the tables presented in the data chapters, we can see that variability is not consistent within demographic categories (across rows). If we look at any particular demographic category, we will find neither homogeneity (no stars in any of the attributes) nor significant difference (at least one star in every attribute) across the attributes, or across the rows in each chapter. For example, if we look at gender, we find that Pearson's two-tailed chi-square test suggests that men and women exhibit similar (homogeneous) knowledge and attitudes in most of the attributes (table columns) measured in the data chapters. In fact, men and women seem homogeneous in thought when mentioning political freedom attributes (Chapter 4, both years), economic freedoms (Chapter 5, both years) and government responsibilities (Chapter 6, 2003 only). Still, there are subdomains where men and women do think differently—hold different knowledge or attitudes about the subdomain—and the difference is statistically significant (see Chapter 3, both years, and Chapter 6, 2003 only).

Looking down the columns of the tables, we see that there are some attributes in each data chapter where the interviewees think the same no matter what the demographic category. That is, there are no stars in some of the columns of each chapter. Still, the columns that do exhibit heterogeneity (stars) do not show consistent patterns of such within chapters or among chapters. For example, Chapter 3 (human rights) shows the same pattern of variability for 'human rights are linked to democracy,' 'human rights were not realized during socialism' and 'human rights mean political freedom' but not in the other columns. I believe the lack of patterning by demographic category (along the rows) or attribute (down the columns) suggests that people are more complex than their demography.

On a final note, I would add that although anthropologists and some political scientists like the ones quoted in this chapter recognize that people define democracy differently, some social scientists express the hope that all nations will adopt liberal democracy. Some even bemoan the fact that uniformity in democratic ideas and practice will never be achieved. This research suggests that there will always be different versions of democracy. Yet these differences do not block people from connecting democratic governance with some of the universal emotions and deeply held values that are important to them. There does not need to be a universal definition or practice of democracy for this to take place. Indeed, national and cultural differences will always figure into people's thoughts. Democracy can and should remain malleable. If people's ideas and practices of democracy ever become uniform, it will be because they are imposed from some overarching administration. Should that happen, there will be no democracy at all.

Appendix

Table A.1 Significant differences within demographic categories concerning major human rights attributes, 1998 and 2003.[a]

	Highly valued				Linked with democracy				Not realized during socialism				Total			
	1998		2003		1998		2003		1998		2003		1998		2003	
	N	%	N	%	N	%	N	%	N	%	N	%	N	%	N	%
Location																
Khovd	124	30.8	84	38.5	99	24.6	76	34.9	34	8.5	11	5.0	125	31.1	88	40.4
Ulaanbaatar	206***	44.3	58*	29.3	150*	32.3	55	27.8	28	6.0	9	4.5	207***	44.5	62	31.3
Residence																
Rural	32	24.6	18	28.6	26	20.0	16	25.4	12	9.2	6	9.5	32	24.6	18	28.6
Urban	298***	40.4	123	35.3	223*	30.3	114	32.8	50	6.8	14	4.0	300***	40.7	131	37.6
Gender																
Female	145	34.7	55	30.9	105	25.1	47	26.4	25	6.0	9	5.1	146	34.9	58	32.6
Male	185*	41.2	86	36.9	144*	32.1	83*	35.6	37	8.2	11	4.7	186*	41.4	91	39.1
Age group																
17–26	114	40.9	42	29.8	92	33.0	43	30.5	18	6.5	10	7.1	114	40.9	45	31.9
27–39	105	39.0	35	33.3	75	27.9	30	28.6	19	7.1	3	2.9	107	39.8	38	36.2
40–54	75	35.5	32	36.8	54	25.6	28	32.2	14	6.6	3	3.4	75	35.5	34	39.1
55+	36	33.6	32	41.0	28	26.2	29	37.2	11	10.3	4	5.1	36	33.6	32	41.0
Formal education completed																
Less than high school	51	27.4	15	18.3	40	21.5	13	15.9	19	10.2	2	2.4	51	27.4	15	18.3
Vocational or high school	103	36.3	30	28.8	80	28.2	29	27.9	16	5.6	4	3.8	103	36.3	32	30.8
Technical college	25	30.5	21	31.3	22	26.8	17	25.4	6	7.3	4	6.0	25	30.5	23	34.3
Baccalaureate+	151***	47.9	75***	47.5	107*	34.0	71***	44.9	21	6.7	10	6.3	153***	48.6	79***	50.0

(cont'd)

Table A.1 (continued)

	Highly valued				Linked with democracy				Not realized during socialism				Total			
	1998		2003		1998		2003		1998		2003		1998		2003	
	N	%	N	%	N	%	N	%	N	%	N	%	N	%	N	%
Occupation																
Unemployed	31	31.6	19	38.8	28	28.6	17	34.7	5	5.1	3	6.1	31	31.6	19	38.8
Student	55	44.7	17	37.0	48	39.0	18	39.1	8	6.5	1	2.2	55	44.7	19	41.3
Pensioner	31	34.8	11	22.9	25	28.1	10	20.8	9	10.1	2	4.2	31	34.8	12	25.0
Government worker	109	48.9	45	37.2	69	30.9	40	33.1	13	5.8	5	4.1	109	48.9	48	39.7
NGO worker	NA	NA	11	45.8	NA	NA	9	37.5	NA	NA	2	8.3	NA	NA	11	45.8
In business	67	31.9	25	42.4	54	25.7	24	40.7	10	4.8	4	6.8	69	32.9	27	45.8
Herder/farmer	31***	27.7	13	20.3	20*	17.9	12	18.8	16*	14.3	3	4.7	31***	27.7	13*	20.3
Ethnic identity																
Kazakh	29	46.0	8	22.9	28	44.4	7	20.0	10	15.9	2	5.7	29	46.0	8	22.9
Oirad	82	31.1	51	37.2	61	23.1	45	32.8	21	8.0	7	5.1	83	31.4	54	39.4
Other Mongols	5	50.0	7	35.0	3	30.0	7	35.0	0	0.0	1	5.0	5	50.0	7	35.0
Khalkh	214*	40.4	73	34.3	157**	29.6	69	32.4	31*	5.8	10	4.7	215*	40.6	78	36.6

In a two-tailed chi-square test, $*p \leq .05$, $**p \leq .01$, $***p \leq .001$. Location, residence and gender = 1 df; age group, education and ethnicity = 3 df; occupation = 5 df for 1998 and 6 df for 2003.

[a]Number, percent and statistical significance of differences within demographic categories.

Table A.2 Significant differences within demographic categories concerning subdomains of human rights, 1998 and 2003[a]

	Political freedom				Economic freedom				Right to political participation				Equality			
	1998		2003		1998		2003		1998		2003		1998		2003	
	N	%	N	%	N	%	N	%	N	%	N	%	N	%	N	%
Location																
Khovd	82	20.4	16	7.3	57	14.2	60	27.5	46	11.4	12	5.5	5	1.2	11	5.0
Ulaanbaatar	92	19.8	26*	13.1	99**	21.3	58	29.3	31*	6.7	19	9.6	22**	4.7	18	9.1
Residence																
Rural	20	15.4	3	4.8	16	25.4	0	0.0	7	5.4	4	6.3	4	3.1	6	9.5
Urban	154	20.9	39	11.2	140	29.0	28*	3.8	70	9.5	27	7.8	23	3.1	22	6.3
Gender																
Female	76	18.2	17	9.6	68	16.3	46	25.8	32	7.7	14	7.9	15	3.6	13	7.3
Male	98	21.8	25	10.7	88	19.6	71	30.5	45	10.0	17	7.3	12	2.7	15	6.4
Age group																
17–26	64	22.9	15	10.6	57	20.4	33	23.4	27	9.7	9	6.4	13	4.7	13	9.2
27–39	56	20.8	7	6.7	47	17.5	32	30.5	24	8.9	9	8.6	7	2.6	9	8.6
40–54	33	15.6	11	12.6	35	16.6	29	33.3	18	8.5	4	4.6	6	2.8	2	2.3
55+	21	19.6	9	11.5	17	15.9	23	29.5	8	7.5	9	11.5	1	0.9	4	5.1
Formal education completed																
Less than high school	30	16.1	4	4.9	27	14.5	14	17.1	11	5.9	2	2.4	5	2.7	5	6.1
Vocational or high school	59	20.8	12	11.5	45	15.8	27	26.0	24	8.5	8	7.7	13	4.6	10	9.6
Technical college	12	14.6	6	9.0	11	13.4	16	23.9	7	8.5	4	6.0	2	2.4	2	3.0
Baccalaureate+	73	23.2	20	12.7	73*	23.2	60**	38.0	35	11.1	17	10.8	7	2.2	11	7.0

(cont'd)

Table A.2 (continued)

	Political freedom				Economic freedom				Right to political participation				Equality			
	1998		2003		1998		2003		1998		2003		1998		2003	
	N	%	N	%	N	%	N	%	N	%	N	%	N	%	N	%
Occupation																
Unemployed	20	20.4	5	10.2	18	18.4	15	30.6	9	9.2	2	4.1	6	6.1	3	6.1
Student	34	27.6	8	17.4	31	25.2	13	28.3	15	12.2	6	13.0	5	4.1	4	8.7
Pensioner	12	13.5	3	6.3	11	12.4	13	27.1	6	6.7	3	6.3	1	1.1	0	0.0
Government worker	48	21.5	12	9.9	48	21.5	35	28.9	25	11.2	11	9.1	5	2.2	9	7.4
NGO worker	NA	NA	3	12.5	NA	NA	7	29.2	NA	NA	3	12.5	NA	NA	2	8.3
In business	32	15.2	8	13.6	32	15.2	21	35.6	12	5.7	4	6.8	6	2.9	4	6.8
Herder/farmer	23	20.5	3	4.7	14*	12.5	13	20.3	6	5.4	2	3.1	4	3.6	6	9.4
Ethnic identity																
Kazakh	21	33.3	4	11.4	12	19.0	4	11.4	10	15.9	1	2.9	1	1.6	1	2.9
Oirad	49	18.6	7	5.1	34	12.9	36	26.3	28	10.6	9	6.6	4	1.5	5	3.6
Other Mongols	4	40.0	1	5.0	2	20.0	7	35.0	2	20.0	2	10.0	0	0.0	3	15.0
Khalkh	100*	18.9	30	14.1	108	20.4	69	32.4	37*	7.0	19	8.9	22	4.2	18	8.5

In a two-tailed chi-square test, *p≤.05, **p≤.01, ***p≤.001. Location, residence and gender=1 df; age group, education and ethnic identity=3 df; occupation=5 df in 1998 and 6 df in 2003.
[a]Number, percent and statistical significance of differences within demographic categories.

Table A.3 Significant differences within demographic categories regarding the association of deeply held values with human rights, 1998 and 2003[a]

	Personal dignity				National dignity				Self-determination			
	1998		2003		1998		2003		1998		2003	
	N	%	N	%	N	%	N	%	N	%	N	%
Location												
Khovd	100	24.9	29	13.3	36	9.0	31	14.2	4	1.0	13	6.0
Ulaanbaatar	120	25.8	43*	21.7	63*	13.5	20	10.1	22***	4.7	17	8.6
Residence												
Rural	24	18.5	12	19.0	6	4.6	7	11.1	0	0.0	3	4.8
Urban	196*	26.6	59	17.0	93**	12.6	44	12.6	26*	3.5	27	7.8
Gender												
Female	90	21.5	28	15.7	48	11.5	17	9.6	12	2.9	10	5.6
Male	130*	29.0	43	18.5	51	11.4	34	14.6	14	3.1	20	8.6
Age group												
17–26	79	28.3	23	16.3	30	10.8	22	15.6	18	6.5	11	7.8
27–39	73	27.1	22	21.0	34	12.6	10	9.5	4	1.5	8	7.6
40–54	44	20.9	15	17.2	26	12.3	8	9.2	3	1.4	4	4.6
55+	24	22.4	11	14.1	9	8.4	11	14.1	1***	0.9	7	9.0
Formal education completed												
Less than high school	35	18.8	8	9.8	12	6.5	9	11.0	6	3.2	3	3.7
Vocational or high school	74	26.1	16	15.4	33	11.6	12	11.5	13	4.6	11	10.6
Technical college	16	19.5	10	14.9	6	7.3	7	10.4	2	2.4	4	6.0
Baccalaureate+	95*	30.2	37*	23.4	48*	15.2	23	14.6	5	1.6	12	7.6

(cont'd)

Table A.3 (continued)

	Personal dignity				National dignity				Self-determination			
	1998		2003		1998		2003		1998		2003	
	N	%	N	%	N	%	N	%	N	%	N	%
Occupation												
Unemployed	20	20.4	10	20.4	8	8.2	7	14.3	3	3.1	6	12.2
Student	40	32.5	12	26.1	22	17.9	9	19.6	14	11.4	5	10.9
Pensioner	17	19.1	5	10.4	10	11.2	5	10.4	2	2.2	4	8.3
Government worker	69	30.9	22	18.2	32	14.3	10	8.3	0	0.0	6	5.0
NGO worker	NA	NA	4	16.7	NA	NA	4	16.7	NA	NA	2	8.3
In business	43	20.5	8	13.6	17	8.1	10	16.9	7	3.3	7	11.9
Herder/farmer	25	22.3	10	15.6	8*	7.1	6	9.4	0***	0.0	0	0.0
Ethnic identity												
Kazakh	23	36.5	4	11.4	9	14.3	3	8.6	1	1.6	2	5.7
Oirad	60	22.7	17	12.4	22	8.3	17	12.4	3	1.1	6	4.4
Other Mongols	3	30.0	4	20.0	2	20.0	3	15.0	0	0.0	4	20.0
Khalkh	134	25.3	45	21.1	66	12.5	27	12.7	22	4.2	18	8.5

In a two-tailed chi-square test, $*p \le .05$, $**p \le .01$, $***p \le .001$. Location, residence and gender=1 df; age group, education and ethnic identity=3 df; occupation=5 df in 1998 and 6 df in 2003.

[a] Number, percent and statistical significance of differences within demographic categories.

Table A.4 Significant differences within demographic categories concerning attributes of political freedom, 1998 and 2003[a]

| | All political freedoms | | | | Freedom from oppression | | | | Democracy brings political freedom | | | |
| | 1998 | | 2003 | | 1998 | | 2003 | | 1998 | | 2003 | |
	N	%	N	%	N	%	N	%	N	%	N	%
Location												
Khovd	149	37.1	132	60.6	12	3.0	8	3.7	40	10.0	26	11.9
Ulaanbaatar	209*	44.9	126	63.6	30*	6.5	6	3.0	39	8.4	34	17.2
Residence												
Rural	33	25.4	30	46.2	2	1.5	1	1.5	5	3.8	5	7.7
Urban	325***	44.1	226**	64.9	40	5.4	13	3.7	74*	10.0	54	15.5
Gender												
Female	170	40.7	110	61.1	21	5.0	7	3.9	37	8.9	24	13.3
Male	188	41.9	146	62.7	21	4.7	7	3.0	42	9.4	35	15.0
Age group												
17–26	118	42.3	89	63.1	12	4.3	5	3.5	28	10.0	23	16.3
27–39	123	45.7	77	73.3	17	6.3	7	6.7	29	10.8	24	22.9
40–54	79	37.4	53	60.9	9	4.3	0	0.0	15	7.1	9	10.3
55+	38	35.5	38**	48.7	4	3.7	2	2.6	7	6.5	4**	5.1
Formal education completed												
Less than high school	51	27.4	31	37.8	4	2.2	2	2.4	13	7.0	11	13.4
Vocational or high school	112	39.4	67	64.4	17	6.0	2	1.9	21	7.4	20	19.2
Technical college	31	37.8	43	64.2	2	2.4	5	7.5	11	13.4	9	13.4
Baccalaureate+	164***	52.1	116***	73.4	19	6.0	5	3.2	34	10.8	20	12.7

(cont'd)

Table A.4 (continued)

	All political freedoms				Freedom from oppression				Democracy brings political freedom			
	1998		2003		1998		2003		1998		2003	
	N	%	N	%	N	%	N	%	N	%	N	%
Occupation												
Unemployed	47	48.0	29	59.2	6	6.1	1	2.0	13	13.3	2	4.1
Student	59	48.0	28	60.9	9	7.3	4	8.7	15	12.2	9	19.6
Pensioner	26	29.2	29	60.4	2	2.2	1	2.1	6	6.7	6	12.5
Government employee	103	46.2	72	59.5	12	5.4	2	1.7	17	7.6	17	14.0
NGO worker	NA	NA	19	79.2	NA	NA	3	12.5	NA	NA	5	20.8
In business	89	42.4	43	72.9	10	4.8	2	3.4	20	9.5	11	18.6
Herder or farmer	29***	25.9	34	53.1	3	2.7	0*	0.0	7	6.3	9	14.1
Ethnic identity												
Kazakh	20	31.7	15	42.9	2	3.2	1	2.9	14	22.2	5	14.3
Oirad	114	43.2	78	56.9	11	4.2	5	3.6	24	9.1	18	13.1
Other Mongols	4	40.0	12	60.0	9	0.0	1	5.0	0	0.0	3	15.0
Khalkh	220	41.5	148**	69.5	29	5.5	7	3.3	41**	7.7	33	15.5

In a two-tailed chi-square test, *p≤.05, **p≤.01, ***p≤.001. Location, residence and gender=1 df; age group, education and ethnic identity=3 df; occupation=5 df in 1998 and 6 df in 2003.

aNumber, percent and statistical significance of differences within demographic categories.

Table A.5 Significant differences within demographic categories concerning major subdomains of political freedom, 1998 and 2003[a]

	Free speech				Religious freedom				Right to protect one's rights			
	1998		2003		1998		2003		1998		2003	
	N	%	N	%	N	%	N	%	N	%	N	%
Location												
Khovd	142	42.5	122	50.2	17	4.2	36	16.5	6	1.5	1	0.5
Ulaanbaatar	192	57.5	121	49.8	48***	10.3	25	12.6	3	0.6	4	2.0
Residence												
Rural	32	24.6	28	43.1	5	3.8	10	15.4	1	0.8	1	1.5
Urban	302***	41.0	213**	61.2	60	8.1	51	14.7	8	1.1	4	1.1
Gender												
Female	161	38.5	103	57.2	29	6.9	28	15.6	4	1.0	1	0.6
Male	173	38.5	138	59.2	36	8.0	33	14.2	5	1.1	4	1.7
Age group												
17–26	113	40.5	84	59.6	23	8.2	23	16.3	3	1.1	3	2.1
27–39	19	44.2	74	70.5	17	6.3	14	13.3	3	1.1	1	1.0
40–54	67	31.8	51	58.6	17	8.1	13	14.9	3	1.4	0	0.0
55+	32.7*	33	42.3**	42.3	8	7.5	11	14.1	0	0.0	1	1.3
Formal education completed												
Less than high school	45	24.2	27	32.9	8	4.3	6	7.3	2	1.1	1	1.2
Vocational or high school	103	36.3	65	62.5	28	9.9	12	11.5	2	0.7	2	1.9
Technical college	29	35.4	38	56.7	3	3.7	10	14.9	1	1.2	1	1.5
Baccalaureate+	157***	49.8	112***	70.9	26	8.3	33*	20.9	4	1.3	1	0.6

(cont'd)

Table A.5 (continued)

	Free speech				Religious freedom				Right to protect one's rights			
	1998		2003		1998		2003		1998		2003	
	N	%	N	%	N	%	N	%	N	%	N	%
Occupation												
Unemployed	44	44.9	23	46.9	9	9.2	13	26.5	0	0.0	0	0.0
Student	55	44.7	27	58.7	16	13.0	1	2.2	2	1.6	0	0.0
Pensioner	22	24.7	28	58.3	7	7.9	7	14.6	0	0.0	0	0.0
Government employee	99	44.4	68	56.2	12	5.4	18	14.9	3	1.3	3	2.5
NGO worker	NA	NA	18	75.0	NA	NA	4	16.7	NA	NA	0	0.0
In business	83	39.5	41	69.5	15	7.1	8	13.6	2	1.0	0	0.0
Herder or farmer	27***	24.1	34	53.1	5	4.5	9	14.1	2	1.8	2	3.1
Ethnic identity												
Kazakh	19	30.2	12	34.3	1	1.6	4	11.4	1	1.6	1	2.9
Oirad	106	40.2	75	54.7	17	6.4	13	9.5	3	1.1	2	1.5
Other Mongols	3	30.0	11	55.0	1	10.0	3	15.0	1	10.0	0	0.0
Khalkh	206	38.9	140**	65.7	46	8.7	40	18.8	4*	0.8	2	0.9

In a two-tailed chi-square test, *p≤.05, **p≤.01, ***p≤.001. Location, residence and gender=1 df; age group, education and ethnic identity=3 df; occupation=5 df in 1998 and 6 df in 2003.
[a]Number, percent and statistical significance of differences within demographic categories.

Table A.6 Significant differences within demographic categories concerning the association of underlying values with political freedom, 1998 and 2003[a]

	Personal dignity				Self-determination				Democratic development			
	1998		2003		1998		2003		1998		2003	
	N	%	N	%	N	%	N	%	N	%	N	%
Location												
Khovd	123	30.6	122	56.0	6	1.5	7	3.2	8	2.0	5	2.3
Ulaanbaatar	150	32.3	93	47.0	12	2.6	4	2.0	9	1.9	4	2.0
Residence												
Rural	26	20.0	28	43.1	1	0.8	0	0.0	2	1.5	0	0.0
Urban	247	33.5	185	53.2	17	2.3	11	3.2	15	2.0	9	2.6
Gender												
Female	136	32.5	89	49.4	9	2.2	7	3.9	8	1.9	3	1.7
Male	137	30.5	124	53.2	9	2.0	4	1.7	9	2.0	6	2.6
Age group												
17–26	98	35.1	78	55.3	9	3.2	3	2.1	8	2.9	4	2.8
27–39	97	36.1	65	61.9	3	1.1	3	2.9	7	2.6	4	3.8
40–54	54	25.6	39	44.8	5	2.4	4	4.6	2	0.9	1	1.1
55+	24	22.4	32*	41.0	1	0.9	1	1.3	0	0.0	0	0.0
Formal education completed												
Less than high school	38	20.4	24	29.3	4	2.2	2	2.4	1	0.5	0	0.0
Vocational or high school	95	33.5	59	56.7	6	2.1	3	2.9	10	3.5	1	1.0
Technical college	23	28.0	36	53.7	2	2.4	2	3.0	0	0.0	1	1.5
Baccalaureate+	117***	37.1	95***	60.1	6	1.9	4	2.5	6	1.9	7	4.4

(cont'd)

Table A.6 (continued)

	Personal dignity				Self-determination				Democratic development			
	1998		2003		1998		2003		1998		2003	
	N	%	N	%	N	%	N	%	N	%	N	%
Occupation												
Unemployed	37	37.8	26	53.1	3	3.1	0	0.0	2	2.0	1	2.0
Student	50	40.7	24	52.2	7	5.7	0	0.0	7	5.7	2	4.3
Pensioner	13	14.6	24	50.0	1	1.1	3	6.3	0	0.0	0	0.0
Government employee	80	35.9	58	47.9	1	0.4	4	3.3	3	1.3	4	3.3
NGO worker	NA	NA	15	62.5	NA	NA	2	8.3	NA	NA	1	4.2
In business	68	32.4	31	52.5	5	2.4	1	1.7	4	1.9	1	1.7
Herder or farmer	20***	17.9	33	51.6	1*	0.9	1	1.6	1*	0.9	0	0.0
Ethnic identity												
Kazakh	16	25.4	13	37.1	2	3.2	2	5.7	0	0.0	1	2.9
Oirad	96	36.4	58	42.3	3	1.1	2	1.5	7	2.7	4	2.9
Other Mongols	3	30.0	12	60.0	0	0.0	1	5.0	0	0.0	0	0.0
Khalkh	158	29.8	127**	59.6	13	2.5	6	2.8	10	1.9	4	1.9

In a two-tailed chi-square test, *p≤.05, **p≤.01, ***p≤.001. Location, residence and gender=1 df; age group, education and ethnic identity=3 df; occupation=5 df in 1998 and 6 df in 2003.
ᵃNumber, percent and statistical significance of differences within demographic categories.

Table A.7 Significant differences within demographic categories concerning people's mention of some subdomains of economic freedom, 1998 and 2003[a]

	Private property				Business or trade				Employment choice			
	1998		2003		1998		2003		1998		2003	
	N	%	N	%	N	%	N	%	N	%	N	%
Location												
Khovd	44	10.9	66	30.3	42	10.4	62	28.4	22	5.5	60	27.5
Ulaanbaatar	77*	16.6	58	29.3	34	7.3	28***	14.1	52**	11.2	43	21.7
Residence												
Rural	20	15.4	18	27.7	14	10.8	11	16.9	4	3.1	17	26.2
Urban	101	13.7	106	30.5	62	8.4	78	22.4	70*	9.5	86	24.7
Gender												
Female	49	11.7	60	33.3	34	8.1	43	23.9	41	9.8	49	27.2
Male	72	16.0	64	27.5	42	9.4	46	19.7	33	7.3	54	23.2
Age group												
17–26	29	10.4	41	29.1	29	10.4	22	15.6	22	7.9	34	24.1
27–39	41	15.2	29	27.6	23	8.6	30	28.6	22	8.2	22	21.0
40–54	36	17.1	32	36.8	15	7.1	19	21.8	18	8.5	29	33.3
55+	15	14.0	20	25.6	9	8.4	18	23.1	12	11.2	18	23.1
Formal education completed												
Less than high school	20	10.8	26	31.7	20	10.8	20	24.4	10	5.4	20	24.4
Vocational or high school	31	10.9	34	32.7	27	9.5	23	22.1	25	8.8	28	26.9
Technical college	10	12.2	14	20.9	7	8.5	12	17.9	8	9.8	17	25.4
Baccalaureate+	60*	19.0	48	30.4	22	7.0	34	21.5	31	9.8	38	24.1

(cont'd)

Table A.7 (continued)

	Private property				Business or trade				Employment choice			
	1998		2003		1998		2003		1998		2003	
	N	%	N	%	N	%	N	%	N	%	N	%
Occupation												
Unemployed	11	11.2	13	26.5	8	8.2	10	20.4	5	5.1	9	18.4
Student	12	9.8	18	39.1	16	13.0	14	30.4	10	8.1	10	21.7
Pensioner	13	14.6	18	37.5	7	7.9	10	20.8	8	9.0	13	27.1
Government worker	36	16.1	35	28.9	14	6.3	24	19.8	24	10.8	23	19.0
NGO worker	NA	NA	4	16.7	NA	NA	6	25.0	NA	NA	5	20.8
In business	29	13.8	18	30.5	21	10.0	12	20.3	23	11.0	21	35.6
Herder/farmer	18	16.1	18	28.1	10	8.9	13	20.3	4	3.6	21	32.8
Ethnic identity												
Kazakh	7	11.1	11	31.4	9	14.3	8	22.9	5	7.9	7	20.0
Oirad	23	8.7	40	29.2	30	11.4	18	13.1	17	6.4	26	19.0
Other Mongols	0	0.0	7	35.0	1	10.0	5	25.0	1	10.0	7	35.0
Khalkh	91**	17.2	63	29.6	36	6.8	156	26.8	51	9.6	63*	29.6

In a two-tailed chi-square test, *p≤.05, **p≤.01, ***p≤.001. Location, residence and gender=1 df; age group, education and ethnic identity=3 df; occupation=5 df in 1998 and 6 df in 2003.
aNumber, percent and statistical significance of differences within demographic categories.

Table A.8 Significant differences within demographic categories concerning people's mention of other subdomains of economic freedom, 1998 and 2003[a]

	Mobility				Education choice				Total economic freedoms			
	1998		2003		1998		2003		1998		2003	
	N	%	N	%	N	%	N	%	N	%	N	%
Location												
Khovd	13	3.2	67	30.7	9	2.2	70	32.1	113	28.1	173	79.4
Ulaanbaatar	25	5.4	47	23.7	47***	10.1	26***	13.1	190***	40.9	142	71.7
Residence												
Rural	4	3.1	20	30.8	2	1.5	21	32.3	35	26.9	47	72.3
Urban	34	4.6	94	27.0	54**	7.3	75	21.6	268*	36.4	266	76.4
Gender												
Female	13	3.1	53	29.4	29	6.9	43	23.9	142	34.0	138	76.7
Male	25	5.6	61	26.2	27	6.0	53	22.7	161	35.9	175	75.1
Age group												
17–26	6	2.2	39	27.7	15	5.4	41	29.1	103	36.9	107	75.9
27–39	12	4.5	27	25.7	18	6.7	23	21.9	94	34.9	81	77.1
40–54	14	6.6	24	27.6	12	5.7	22	25.3	70	33.2	69	79.3
55+	6	5.6	23	29.5	10	9.3	10	12.8	35	32.7	56	71.8
Formal education completed												
Less than high school	6	3.2	18	22.0	5	2.7	15	18.3	56	30.1	63	76.8
Vocational or high school	11	3.9	29	27.9	15	5.3	27	26.0	95	33.5	86	82.7
Technical college	3	3.7	19	28.4	4	4.9	16	23.9	27	32.9	48	71.6
Baccalaureate+	18	5.7	47	29.7	32**	10.2	38	24.1	125	39.7	116	73.4

(cont'd)

Table A.8 (continued)

	Mobility				Education choice				Total economic freedoms			
	1998		2003		1998		2003		1998		2003	
	N	%	N	%	N	%	N	%	N	%	N	%
Occupation												
Unemployed	5	5.1	12	24.5	7	7.1	13	26.5	29	29.6	34	69.4
Student	2	1.6	15	32.6	9	7.3	11	23.9	53	43.1	34	73.9
Pensioner	7	7.9	12	25.0	7	7.9	9	18.8	25	28.1	40	83.3
Government worker	10	4.5	28	23.1	20	9.0	18	14.9	80	35.9	86	71.1
NGO worker	NA	NA	8	33.3	NA	NA	5	20.8	NA	NA	18	75.0
In business	13	6.2	17	28.8	12	5.7	18	30.5	82	39.0	49	83.1
Herder/farmer	1	0.9	21	32.8	0	0.0	21	32.8	31	27.7	51	79.9
Ethnic identity												
Kazakh	2	3.2	8	22.9	2	3.2	4	11.4	21	33.3	22	62.9
Oirad	11	4.2	27	19.7	7	2.7	20	14.6	74	28.0	95	69.3
Other Mongols	1	10.0	9	45.0	1	10.0	8	40.0	5	50.0	18	90.0
Khalkh	24	4.5	67	31.5	46**	8.7	64***	30.0	203*	38.3	173*	81.2

In a two-tailed chi-square test, *p ≤ .05, **p ≤ .01, ***p ≤ .001. Location, residence and gender = 1 df; age group, education and ethnic identity = 3 df; occupation = 5 df in 1998 and 6 df in 2003.
ªNumber, percent and statistical significance of differences within demographic categories.

Table A.9 Significant differences within demographic categories concerning the association of certain deeply held values with economic freedom, 1998 and 2003[a]

	Personal dignity				Economic survival				Opportunity				Self-determination			
	1998		2003		1998		2003		1998		2003		1998		2003	
	N	%	N	%	N	%	N	%	N	%	N	%	N	%	N	%
Location																
Khovd	161	40.0	122	56.0	88	21.9	110	50.5	50	12.4	81	37.2	27	6.7	43	19.7
Ulaanbaatar	207	44.5	94***	47.5	176	37.8	117*	59.1	93	20.0	88	44.4	52	11.2	38**	19.2
Residence																
Rural	39	30.0	28	43.1	38	29.2	39	60.0	24	18.5	29	44.6	4	3.1	15	23.1
Urban	329**	44.6	186	53.4	226	30.7	186	53.4	119	16.1	138	39.7	75*	10.2	66	19.0
Gender																
Female	172	41.1	89	49.4	137	32.8	107	59.4	74	17.7	81	45.0	39	9.3	33	18.3
Male	196	43.7	125	53.6	127	28.3	118	50.6	69	15.4	86	36.9	40	8.9	48	20.6
Age group																
17–26	127	45.5	79	56.0	77	27.6	70	49.6	40	14.3	55	39.0	42	15.1	26	18.4
27–39	131	48.7	65	61.9	89	33.1	62	59.0	47	17.5	44	41.9	18	6.7	22	21.0
40–54	73	34.6	39	44.8	67	31.8	52	59.8	38	18.0	40	46.0	15	7.1	16	18.4
55+	37**	34.6	32*	41.0	31	29.0	41	52.6	18	16.8	29	37.2	4***	3.7	16	20.5
Formal education completed																
Less than high school	55	29.6	24	29.3	52	28.0	51	62.2	38	20.4	41	50.0	16	8.6	12	14.6
Vocational or high school	129	45.4	60	57.7	77	27.1	61	58.7	31	10.9	41	39.4	37	13.0	31	29.8
Technical college	27	32.9	36	53.7	25	30.5	28	41.8	12	14.6	25	37.3	9	11.0	14	20.9
Baccalaureate+	157***	49.8	95***	60.1	110	34.9	85	53.8	62*	19.7	61	38.6	17*	5.4	23*	14.6

(cont'd)

Table A.9 (continued)

| | Personal dignity | | | | Economic survival | | | | Opportunity | | | | Self-determination | | | |
| | 1998 | | 2003 | | 1998 | | 2003 | | 1998 | | 2003 | | 1998 | | 2003 | |
	N	%	N	%	N	%	N	%	N	%	N	%	N	%	N	%
Occupation																
Khovd	161	40.0	122	56.0	88	21.9	110	50.5	50	12.4	81	37.2	27	6.7	43	19.7
Unemployed	43	43.9	26	53.1	21	21.4	29	59.2	8	8.2	22	44.9	11	11.2	61	2.2
Student	61	49.6	24	52.2	39	31.7	27	58.7	21	17.1	20	43.5	27	22.0	10	21.7
Pensioner	23	25.8	24	50.0	21	23.6	27	56.3	7	7.9	18	37.5	5	5.6	11	22.9
Government worker	113	50.7	58	47.9	88	39.5	60	49.6	61	27.4	45	37.2	7	3.1	22	18.2
NGO worker	NA	NA	15	62.5	NA	NA	11	45.8	NA	NA	10	41.7	NA	NA	8	33.3
In business	86	41.0	32	54.2	60	28.6	32	54.2	19	9.0	24	40.7	23	11.0	9	15.3
Herder/farmer	34***	30.4	33	51.6	34*	30.4	38	59.4	26***	23.2	28	43.8	6***	5.4	15	23.4
Ethnic identity																
Kazakh	24	38.1	13	37.1	13	20.6	20	57.1	8	12.7	18	51.4	5	7.9	4	11.4
Oirad	119	45.1	59	43.1	60	22.7	82	59.9	35	13.3	61	44.5	17	6.4	22	16.1
Other Mongols	4	40.0	12	60.0	3	30.0	14	70.0	0	0.0	11	55.0	0	0.0	6	30.0
Khalkh	221	41.7	127*	59.6	188***	35.5	105	49.3	100	18.9	75	35.2	57	10.8	47	22.1

In a two-tailed chi-square test, *p ≤ .05, **p ≤ .01, ***p ≤ .001. Location, residence and gender = 1 df; age group, education and ethnic identity = 3 df; occupation = 5 df in 1998 and 6 df in 2003.
[a]Number, percent and statistical significance of differences within demographic categories.

Table A.10 Significant differences within demographic categories in three attributes of a democratic government, 1998 and 2003[a]

	Not corrupt				Rule of law				Transparent			
	1998		2003		1998		2003		1998		2003	
	N	%	N	%	N	%	N	%	N	%	N	%
Location												
Khovd	21	5.2	31	14.2	6	1.5	26	11.9	11	2.7	35	16.1
Ulaanbaatar	42	9.0	37*	18.7	23*	4.9	55***	27.8	13	2.8	62***	31.3
Residence												
Rural	24	18.5	7	10.8	3	2.3	15	23.1	2	1.5	18	27.7
Urban	39***	5.3	60	17.2	26	3.5	66	19.0	22	3.0	77	22.1
Gender												
Female	24	5.7	29	16.1	9	2.2	33	18.3	12	2.9	40	22.2
Male	39	8.7	38	16.3	20	4.5	48	20.6	12	2.7	55	23.6
Age group												
17–26	11	3.9	15	10.6	6	2.2	27	19.1	10	3.6	40	28.4
27–39	21	7.8	21	20.0	14	5.2	21	20.0	8	3.0	18	17.1
40–54	18	8.5	14	16.1	6	2.8	21	24.1	5	2.4	27	31.0
55+	13*	12.1	16	20.5	3	2.8	12	15.4	1	0.9	12*	15.4
Formal education completed												
Less than high school	23	12.4	12	14.6	1	0.5	11	13.4	2	1.1	18	22.0
Vocational or high school	14	4.9	24	23.1	14	4.9	18	17.3	10	3.5	25	24.0
Technical college	8	9.8	6	9.0	3	3.7	17	25.4	3	3.7	19	28.4
Baccalaureate+	18**	5.7	24	15.2	11	3.5	35	22.2	9	2.9	35	22.2

(cont'd)

Table A.10 (continued)

	Not corrupt				Rule of law				Transparent			
	1998		2003		1998		2003		1998		2003	
	N	%	N	%	N	%	N	%	N	%	N	%
Occupation												
Unemployed	2	2.0	5	10.2	3	3.1	10	20.4	1	1.0	8	16.3
Student	4	3.3	9	19.6	3	2.4	6	13.0	6	4.9	10	21.7
Pensioner	5	5.6	9	18.8	3	3.4	4	8.3	2	2.2	11	22.9
Government worker	14	6.3	23	19.0	6	2.7	31	25.6	5	2.2	32	26.4
NGO worker	NA	NA	1	4.2	NA	NA	6	25.0	NA	NA	4	16.7
In business	11	5.2	9	15.3	11	5.2	10	16.9	7	3.3	14	23.7
Herder/farmer	27***	24.1	11	17.2	3	2.7	12	18.8	2	1.8	15	23.4
Ethnic identity												
Kazakh	10	15.9	7	20.0	1	1.6	13	37.1	2	3.2	11	31.4
Oirad	11	4.2	21	15.3	6	2.3	34	24.8	6	2.3	40	29.2
Other Mongols	1	10.0	4	20.0	0	0	1	5.0	1	10.0	2	10.0
Khalkh	41*	7.7	34	16.0	22	4.2	33*	15.5	15	2.8	41	19.2

In a two-tailed chi-square test, $*p \leq .05$, $**p \leq .01$, $***p \leq .001$. Location, residence and gender=1 df; age group, education and ethnic identity=3 df; occupation=5 df in 1998 and 6 df in 2003.
[a]Number, percent and statistical significance of differences within demographic categories.

Table A.11 Significant differences within demographic categories concerning a democratic government's major responsibilities toward citizens, 1998 and 2003[a]

	Rights and freedoms				Justice (fairness)				Equality			
	1998		2003		1998		2003		1998		2003	
	N	%	N	%	N	%	N	%	N	%	N	%
Location												
Khovd	81	20.1	62	28.4	59	14.7	36	16.5	22	5.5	129	59.2
Ulaanbaatar	124*	26.7	104***	52.5	101**	21.7	67***	33.8	67***	14.4	112	56.6
Residence												
Rural	17	13.1	26	40.0	11	8.5	19	29.2	26	20.0	39	60.0
Urban	188**	25.5	138	39.7	149***	20.2	83	23.9	63***	8.5	200	57.5
Gender												
Female	95	22.7	70	38.9	74	17.7	51	28.3	37	8.9	105	58.3
Male	110	24.5	94	40.3	86	19.2	51	21.9	52	11.6	134	57.5
Age group												
17–26	70	25.1	59	41.8	42	15.1	34	24.1	29	10.4	99	70.2
27–39	71	26.4	42	40.0	52	19.3	29	27.6	25	9.3	61	58.1
40–54	44	20.9	30	34.5	51	24.2	26	29.9	23	10.9	39	44.8
55+	20	18.7	34	43.6	15*	14.00	14	17.9	12	11.2	38***	48.7
Formal education completed												
Less than high school	27	14.5	17	20.7	13	7.0	14	17.1	26	14.0	57	69.5
Vocational or high school	68	23.9	39	37.5	46	16.2	20	19.2	26	9.2	56	53.8
Technical college	13	15.9	32	47.8	14	17.1	23	34.3	7	8.5	39	58.2
Baccalaureate+	97***	30.8	77***	48.7	87***	27.6	46*	29.1	30	9.5	85	53.8

(cont'd)

Table A.11 (continued)

	Rights and freedoms				Justice (fairness)				Equality			
	1998		2003		1998		2003		1998		2003	
	N	%	N	%	N	%	N	%	N	%	N	%
Occupation												
Unemployed	22	22.4	21	42.9	18	18.4	10	20.4	7	7.1	29	59.2
Student	38	30.9	15	32.6	16	13.0	14	30.4	11	8.9	31	67.4
Pensioner	17	19.1	21	43.8	13	14.6	7	14.6	7	7.9	29	60.4
Government worker	53	23.8	48	39.7	71	31.8	32	26.4	23	10.3	68	56.2
NGO worker	NA	NA	11	45.8	NA	NA	5	20.8	NA	NA	14	58.3
In business	53	25.2	19	32.2	33	15.7	13	22.0	13	6.2	30	50.8
Ethnic identity												
Herder/farmer	19	17.0	27	42.2	9***	8.0	20	31.3	26***	23.2	36	56.3
Kazakh	15	23.8	12	34.3	3	4.8	13	37.1	6	9.5	32	91.4
Oirad	51	19.3	60	43.8	48	18.2	45	32.8	17	6.4	74	54.0
Other Mongols	5	50.0	7	35.0	5	50.0	4	20.0	1	10.0	13	65.0
Khalkh	134	25.3	84	39.4	104*	19.6	39*	18.3	65	12.3	115***	54.0

In a two-tailed chi-square test, *p≤.05, **p≤.01, ***p≤.001. Location, residence and gender=1 df; age group, education and ethnic identity=3 df; occupation=5 df in 1998 and 6 df in 2003.
[a]Number, percent and statistical significance of differences within demographic categories.

Table A.12 Significant differences within demographic categories regarding democratic government support of citizens' transition to the market economy, 1998 and 2003[a]

	Law and order				Access to education				Social safety net			
	1998		2003		1998		2003		1998		2003	
	N	%	N	%	N	%	N	%	N	%	N	%
Location												
Khovd	17	4.2	19	8.7	21	5.2	20	9.2	0	0	15	6.9
Ulaanbaatar	28	6.0	26	13.1	61***	13.1	13	6.6	32***	6.9	13	6.6
Residence												
Rural	6	4.6	7	10.8	8	6.2	6	9.2	5	3.8	5	7.7
Urban	39	5.3	38	10.9	74	10.0	27	7.8	27	3.7	23	6.6
Gender												
Female	21	5.0	15	8.3	53	12.7	12	6.7	15	3.6	15	8.3
Male	24	5.3	30	12.9	29*	6.5	21	9.0	17	3.8	13	5.6
Age group												
17–26	11	3.9	7	5.0	22	7.9	12	8.5	7	2.5	12	8.5
27–39	11	4.1	11	10.5	32	11.9	7	6.7	8	3.0	3	2.9
40–54	17	8.1	8	9.2	19	9.0	7	8.0	7	3.3	3	3.4
55+	6	5.6	18***	23.1	8	7.5	7	9.0	10*	9.3	10*	12.8
Formal education completed												
Less than high school	13	7.0	10	12.2	15	8.1	5	6.1	6	3.2	5	6.1
Vocational or high school	16	5.6	13	12.5	24	8.5	9	8.7	10	3.5	6	5.8
Technical college	6	7.3	9	13.4	3	3.7	4	6.0	1	1.2	6	9.0
Baccalaureate+	10	3.2	12	7.6	40*	12.7	15	9.5	15	4.8	11	7.0

(cont'd)

Table A.12 (continued)

	Law and order				Access to education				Social safety net			
	1998		2003		1998		2003		1998		2003	
	N	%	N	%	N	%	N	%	N	%	N	%
Occupation												
Unemployed	12	12.2	6	12.2	3	3.1	5	10.2	2	2.0	3	6.1
Student	2	1.6	6	13.0	7	5.7	4	8.7	1	0.8	4	8.7
Pensioner	10	11.2	6	12.5	8	9.0	4	8.3	8	9.0	1	2.1
Government worker	2	0.9	14	11.6	39	17.5	5	4.1	6	2.7	11	9.1
NGO worker	NA	NA	2	8.3	NA	NA	2	8.3	NA	NA	0	0
In business	12	5.7	5	8.5	18	8.6	5	8.5	10	4.8	3	5.1
Herder/farmer	7***	6.3	6	9.4	7***	6.3	8	12.5	5*	4.5	5	7.8
Ethnic identity												
Kazakh	4	6.3	6	17.1	2	3.2	3	8.6	0	0	3	8.6
Oirad	9	3.4	18	13.1	21	8.0	7	5.1	4	1.5	6	4.4
Other Mongols	0	0.0	3	15.0	0	0	4	20.0	0	0	0	0
Khalkh	32	6.0	16	7.5	59	11.1	19	8.9	28*	5.3	19	8.9

In a two-tailed chi-square test, * p ≤ .05, ** p ≤ .01, *** p ≤ .001. Location, residence and gender = 1 df; age group, education and ethnic identity = 3 df; occupation = 5 df in 1998 and 6 df in 2003.
ªNumber, percent and statistical significance of differences within demographic categories.

Table A.13 Significant differences within demographic categories regarding people's underlying values when discussing government responsibilities, 1998 and 2003[a]

	Personal dignity				Justice (fairness)				Equality			
	1998		2003		1998		2003		1998		2003	
	N	%	N	%	N	%	N	%	N	%	N	%
Location												
Khovd	65	16.2	57	26.1	61	15.2	44	20.2	25	6.2	115	52.8
Ulaanbaatar	86	18.5	35*	17.7	103**	22.2	78***	39.4	63***	13.5	97	49.0
Residence												
Rural	14	10.8	9	13.8	12	9.2	20	30.8	20	15.4	33	50.8
Urban	137*	18.6	82	23.6	152**	20.6	101	29.0	68*	9.2	177	50.9
Gender												
Female	68	16.3	36	20.0	75	17.9	59	32.8	36	8.6	92	51.1
Male	83	18.5	55	23.6	89	19.8	62	26.6	52	11.6	118	50.6
Age group												
17–26	56	20.1	34	24.1	43	15.4	40	28.4	31	11.1	90	63.8
27–39	50	18.6	26	24.8	53	19.7	33	31.4	26	9.7	51	48.6
40–54	30	14.2	16	18.4	52	24.6	31	35.6	22	10.4	33	37.9
55+	15	14.0	15	19.2	16*	15.0	18	23.1	9	8.4	36***	46.2
Formal education completed												
Less than high school	20	20.1	10	12.2	14	7.5	15	18.3	26	14.0	44	53.7
Vocational or high school	54	18.6	29	27.9	48	16.9	26	25.0	26	9.2	52	50.0
Technical college	5	14.2	18	26.9	14	17.1	25	37.3	5	6.1	37	55.2
Baccalaureate+	72 ***14.0		34	21.5	88 ***27.9		56 *	35.4	31	9.8	77	48.7

(cont'd)

Table A.13 (continued)

	Personal dignity				Justice (fairness)				Equality			
	1998		2003		1998		2003		1998		2003	
	N	%	N	%	N	%	N	%	N	%	N	%
Occupation												
Unemployed	13	10.8	13	26.5	18	18.4	13	26.5	9	9.2	27	55.1
Student	31	19.0	10	21.7	17	13.8	14	30.4	12	9.8	26	56.5
Pensioner	10	6.1	10	20.8	14	15.7	8	16.7	3	3.4	27	56.3
Government worker	47	22.9	27	22.3	72	32.3	43	35.5	22	9.9	58	47.9
NGO worker	NA		7	29.2	NA	NA	5	20.8	NA	NA	13	54.2
In business	33	13.3	12	20.3	33	15.7	15	25.4	18	8.6	24	40.7
Herder/farmer	14*	25.2	11	17.2	10***	8.9	22	34.4	23**	20.5	33	51.6
Ethnic identity												
Kazakh	14	22.2	6	17.1	4	6.3	14	40.0	8	12.7	28	80.0
Oirad	38	14.4	21	15.3	49	18.6	53	38.7	14	5.3	62	45.3
Other Mongols	3	30.0	3	15.0	5	50.0	4	20.0	1	10.0	10	50.0
Khalkh	96	18.1	59	27.7	106**	20.0	48**	22.5	65*	12.3	107**	50.2

In a two-tailed chi-square test, *p≤.05, **p≤.01, ***p≤.001. Location, residence and gender=1 df; age group, education and ethnic identity=3 df; occupation=5 df in 1998 and 6 df in 2003.
ᵃNumber, percent and statistical significance of differences within demographic categories.

Table A.14 Significant differences within demographic categories concerning participation in elections, 1998 and 2003[a]

	Vote (duty)				Vote (right)				Total			
	1998		2003		1998		2003		1998		2003	
	N	%	N	%	N	%	N	%	N	%	N	%
Location												
Khovd	5	1.2	36	16.5	81	20.1	84	38.5	82	20.4	89	40.8
Ulaanbaatar	32***	6.9	44	22.2	97	20.9	98*	49.5	113	24.3	108**	54.5
Residence												
Rural	2	1.5	8	12.3	13	10.0	23	35.4	14	10.8	26	40.0
Urban	35	4.7	71	20.4	165***	22.4	157	45.1	181***	24.6	169	48.6
Gender												
Female	23	5.5	32	17.8	91	21.8	80	44.4	102	24.4	86	47.8
Male	14	3.1	47	20.2	87	19.4	100	42.9	93	20.7	109	46.8
Age group												
17–26	18	6.5	28	19.9	62	22.2	59	41.4	70	25.1	63	44.7
27–39	11	4.1	14	13.3	58	21.6	48	45.7	62	23.0	50	47.6
40–54	6	2.8	24	27.6	41	19.4	39	44.8	45	21.3	45	51.7
55+	2	1.9	13	16.7	17	15.9	35	44.9	18	16.8	37	47.4
Formal education completed												
Less than high school	3	1.6	10	12.2	17	9.1	20	24.4	19	10.2	22	26.8
Vocational or high school	12	4.2	27	26.0	59	20.8	48	46.2	62	21.8	51	49.0
Technical college	1	1.2	10	14.9	17	20.7	29	43.3	17	20.7	30	44.8
Baccalaureate+	21*	6.7	32	20.3	85***	27.0	84***	53.2	97***	30.8	92***	58.2

(cont'd)

Table A.14 (continued)

	Vote (duty)				Vote (right)				Total			
	1998		2003		1998		2003		1998		2003	
	N	%	N	%	N	%	N	%	N	%	N	%
Occupation												
Unemployed	3	3.1	11	22.4	24	24.5	19	38.8	26	26.5	21	42.9
Student	11	8.9	7	15.2	39	31.7	18	39.1	43	35.0	19	41.3
Pensioner	1	1.1	12	25.0	14	15.7	25	52.1	14	15.7	26	54.2
Government worker	12	5.4	27	22.3	54	24.2	57	47.1	59	26.5	63	52.1
NGO worker	NA	NA	7	29.2	NA	NA	13	54.2	NA	NA	13	54.2
In business	8	3.8	7	11.9	30	14.3	25	42.4	35	16.7	27	45.8
Herder/farmer	2*	1.8	7	10.9	11***	9.8	23	35.9	12***	10.7	25	39.1
Ethnic identity												
Kazakh	0	.0	5	14.3	14	22.2	15	42.9	14	22.2	16	45.7
Oirad	4	1.5	20	14	54	20.5	59	43.1	55	20.8	66	48.2
Other Mongols	1	10.0	2	10.0	3	30.0	4	20.0	3	30.0	4	20.0
Khalkh	32**	6.0	51	23.9	107	20.2	99	46.5	123	23.2	105	49.3

In a two-tailed chi-square test, *p ≤ .05, **p ≤ .01, ***p ≤ .001. Location, residence and gender = 1 df; age group, education and ethnic identity = 3 df; occupation = 5 df in 1998 and 6 df in 2003.
ªNumber, percent and statistical significance of differences within demographic categories.

Table A.15 Significant differences within demographic categories concerning civil society and access to information, 1998 and 2003[a]

	Civil society				Access to information (duty)				Access to information (right)			
	1998		2003		1998		2003		1998		2003	
	N	%	N	%	N	%	N	%	N	%	N	%
Location												
Khovd	0	.0	4	1.8	27	6.7	35	16.1	6	1.5	23	10.6
Ulaanbaatar	0	.0	0	.0	35	7.5	42	21.2	18*	3.9	23	11.6
Residence												
Rural	0	.0	0	.0	14	10.8	9	13.8	3	2.3	5	7.7
Urban	0	.0	4	1.1	48	6.5	66	19.0	21	2.8	40	11.5
Gender												
Female	0	.0	2	1.1	36	8.6	35	19.4	12	2.9	24	13.3
Male	0	.0	2*	.9	26	5.8	40	17.2	12	2.7	21	9.0
Age group												
17–26	0	.0	0	.0	20	7.2	29	20.6	5	1.8	15	10.6
27–39	0	.0	1	1.0	19	7.1	16	15.2	11	4.1	10	9.5
40–54	0	.0	1	1.1	17	8.1	21	24.1	7	3.3	15	17.2
55+	0	.0	1	1.3	6	5.6	10	18.5	1	.9	5	6.4
Formal education completed												
Less than high school	0	.0	0	.0	15	8.1	12	14.6	2	1.1	4	4.9
Vocational or high school	0	.0	1	1.0	14	4.9	22	21.2	7	2.5	15	14.4
Technical college	0	.0	0	.0	8	9.8	9	13.4	0	.0	7	10.4
Baccalaureate+	0	.0	2	1.3	25	7.9	33	20.9	15*	4.8	19	12.0

(cont'd)

Table A.15 (continued)

	Civil society				Access to information (duty)				Access to information (right)			
	1998		2003		1998		2003		1998		2003	
	N	%	N	%	N	%	N	%	N	%	N	%
Occupation												
Unemployed	0	.0	0	.0	3	3.1	8	16.3	3	3.1	5	10.2
Student	0	.0	0	.0	10	8.1	7	15.2	4	3.3	5	10.9
Pensioner	0	.0	0	.0	12	13.5	11	22.9	4	4.5	7	14.6
Government worker	0	.0	4	3.3	19	8.5	25	20.7	9	4.0	10	8.3
NGO worker	NA	NA	0	.0	NA	NA	3	12.5	NA	NA	3	12.5
In business	0	.0	0	.0	8	3.8	11	18.6	2	1.0	9	15.3
Herder/farmer	0	.0	0	.0	10*	8.9	10	15.6	2	1.8	6	9.4
Ethnic identity												
Kazakh	0	.0	0	.0	4	6.3	6	17.1	0	.0	3	8.6
Oirad	0	.0	0	.0	19	7.2	29	21.2	4	1.5	16	11.7
Other Mongols	0	.0	0	.0	1	10.0	3	15.0	0	.0	2	10.0
Khalkh	0	.0	2	.9	38	7.2	36	16.9	20	3.8	23	10.8

In a two-tailed chi-square test, * p ≤ .05, ** p ≤ .01, *** p ≤ .001. Location, residence and gender = 1 df; age group, education and ethnic identity = 3 df; occupation = 5 df in 1998 and 6 df in 2003.
[a] Number, percent and statistical significance of differences within demographic categories.

Table A.16 Significant differences within demographic categories concerning citizens' political activity, 1998 and 2003[a]

	Politically active (duty)				Politically active (right)				Total politically active				Politically passive			
	1998		2003		1998		2003		1998		2003		1998		2003	
	N	%	N	%	N	%	N	%	N	%	N	%	N	%	N	%
Location																
Khovd	25	6.2	46	21.1	82	20.4	86	39.4	99	24.6	100	45.9	30	7.5	3	1.4
Ulaanbaatar	52*	11.2	56	28.3	79	17.0	98*	49.5	118	25.4	113*	57.1	39	8.4	21***	10.6
Residence																
Rural	6	4.6	13	20.0	12	9.2	21	32.3	17	13.1	29	44.6	8	6.2	4	6.2
Urban	71*	9.6	88	25.3	149**	20.2	162*	46.6	200***	27.1	183	52.6	61	8.3	18	5.2
Gender																
Female	41	9.8	40	22.2	80	19.1	81	45.0	110	26.3	88	48.9	31	7.4	7	3.9
Male	36	8.0	61	26.2	81	18.0	102	43.8	107	23.8	124	53.2	38	8.5	15	6.4
Age group																
17–26	32	11.5	36	25.5	54	19.4	60	42.6	75	26.9	69	48.9	28	10.0	9	6.4
27–39	21	7.8	20	19.0	60	22.3	50	47.6	75	27.9	57	54.3	11	4.1	3	2.9
40–54	18	8.5	26	29.9	33	15.6	37	42.5	48	22.7	45	51.7	16	7.6	2	2.3
55+	6	5.6	18	23.1	14	13.1	36	46.2	19	17.8	39	50.0	14*	13.1	10*	12.8
Formal education completed																
Less than high school	10	5.4	13	15.9	19	10.2	20	24.4	27	14.5	24	29.3	14	7.5	2	2.4
Vocational or high school	20	7.0	36	34.6	48	16.9	45	43.3	61	21.5	55	52.9	28	9.9	8	7.7
Technical college	2	2.4	11	16.4	18	22.0	32	47.8	18	22.0	35	52.2	4	4.9	6	9.0
Baccalaureate+	45***	14.3	40**	25.3	76***	24.1	86***	54.4	111***	35.2	96***	60.8	23	7.3	8	5.1

(cont'd)

Table A.16 (continued)

	Politically active (duty)				Politically active (right)				Total politically active				Politically passive			
	1998		2003		1998		2003		1998		2003		1998		2003	
	N	%	N	%	N	%	N	%	N	%	N	%	N	%	N	%
Occupation																
Unemployed	4	4.1	14	28.6	25	25.5	24	49.0	26	26.5	27	55.1	3	3.1	1	2.0
Student	18	14.6	8	17.4	33	26.8	18	39.1	45	36.6	20	43.5	16	13.0	0	.0
Pensioner	4	4.5	13	27.1	11	12.4	27	56.3	14	15.7	28	58.3	17	19.1	1	2.1
Government worker	27	12.1	37	30.6	54	24.2	52	43.0	74	33.2	66	54.5	7	3.1	7	5.8
NGO worker	NA	NA	8	33.3	NA	NA	13	54.2	NA	NA	13	54.2	NA	NA	1	4.2
In business	18	8.6	9	15.3	21	10.0	26	44.1	37	17.6	30	50.8	20	9.5	7	11.9
Herder/farmer	6*	5.4	11	17.2	11***	9.8	22	34.4	15***	13.4	27	42.2	4***	3.6	4	6.3
Ethnic identity																
Kazakh	3	4.8	7	20.0	15	23.8	11	31.4	17	27.0	14	40.0	9	14.3	2	5.7
Oirad	16	6.1	30	21.9	52	19.7	56	40.9	63	23.9	69	50.4	19	7.2	12	8.8
Other Mongols	1	10.0	3	15.0	1	10.0	6	30.0	2	20.0	7	35.0	0	.0	0	.0
Khalkh	57	10.8	59	27.7	93	17.5	106	49.8	135	25.5	116	54.5	41	7.7	10	4.7

In a two-tailed chi-square test, *p≤.05, **p≤.01, ***p≤.001. Location, residence and gender=1 df; age group, education and ethnic identity=3 df; occupation=5 df in 1998 and 6 df in 2003.
aNumber, percent and statistical significance of differences within demographic categories.

Table A.17 Significant differences within demographic categories regarding the perception of citizens' participation in governance and their deeply held values, 1998 and 2003[a].

	Personal dignity				Justice				Equality			
	1998		2003		1998		2003		1998		2003	
	N	%	N	%	N	%	N	%	N	%	N	%
Location												
Khovd	3	.7	0	.0	2	.5	2	.9	4	1.0	3	1.4
Ulaanbaatar	8	1.7	4*	2.0	2	.4	4	2.0	13	2.8	7	3.5
Residence												
Rural	3	2.3	1	1.5	1	.8	1	1.5	2	1.5	0	.0
Urban	8	1.1	3	.9	3	.4	5	1.4	15	2.0	10	2.9
Gender												
Female	2	.5	0	.0	2	.5	3	1.7	9	2.2	2	1.1
Male	9*	2.0	4	1.7	2	.4	3	1.3	8	1.8	8	3.4
Age group												
17–26	1	.4	1	.7	1	.4	2	1.4	6	2.2	2	1.4
27–39	4	1.5	1	1.0	2	.7	1	1.0	2	.7	1	1.0
40–54	6	2.8	0	.0	1	.5	2	2.3	7	3.3	1	1.1
55+	0	.0	2	2.6	0	.0	1	1.3	2	1.9	6**	7.7
Formal education completed												
Less than high school	2	1.1	0	.0	0	.0	1	1.2	3	1.6	4	4.9
Vocational or high school	3	1.1	1	1.0	0	.0	2	1.9	8	2.8	3	2.9
Technical college	0	.0	1	1.5	1	1.2	1	1.5	2	2.4	1	1.5
Baccalaureate+	6	1.9	2	1.3	3	1.0	2	1.3	4	1.3	2	1.3

(cont'd)

Table A.17 (continued)

	Personal dignity				Justice				Equality			
	1998		2003		1998		2003		1998		2003	
	N	%	N	%	N	%	N	%	N	%	N	%
Occupation												
Unemployed	0	.0	0	.0	0	.0	0	.0	0	.0	0	.0
Student	0	.0	2	4.3	0	.0	0	.0	5	4.1	1	2.2
Pensioner	1	1.1	1	2.1	1	1.1	1	2.1	2	2.2	2	4.2
Government worker	3	1.3	1	.8	2	.9	3	2.5	4	1.8	3	2.5
NGO worker	NA	NA	0	.0	NA	NA	0	.0	NA	NA	2	8.3
In business	5	2.4	0	.0	1	.5	2	3.4	4	1.9	1	1.7
Herder/farmer	2	1.8	0	.0	0	.0	0	.0	2	1.8	1	1.6
Ethnic identity												
Kazakh	1	1.6	0	.0	0	.0	1	2.9	1	1.6	1	2.9
Oirad	1	.4	0	.0	1	.4	2	1.5	3	1.1	3	2.2
Other Mongols	0	.0	0	.0	0	.0	0	.0	0	.0	0	.0
Khalkh	9	1.7	4	1.9	3	.6	3	1.4	13	2.5	6	2.8

In a two-tailed chi-square test, $^*p \leq .05$, $^{**}p \leq .01$, $^{***}p \leq .001$. Location, residence and gender=1 df; age group, education and ethnic identity=3 df; occupation=5 df in 1998 and 6 df in 2003.
[a]Number, percent and statistical significance of differences within demographic categories.

Endnotes

CHAPTER ONE

1 There are many spellings of Chinggis Khaan: Chinggis Khan, Genghis Khan, Jinghiz Khan, Chingiz Khan and more. The spelling closest to Mongolian is Chinggis Khaan; therefore, I use it in this book.

2 The UN definition of literacy is the ability to read with understanding and write a simple, short statement (United Nations Statistics Division 2011).

3 Mongolian names are in flux. Traditionally, people use only their given name or their father's name, as in John Johnson (son of John). In Mongolian, the father's name precedes the given name and is in the genitive form, ending in 'iin' or 'yn.' So, for example, Idshin-norov is the Director's given name, and he is the son of Sandu, or Sanduiin. This becomes confusing as people leave their aimags and move to a big city like Ulaanbaatar. I have been in conversations where it has taken two Mongolians a few minutes to figure out if the Oyuna they know is the daughter of Bat-Tsetseg, the one who works in the Khaan Bank, or a different Oyuna [the names are imagined here]. More recently, people have been switching to the Western way of naming. They take their father's name and make it a family name. So, for example, the daughter of Altangerel, who attended university in the United States, calls herself Tuya Altangerel rather than Altangereliin Tuya. I have tried to honor people's names, using the forms I know them by.

4 Bourdieu's concept of *habitus* is really based on the idea that people's current behavior (actions and thoughts) is greatly influenced by their ideas about their future lives (Bourdieu 1990:53–65).

5 In quota sampling, researchers find possible interviewees who match the demographic subcategories that need to be covered (Bernard 2006:187–89). When I was trained in cognitive methodology at the Summer Institute in Research Methods, supported by the National Science Foundation (1991), Stephen Borgatti told the class that the goal was to interview at least 20 people in each subcategory.

6 Thanks to Carol Ember for walking me through this process and Paul Hooper for checking it.

CHAPTER TWO

1 More than 80 percent of people living in Mongolia today are Khalkh Mongols. In fact, the term Mongol often refers to the Khalkh rather than the other 18 branches of the Mongolian people.

2 Ulaanbaatar 1998 Os024 refers to an interview in Ulaanbaatar in 1998. It is the twenty-fourth interview conducted by Os (Olziesekhan).

3 In 1919, the new Soviet Russia asked Ivan Maiiski to survey Mongolia's population—its economy, political structure and demographic characteristics. The expedition that he led surveyed the four eastern aimags and then the western ones.

4 Larson, a Swedish missionary who lived in Outer Mongolia 1893–1900, wrote that every adult owes "one moon [month] of annual service to the ruler" (Larson 1930:9–10).

5 Some Russians also settled in Mongolian territory, both east and west. They raised crops and livestock, mined gold and engaged in trade (Boikova 2002:13). Unlike the Chinese, most Russians came with their families and formed bonds with their Mongolian neighbors (ibid.:16).

6 While we talk in terms of kin being of the same blood, Mongolians talk about people of the same descent or class being of the same bone. The lower classes belong to the black bone; the nobility belong to the white bone.

7 Actually, it was the only territory of the Manchu Dynasty that managed to attain independence. Tibet, Inner Mongolia and Xinjiang remain provinces of China (Nakami et al. 2005:362).

8 Tsedenbal, dictator of Mongolia (1952–1984), invokes the goal of economic and social development via 'non-capitalist development' many times in his written work (Tsedenbal 1967).

9 Ma Ho-t'ien was a 'political agent' for the Kuomintang, an organization that sought to establish a socialist government in China following the 1912 revolution, according to his translator, John De Francis (1949:v). Like the Mongolian People's Revolutionary Party, the Kuomintang was supported by the Soviet Comintern.

10 Lukin (2000:113) writes, "Official dogmas were instilled into everyone from infancy with the goal of transforming the entire Soviet population into model Communist citizens."

11 If less than 1 percent of Mongolians were literate, who taught the early students? Mongols from Russia and China, writes Ma Ho-t'ien (1949:79), who visited several schools in Ulaanbaatar.

CHAPTER THREE

1 'Truth' in Russian is *pravda*. The Russian newspaper of that name was an arm of the Soviet government.

CHAPTER FOUR

1 Globe International in Mongolia (*http://www.globeinter.org.mn/old/en/index.php*) is not to be confused with Globe International in Pensacola, Florida, which is a fundamentalist organization.

CHAPTER FIVE

1 *Ulzii* is the Mongolian word for the Chinese symbol of long life.

2 DeGlopper (1991:75) goes even further, writing that a nomadic ethos "values mobility and the ability to cope with problems by moving away from threats or toward resources and ... disparages permanent settlement, cultivation of the earth, and accumulation of objects."

3 Herders who kept their children (especially the boys) home from school needed them to help with the animals. As a result, school enrollment rates dropped over the 1990s, especially in 1998 (Bajiikhuu, Tegshjargal and G. Orsoo 2000:177).

4 In 1998, the GDP per capita (current US dollars) of Mongolia's neighbors, China and the Russian Federation, were US$820.90 and US$1,844.50, respectively; the United States was US$31,687.10. By 2003, the GDP per capita in China was US$1,273.60, the Russian Federation was US$2,976.10 and the United States was US$38,224.70 (World Bank 2012).

5 This pension-age Oirad herder is referring to the classic five-animal herd in Mongolia: camels, horses, cattle (cows and/or yaks), goats and sheep. Before socialism, these animals grazed together.

CHAPTER SIX

1 Humphrey (2002:128) writes that Russians distinguish between three different kinds of bribery: "It is a payment improperly accepted to influence public duties that are meant to be performed for free; it is intentionally involuntarily taken/offered; and it creates a particular, usually short-lived, 'negative' social relation between the giver and taker.... What counts as bribery differs in different cultures, that a tension often exists between laws on bribery and the actually applied moral views of a community, and that the seriousness with which bribery is condemned varies from society to society and historically within one country."

2 This means that if the democratic government is run by the former socialist officials, then it will exhibit totalitarian tendencies, too.

3 Anderson and Anderson LLP (2011), an international law firm operating in Ulaanbaatar, corroborates Liberty Center's evidence.

4 The maternal mortality rate is the death rate of pregnant women and nursing mothers no matter what the cause of death.

5 GTZ is now GIZ (*Deutsche Gesellschaft für Internationale Zusammenarbeit*). Its mission: "We are a government-owned corporation with international operations. We implement commissions for the German federal government and other national and international, public and private-sector clients. We further political, economic, ecological and social development worldwide, and so improve people's living conditions. We provide services that support complex development and reform processes."

CHAPTER SEVEN

1 This is the classic definition of civic duty (see Dagger 2010).

2 To be fair, the Mongolian numbers show a steady decline in voting participation. In the first free election for parliament (1990), 98 percent of qualified citizens voted. In 1992, 95.5 percent voted. In 1996, voter turnout started to drop, to 88.4 percent. By 2004, 81.4 percent participated in the election.

3 Again, the Mongolian situation is not unique. A 37-year-old rock musician interviewed in Hungary describes the process whereby the former Communist Party keeps control of the media in that nation:

> Milun: You don't seem to see much change going on out there.
> Grandpierre: Nothing. These people in charge of many domains like the radio and TV were selected under the old system because of their cultural ideology, and these people are still there. These are people who have no new ideas, they don't really even want to work, they simply want to keep getting their paychecks. So all these people with no real ideas or abilities depend on each other for the system to continue. But now there will be a new media law.... I hope it will force them to state what the most basic tasks of the television and radio are. And then if people do not do these things, it will be possible to have been kicked out. Kicked out if they are not representing the real world to the people—by "real" I mean not only the lying and cheating that is going on, but some kind of culture, some kind of interesting things. The people in this country need to get some information about how to live another future. Not the future that the Party had in mind. In that era as everybody knows, the idea was only to push the people more deeply down. To stop them from doing anything outside of the prescribed 'norm' (Milun 1993:65–66).

CHAPTER EIGHT

1 Mongolians tell me that the high Mandarin collar may be Chinese, but Mongolians wore similar robes without collars even in the time of Chinggis Khaan. I have seen a few traditional Mongolian deels on the street, but most people I saw wore deels with Mandarin collars.

References

"Attitudes and Reactions of the People." In *Subcontractor's Monograph: Mongolian People's Republic, HRAF-39, Wash-1*, edited by William B. Ballis and Robert A. Rupen. 427–37. New Haven, CT: Human Relations Area Files, 1956.

The Constitution of Mongolia. Ulaanbaatar Mongolia, 1992. http://www.servat.unibe.ch/icl/mg00000_.html. Accessed October 12, 2012.

Academy of Sciences MPR. *Information Mongolia.* Oxford, UK: Pergamon, 1990.

Altangerel, Munkhtuya. "My Mongolia." In *Modern Mongolia: Reclaiming Genghis Khan*, edited by Paula L.W. Sabloff. 1–29. Philadelphia: University of Pennsylvania Museum of Archaeology and Anthropology, 2001.

Altman, Andrew. "Civil Rights." In *The Stanford Encyclopedia of Philosophy*, edited by Edward N. Zalta. http://plato.stanford.edu/archives/sum2009/entries/civil-rights/. Accessed April 28, 2012.

Anderson and Anderson LLP. "Land Law of Mongolia." In *Newsletter* (2011). Published electronically February 10, 2011. http://www.anallp.com/land-law-of-mongolia/.

Asian Development Bank. *Mongolia: A Centrally Planned Economy in Transition.* Oxford: Oxford University Press, 1992.

Atwood, Christopher. *Encyclopedia of Mongolia and the Mongol Empire.* New York: Facts on File, Inc., 2004.

Axelbank, Albert. *Mongolia: This Beautiful World.* Palo Alto, CA: Kodansha International, 1971.

Baabar (Bat-Erdene Batbayar). *Twentieth Century Mongolia*, edited by Christopher Kaplonski. Translated by D. Sühjargalmaa, S. Burenbayar, H. Hulan and N. Tuya. Cambridge, UK: White Horse Press, 1999.

Ballis, William B. "The Constitutional System and Structure of Government." In *Subcontractor's Monograph: Mongolian People's Republic, HRAF-39, Wash-1*, edited by William B. Ballis and Robert A. Rupen. 509–31. New Haven, CT: Human Relations Area Files, 1956a.

———. "Political Dynamics." In *Subcontractor's Monograph: Mongolian People's Republic, HRAF-39, Wash-1*, edited by William B. Ballis and Robert A. Rupen. 532–49. New Haven, CT: Human Relations Area Files, 1956b.

Ballis, William B. and Noburu Hiraga. "Public Order and Safety." In *Subcontractor's Monograph: Mongolian People's Republic, HRAF-39, Wash-1*, edited by William B. Ballis and Robert A. Rupen. 550–65. New Haven, CT: Human Relations Area Files, 1956.

Barber, Benjamin. "Adapting to the Culture of Democracy." In *Democracy Is a Discussion*, edited by Sondra Myers. 22. New London, CT: Connecticut College, 1998.

Barfield, Thomas. *The Perilous Frontier: Nomadic Empires and China.* Oxford, UK: Basil Blackwell, 1989.

Bar-Yosef, Ofer. "The Upper Paleolithic Revolution." In *Annual Review of Anthropology*, edited by William H. Durham, Jean Comaroff, and Jane Hill. 363–93. Palo Alto, CA: Annual Reviews, 2002.

Bat Ochir, L. and D. Dashjamts. "Sükhbaatar the Supreme Hero." In *Mongolian Heroes of the Twentieth Century*, edited by Urgunge Onon. 143–44. New York: AMS, 1976.

Batchuluun, Yembuu and Khulan Munkh-Erdene. "Paper Commissioned for the EFA Global Monitoring Report 2006, Literacy for Life." In *Education for All, Global Monitoring Report*, 19: UNESCO, 2005.

Bawden, C. R. *The Modern History of Mongolia*. London and New York: Kegan Paul International, 1989.

Beck, Ulrich. "Living in the World Risk Society." *Hobhouse Memorial Public Lecture delivered Wednesday 15th February*. London School of Economics and Political Science, 2006.

Bernard, H. Russell. *Research Methods in Anthropology*. 4th ed. Lanham, MD: Altamira, 2006.

Berns, Gregory and Scott Atran. "The Biology of Cultural Conflict." *Philosophical Transactions of the Royal Society B* 367 (2012): 633–39.

Bilefsky, Dan and Jan Krcmar. "Czech Wounds Still Open, Communists Face a Ban." *New York Times*, December 27, 2009, 10.

Bloch, Maurice. "Language, Anthropology and Cognitive Science." *Man* 26 (1991): 183–98.

———. "Reconciling Social Science and Cognitive Science Notions of the 'Self.'" *Speech Presented to the Department of Anthropology, London School of Economics*. London, UK, 2010.

———. "What Goes without Saying: The Conceptualization of Zafimaniry Society." In *Conceptualising Society*, edited by Adam Kuper. 127–46. New York: Routledge, 1992.

Boikova, Elena. "Russians in Mongolia in the Late 19th-Early 20th Centuries." *Mongolian Studies* 25 (2002):13–19.

Bourdieu, Pierre. *The Logic of Practice*. Stanford, CA: Stanford University Press, 1990.

———. *Practical Reason: On the Theory of Action*. Stanford, CA: Stanford University Press, 1998.

Bratton, Michael. "Democratic Attitudes and Political Participation: An Exploratory Comparison across World Regions." In *Congress of the International Political Science Association*. Santiago, Chile, 2009.

Breslauer, George. "Introduction" In *Postcommunism and the Theory of Democracy*, edited by Richard Anderson, Jr., Steven Fish, Stephen E. Hanson and Philip G. Roeder. 1–10. Princeton, NJ: Princeton University Press, 2001.

Brink-Danan, Marcy. "'I Vote, Therefore I Am:' Rituals of Democracy and the Turkish Chief Rabbi." *PoLAR (Political and Legal Anthropology Review)* 32, no. 1 (2009): 5–27.

Brown, Donald E. "Human Universals and Their Implications." In *Being Humans: Anthropological Universality and Particularity in Transdisciplinary Perspectives*, edited by N. Roughley. 156–74. New York: Walter de Gruyter, 2000.

———. "Human Universals, Human Nature and Human Culture." *Daedalus* 133 (Fall 2004): 47–54.

Brown, William and Urgunge Onon. *History of the Mongolian People's Republic*. Cambridge, MA: Harvard University Press, 1976.

Bruun, Ole. *Precious Steppe: Mongolian Nomadic Pastoralists in Pursuit of the Market.* Lanham, MD: Lexington Books, 2006.

Bruun, Ole and Ole Odgaard. "A Society and Economy in Transition." In *Mongolia in Transition: Old Patterns, New Challenges,* edited by Ole Bruun and Ole Odgaard. 23–41. London: Curzon, 1996.

Campbell, C.W. *Travels in Mongolia, 1902: A Journey by C.W. Campbell, the British Consul in China.* London: The Stationery Office, 2000.

Carothers, Thomas. "The End of the Transition Paradigm." *Journal of Democracy* 13, no. 1 (2002): 5–21.

Carter, Ian. "Positive and Negative Liberty." In *The Stanford Encyclopedia of Philosophy,* edited by Edward N. Zalta. Stanford, CA, 2007. http://plato.stanford.edu/archives/spr2003/entries/liberty-positive-negative/.

Cernea, Michael, ed. *Putting People First: Sociological Variables in Rural Development.* 2nd ed. Oxford: Oxford University Press for the World Bank, 1985.

Christiano, Tom. "Democracy." In *The Stanford Encyclopedia of Philosophy,* edited by Edward N. Zalta, 2006. http://plato.stanford.edu/archives/fall2008/entries/democracy/.

CIA (Central Intelligence Agency). "American People—1989." In *The World Factbook* (2003a). http://www.theodora.com/wfb1989/united_states/united_states_people. html.

———. "Chinese People—1989." In *The World Factbook* (2003b). http://www.theodora. com/wfb1989/china/china_people.html.

———. "Mongolian Literacy Rate." In *Twenty-one Years of World Facts: Countries of the World,* 2009. http://www.theodora.com/wfb1989/mongolia/mongolia_people. html.

Clemens, Walter, Jr. *The Baltic Transformed: Complexity Theory and European Security.* Lanham, MD: Rowman and Littlefield, 2001.

Colwin, John. *Twice around the World: Some Memoirs of Diplomatic Life in North Vietnam and Outer Mongolia.* London: Leo Cooper, 1991.

Constitution Society. "Rights and Responsibilities." http://www.usconstitution.net/consttop_resp.html.

Creed, Gerald W. "Deconstructing Socialism in Bulgaria." In *Uncertain Transition: Ethnographies of Change in the Postsocialist World,* edited by Michael Burawoy and Katherine Verdery. 223–43. Lanham, MD: Rowman and Littlefield, 1999.

D'Andrade, Roy. *The Development of Cognitive Anthropology.* Cambridge: Cambridge University Press, 1995.

Dagger, Richard. "Political Obligation." In *The Stanford Encyclopedia of Philosophy,* edited by Edward N. Zalta, 2010. http://plato.stanford.edu/archives/sum2010/entries/political-obligation/.

De Francis, John. "Translator's Preface." In *Chinese Agent in Mongolia (Ma Ho-T'ien).* Baltimore, MD: The Johns Hopkins Press, 1949.

DeGlopper, Donald. "The Society and Environment." In *Mongolia: A Country Study,* edited by Robert Worden and Andrea Matles-Savada. Headquarters, US Department of the Army, 1991.

Dembour, Marie-Bénédicte. "Following the Movement of a Pendulum: Between Universalism and Relativism." In *Culture and Rights: Anthropological Perspectives,* edited by

Jane Cowan, Marie-Bénédicte Dembour and Richard Wilson. 56–79. Cambridge: Cambridge University Press, 2001.

Derevianko, Anatoly and Sergei Markin. "The Middle and Upper Paleolithic of the Altai." *Antropozoikum* 23 (1999): 157–66.

Diamond, Larry. "Is the Third Wave Over?" *Journal of Democracy* 7, no. 3 (1996): 20–37.

———. *The Spirit of Democracy.* New York: Times Books, 2008.

Djanaeva, Nurgul. *Kyrgyzstan Women in Transition.* Bishkek, Kyrgyzstan: Nurgul Djanaeva, 2002.

Dryzek, John, Leslie Templeman Holmes with Sinisa Nikolin. "Yugoslavia." In *Post-Communist Democratization: Political Discourse across Thirteen Countries,* edited by John Dryzek and Leslie T. Holmes. 57–78. Cambridge: Cambridge University Press, 2002.

Dryzek, John and Leslie Templeman Holmes. *Post-Communist Democratization: Political Discourses across Thirteen Countries.* Cambridge: Cambridge University Press, 2002.

Ekman, Paul. "Basic Emotions." In *Handbook of Cognition and Emotion,* edited by T. Dalgleish and M. Power. Chichester, UK: Wiley, 1999.

Ekman, Paul, and W. V. Friesen. "The Repertoire of Nonverbal Behavior: Categories, Origins, Usage, and Coding." *Semiotica* 1 (1969): 49–98.

El-Naggar, Mona. "Egyptian Youths Drive the Revolt against Mubarak." *New York Times,* January 27, 2011.

Fahim, Kareem, and Mona El-Naggar. "Violent Clashes Mark Protests against Mubarak's Rule." *New York Times,* January 26, 2011.

Friters, Gerard M. *Outer Mongolia and Its International Position.* Baltimore, MD: The Johns Hopkins Press, 1949.

Frohlich, Bruno and David Hunt. "A History Not to Be Forgotten: Mass Burials in Mongolia." *AnthroNote* 27, no. 1 (2006): 1–5.

Ganbold@magicnet.mn. "The Collectivization Movement." In *Email Daily News* 253 (2000).

Giordano, Christian and Dobrinka Kostova. "The Social Production of Mistrust." In *Postsocialism: Ideals, Ideologies and Practices in Eurasia,* edited by C.M. Hann. 74–91. London: Routledge, 2002.

GIZ (Deutsche Gesellschaft für Internationale Zusammenarbeit). "Mission Statement." http://www.gtz.de/en/unternehmen/1716.htm. Accessed November 23, 2012.

Goldstein, Melvin and Cynthia Beall. *The Changing World of Mongolia's Nomads.* Berkeley: University of California Press, 1994.

Goodale, Mark. "Introduction: Locating Rights, Envisioning Law between the Global and the Local." In *The Practice of Human Rights: Tracking Law between the Global and the Local,* edited by Mark Goodale and Sally Merry. 1–48. Cambridge: Cambridge University Press, 2007.

Goodenough, Ward. *Cooperation in Change: An Anthropological Approach to Community Development.* New York: Russell Sage Foundation, 1963.

Grant, Bruce. "Dirges for Soviets Passed." In *Perilous States: Conversations on Culture, Politics, and Nation,* edited by George Marcus. 17–51. Chicago: University of Chicago Press, 1993.

Hann, Chris. *"Not the Horse We Wanted!": Postsocialism, Neoliberalism, and Eurasia.* Halle

Studies in the Anthropology of Eurasia, edited by Richard Rottenburg, Chris Hann, and Burkhard Schnepel. Vol. 10, Munster, Germany: Lit Verlag, 2006.

Haslund, Henning. *In Secret Mongolia.* Kempton, IL: Adventures Unlimited, 1995.

Hemment, Julie. *Empowering Women in Russia: Activism, Aid, and NGOs.* Bloomington, IN: Indiana University Press, 2007.

Hirabayashi, James. "Social Structure." In *Subcontractor's Monograph: Mongolian People's Republic, HRAF-39, Wash-1,* edited by William B. Ballis and Robert A. Rupen. 183–219. New Haven, CT: Human Relations Area Files, 1956.

Hirabayashi, James, Robert A. Rupen and Nicholas Poppe. "Social Values and Patterns of Living." In *Subcontractor's Monograph: Mongolian People's Republic, HRAF-39, Wash-1,* edited by William and Robert A. Rupen Ballis. 241–57. New Haven, CT: Human Relations Area Files, 1956.

Holzman, F. R. "Taxation." In *Subcontractor's Monograph: Mongolian People's Republic, HRAF-39, Wash-1,* edited by William Ballis and Robert A. Rupen. 873–905. New Haven, CT: Human Relations Area Files, 1956.

Honeychurch, William. "States on Horseback: The Rise of Inner Asian Confederations and Empires." In *Archaeology of Asia,* edited by Miriam T. Stark. Oxford, UK: Blackwell, 2006.

Honeychurch, William and Chunag Amartuvshin. "Hinterlands, Urban Centers, and Mobile Settings: The 'New' Old World Archaeology from the Eurasian Steppe." *Asian Perspectives* 46, no. 1 (2007): 36–64.

Huc, E. *Souvenirs of a Journey through Tartary, Tibet and China during the Years 1844, 1845 and 1846.* Vols. 1–2, Peking: Lazarist Press, 1931.

Humphrey, Caroline. *Marx Went Away but Karl Stayed Behind.* Ann Arbor: University of Michigan Press, 1998.

———. *The Unmaking of Soviet Life: Everyday Economies after Socialism.* Ithaca, NY: Cornell University Press, 2002.

Huntington, Samuel P. "Democracy's Third Wave." *Journal of Democracy* 2, no. 2 (1991): 12–34.

Idea Institute for Democracy and Electoral Assistance. "Voter Turnout Data for Mongolia." http://www.idea.int/vt/country_view.cfm?CountryCode=MN. Accessed September 4, 2012.

Ignatieff, Michael. "Who Are Americans to Think That Freedom Is Theirs to Spread?" *New York Times,* June 26, 2005. http://www.nytimes.com/2005/06/26/magazine/26EXCEPTION.html?_r=0. Accessed January 28, 2013.

Ikenberry, John. "Why Export Democracy? The 'Hidden Grand Strategy' of American Foreign Policy." *The Wilson Quarterly* 23, no. 2 (1999): 56–65.

InfoMongolia.com. "Ulaanbaatar General Information." http://www.infomongolia.com/ct/ci/208/137/. Accessed April 16, 2012.

InfoPlease. "National Voter Turnout in Federal Elections: 1960–2010." Pearson Education, publishing as Infoplease, http://www.infoplease.com/ipa/A0781453.html. Accessed April 16, 2012.

Inglehart, Ronald, Bi Pura nen, Chris Welzel et al. *Values Change the World: World Values Survey.* World Values Survey Association, 2012. http://www.worldvaluessurvey.org/wvs/articles/folder_published/article_base_110/files/WVSbrochure6-2008_11.pdf.

Inglehart, Ronald, Roberto Foa, Christopher Peterson, and Christian Welzel. "Development, Freedom, and Rising Happiness: A Global Perspective (1981–2007)." *Perspectives on Psychological Science* 3, no. 4 (2008): 264–85.

Jones Luong, Pauline. *Institutional Change and Political Continuity in Post-Soviet Central Asia: Power, Perceptions, and Pacts.* Cambridge: Cambridge University Press, 2002.

Jones, Peter. "Group Rights." In *The Stanford Encyclopedia of Philosophy,* edited by Edward N. Zalta, 2008. http://plato.stanford.edu/archives/win2008/entries/rights-group/.

Jurmed, Zanaa. "Democracy in the 21st Century: New Challenges and New Opportunities." In *Report to the United Nations by the Director of the National CEDAW-Watch Network Center in Mongolia.* Ulaanbaatar, Mongolia, 1999.

Kalb, Don. "Afterword: Globalism and Post-Socialist Prospects." In *Postsocialism: Ideals, Ideologies and Practices in Eurasia,* edited by C.M. Hann. 317–34. Cambridge: Cambridge University Press, 2002.

Karamisheff (Karamyshev), W. (V.). *Mongolia and Western China: Social and Economic Study.* Tientsin, China: La Librairie Francaise, 1925.

Kaser, Michael. "Economic Developments." In *Mongolia Today,* edited by Shirin Akiner. 94–113. London: Kegan Paul International, 1991.

Keane, John. *Civil Society: Old Images, New Visions.* Stanford: Stanford University Press, 1998.

Konrad Adenauer Foundation. "Update on Democracy." Ulaanbaatar, Mongolia, e-mail to listserv, 2002.

Krueger, John R., Nicholas Poppe, and Martin Kilcoyne. "Education." In *Subcontractor's Monograph: Mongolian People's Republic, HRAF-39, Wash-1,* edited by William B. Ballis and Robert A. Rupen. 286–307. New Haven, CT: Human Relations Area Files, 1956.

Kuran, Timur. *Private Truths, Public Lies: The Social Consequences of Preference Falsification.* Cambridge, MA: Harvard University Press, 1995.

Lakoff, George. *Moral Politics: What Conservatives Know That Liberals Do Not.* Chicago: University of Chicago Press, 1996.

———. *The Political Mind.* New York: The Penguin Group, 2008.

———. *Women, Fire and Dangerous Things.* Chicago: University of Chicago Press, 1987.

Landman, Todd, Marco Larizza, et al. *The State of Democracy in Central Asia: A Comparative Study.* Ulaanbaatar, Mongolia: United Nations Development Programme for Human Rights Centre, University of Essex, 2006.

Larson, Frans August. *Larson, Duke of Mongolia.* Boston: Little, Brown and Company, 1930.

Lattimore, Owen. "Introduction: Mongolia's Place in the World." In *Outer Mongolia and Its International Position,* edited by Gerard M. Friters. Baltimore, MD: The Johns Hopkins Press, 1949.

Lenin, V.I. "The State and Revolution: The Marxist Theory of the State and the Tasks of the Proletariat in the Revolution " In *Collected Works of V. I. Lenin.* Moscow: Progress Publishers, (1918) 1993. http://www.marxist.com/classics-old/lenin/staterev.html.

———._. "Thesis and Report on Bourgeois Democracy and the Dictatorship of the Proletariat, March 4, 1919." In *Collected Works of V. I. Lenin.* Moscow: Progress Publishers, (1920) 1966. http://www.marxists.org/archive/lenin/works/1919/mar/comintern.htm.

Liberty Center. "Demand for National TV to Show the Truth on Mass Arrest Increases." *Newsletter* (2002b). Published electronically November 15, 2002. www.libertycenter. org.mn/.

———. "First Mass Demonstration for Private Land Is Going to Be Held Despite Numerous Obstacles." *Newsletter* (2002a). Published electronically November 4, 2002. www. libertycenter.org.mn/land_demonstration.htm.

———. "Local Bureaucracy Shuts the Land Privatization Hopes Down." *Newsletter* (2003a). Published electronically March 5, 2003. http://www. libertycenter. org. mn/law_eng. htm.

———. "Mongolia's Land Privatization Concern: City Mayor Seizes Land from Poor Families." *Newsletter* (2003c). Published electronically July 2, 2003. http://www. libertycenter.org.mn/law_eng.htm.

———. "Ruling Party Demands to Punish a Journalist for His Investigative Articles." *Newsletter* (2003d). Published electronically April 25, 2003. http://www.liberty-center.org.mn/alerts.htm.

———. "Rural Media Almost in a Deadlock of Government Censorship." In *Liberty Center Missive* (2003b). Published electronically February 10, 2003. http://www. libertycenter.org.mn/alerts.htm.

Lipset, Seymour Martin. "Some Social Requisites of Democracy: Economic Development and Political Legitimacy." *American Political Science Review* 53, no. 1 (1959): 69–105.

Lipset, Seymour Martin, Kyoung-Ryung Seong, and John Charles Torres. "A Comparative Analysis of the Social Requisites of Democracy." *International Social Science Journal* 136 (1993): 155–76.

Liu, Xiaoyuan. *Reins of Liberation: An Entangled History of Mongolian Independence, Chinese Territoriality, and Great Power Hegemony, 1911–1950.* Stanford: Stanford University Press, 2006.

Lizza, Ryan. "The Consequentialist: How the Arab Spring Remade Obama's Foreign Policy." *The New Yorker* (May 2, 2011): 44–55.

Lukin, Alexander. *The Political Culture of the Russian 'Democrats.'* Oxford: Oxford University Press, 2000.

Ma Ho-t'ien. *Chinese Agent in Mongolia.* Translated by John De Francis. Baltimore, MD: The Johns Hopkins Press, 1949.

Maiskii, Ivan M. *Contemporary Mongolia (Gosudarstvernoe Izdatel'stva).* Translated by Mrs. Dayton and J. Kunitz. New Haven, CT: Human Relations Area Files, (1921) 1956.

Mandel, Ruth. "Seeding Civil Society." In *Postsocialism: Ideals, Ideologies and Practices in Eurasia,* edited by C.M. Hann. 279–96. Cambridge: Cambridge University Press, 2002.

Marx, Karl and Friedrich Engels. "Manifesto of the Communist Party." In *The Marx-Engels Reader,* edited by Robert C. Tucker. 469-500. New York: W.W. Norton, (1848) 1978.

Mend-Ooyo, G. *Golden Hill.* Translated by Simon Wickham-Smith. Ulaanbaatar, Mongolia: Munkhin Useg, 2007.

Merry, Sally. "Changing Rights, Changing Culture." In *Culture and Rights: Anthropological Perspectives,* edited by Jane Cowan, Marie-Bénédicte Dembour, and Richard Wilson. Cambridge: Cambridge University Press, 2001.

Michnik, Adam. "Gray Is Beautiful: Thoughts on Democracy in Central Europe." In *De-*

mocracy Is a Discussion, edited by Sondra Myers. 25–27. New London: Connecticut College, 1998.

Mill, John Stuart. *On Liberty.* Constitution Society: P. F. Collier & Son, (1860) 1993. http://www.constitution.org/jsm/liberty.htm.

Milun, Kathryn. "Returning to Eastern Europe." In *Perilous States: Conversations on Culture, Politics, and Nation,* edited by George Marcus. 53–79. Chicago: University of Chicago Press, 1993.

Morgan, David. *The Mongols.* Oxford, UK: Basil Blackwell, 1986.

Murphy, G. G. S. "Industrial Potential." In *Subcontractor's Monograph: Mongolian People's Republic, HRAF-39, Wash-1,* edited by William B. Ballis and Robert A. Rupen. 828–72. New Haven, CT: Human Relations Area Files, 1956.

Myers, Sondra, ed. *The Challenges and Promise of a New Democratic Era.* Vol. 2 of *Democracy Is a Discussion.* New London: Connecticut College, 1998.

Nakami, Tatsuo. "The Mongol Summer in 1911: The Qing-Manchu Amban, the Russian Consul, and the Mongol Secret Mission." In *Mongol Sodlalin Oguulliin Tuuver (Mongolian Studies).* 48–54. Ulaanbaatar, Mongolia: Bembi San, 2006.

Nasan Dashdendeviin, Bumaa. "The Twentieth Century: From Domination to Democracy." In *Modern Mongolia: Reclaiming Genghis Khan,* edited by Paula L.W. Sabloff. 31–63. Philadelphia: University of Pennsylvania Museum of Archaeology and Anthropology, 2001.

National Statistical Office of Mongolia. *1998 Mongolian Statistical Yearbook.* Ulaanbaatar, Mongolia: National Statistical Office of Mongolia, 1999.

———. *1999 Mongolian Statistical Yearbook.* Ulaanbaatar, Mongolia: National Statistical Office of Mongolia, 2000.

———. *2003 Mongolian Statistical Yearbook.* Ulaanbaatar, Mongolia: National Statistical Office of Mongolia, 2004.

Natsagdorj, Sh. "Arad Ayush the Commoner." In *Mongolian Heroes of the Twentieth Century,* edited by Urgunge Onon. 15–19. New York: AMS, 1976.

Nickel, James. "Human Rights." In *The Stanford Encyclopedia of Philosophy,* edited by Edward N. Zalta, 2010. http://plato.stanford.edu/archives/fall2010/entries/rights-human/.

Nugent, David. "Democracy Otherwise: Struggles over Popular Rule in the Northern Peruvian Andes." In *Democracy: Anthropological Approaches,* edited by Julia Paley. 21–62. Santa Fe, NM: School for Advanced Research Press, 2008.

Obama, Barack. "Full Text of Obama's Speech to AIPAC." *International Business Times,* March 4, 2012. http://www.ibtimes.com/full-text-obama-aipac-2012-speech-420078.

Pagden, Anthony. "Imperialism, Liberalism and the Quest for Perpetual Peace." *Daedalus* (Spring 2005): 46–57.

Paley, Julia. "Toward an Anthropology of Democracy." In *Annual Review of Anthropology.* 469–96. Palo Alto, CA: Annual Reviews, Inc., 2002.

Petro, Nicolai. *The Rebirth of Russian Democracy: An Interpretation of Political Culture.* Cambridge, MA: Harvard University Press, 1995.

Pinker, Steven. *The Blank Slate: The Modern Denial of Human Nature.* New York: Penguin Books, 2002.

Plank, Dale. "Health and Sanitation." In *Subcontractor's Monograph: Mongolian People's Republic, HRAF-39, Wash-1,* edited by William B. Ballis and Robert A. Rupen. 405–18. New Haven, CT: Human Relations Area Files, 1956d.

———. "Labor Relations and Organization." In *Subcontractor's Monograph: Mongolian People's Republic, HRAF-39, Wash-1,* edited by William B. Ballis and Robert A. Rupen. 404. New Haven, CT: Human Relations Area Files, 1956c.

———. "Public Welfare." In *Subcontractor's Monograph: Mongolian People's Republic, HRAF-39, Wash-1,* edited by William B. Ballis and Robert A. Rupen. 419–26. New Haven, CT: Human Relations Area Files, 1956b.

———. "Religion." In *Subcontractor's Monograph: Mongolian People's Republic, HRAF-39, Wash-1,* edited by William B. Ballis and Robert A. Rupen. 308–73. New Haven, CT: Human Relations Area Files, 1956a.

Prejevalsky, N. *Mongolia: The Tangut Country and the Solitudes of Northern Tibet.* Translated by E. Delmar Morgan and Henry Yule. Vol. 1. New Delhi, India: Asian Educational Services, (1876) 1991.

Pye, Lucian. "Political Culture Revisited." *Political Psychology* 12, no. 3 (1991): 487–508.

Quinn, Naomi. "Event Sequencing as an Organizing Cultural Principle." Paper presented at the *Society for Anthropological Sciences Annual Meeting.* Albuquerque, NM, 2010.

———. "How to Reconstruct Schemas People Share, from What They Say." In *Finding Culture in Talk: A Collection of Methods,* edited by Naomi Quinn. 35–81. New York: Palgrave MacMillan, 2005.

Ramstedt, Gustav John. *Seven Journeys Eastward, 1898–1912.* Mongolia Society, Occasional Paper 9. Bloomington, IN: Mongolia Society, 1978.

Ratchnevsky, Paul. *Genghis Khan: His Life and Legacy.* Edited and translated by Thomas Nivison Haining. Oxford, UK: Blackwell, 1991.

Renteln, Alison Dundes. *International Human Rights: Universalism versus Relativism.* Frontiers of Anthropology. Vol. 6. Newbury Park, CA: Sage, 1990.

Riasanovsky, Valentin A. *Fundamental Principles of Mongol Law.* London: K. Paul, Trench, Tribner and Co., 1937.

Ries, Nancy. "Potato Ontology: Surviving Postsocialism in Russia." *Cultural Anthropology* 24, no. 2 (2009): 181–212.

Rinchin, Narangerel. "Mongolia: Human Rights Education in Schools." In *Mongolia: Human Rights Education in Asian Schools.* Osaka, Japan: Asia-Pacific Human Rights Information Center, 2000. www.hurights.or.jp/pub/hreas/3/03rinchin.pdf.

Rindermann, Heiner. "Relevance of Education and Intelligence for the Political Development of Nations: Democracy, Rule of Law and Political Liberty." *Intelligence* 36 (2008): 306–22.

Rossabi, Morris. *Modern Mongolia: From Khans to Commissars to Capitalists.* Berkeley: University of California Press, 2005.

Rousseau, Jean-Jacques. *A Discourse on Political Economy.* Constitution Society, (1755) 1998. www.constitution.org/jjr/polecon.htm.

Rupen, Robert A. *How Mongolia Is Really Ruled: A Political History of the Mongolian People's Republic 1900–1978.* Stanford, CA: Hoover Institution, Stanford University, 1979.

———. *The Mongolian People's Republic: Integration and Community Building among the*

Fourteen Communist Party-States, edited by Jan F. Triska. Vol. 2. Stanford, CA: The Hoover Institution on War, Revolution, and Peace; Stanford University, 1966.

———. *Mongols of the Twentieth Century,* Parts 1 and 2. Uralic and Altaic Series. Vol. 37, Bloomington: Indiana University Press, 1964.

Sabloff, Paula L.W. "Capitalist Democracy Discourse among Mongolian Herders." *Human Organization* 69, no. 1 (2010): 86–96.

———. "Democracy and Risk: Mongolians' Perspectives." In *Change in Democratic Mongolia: Social Relations, Health, Mobile Pastoralism, and Mining,* edited by Julian Dierkes. 55–82. Leiden, The Netherlands: Brill, 2012.

———. "Differential Distribution of Political Knowledge in Two Regions of Mongolia: National Science Foundation Grant Proposal Funded 1998." *PoLAR (Political and Legal Anthropology Review)* 22, no. 1 (1999): 123–27.

———. "Genghis Khan, Father of Mongolian Democracy." In *Modern Mongolia: Reclaiming Genghis Khan,* edited by Paula L.W. Sabloff. 91–119. Philadelphia: University of Pennsylvania Museum of Archaeology and Anthropology, 2001.

———, ed. *Mapping Mongolia: Situating Mongolia in the World from Geologic Time to the Present.* Vol. 2, Penn Museum International Research Conferences, series editor Holly Pittman. Philadelphia: University of Pennsylvania Museum of Archaeology and Anthropology, 2011.

Salzman, P. "Multi-Resource Nomadism in Iranian Baluchistan." In *Perspectives on Nomadism,* edited by W. Irons and N. Dyson-Hudson. Leiden, The Netherlands: E.J. Brill, 1972.

Sambuu, Jamsrangiin. *Herdsman to Statesman: The Autobiography of Jamsrangiin Sambuu of Mongolia.* Translated by Mary Rossabi. Lanham, MD: Rowman Littlefield, 2010.

Sampson, Steven. "Beyond Transition: Rethinking Elite Configurations in the Balkans." In *Postsocialism: Ideals, Ideologies and Practices in Eurasia,* edited by C.M. Hann. 297–316. Cambridge: Cambridge University Press, 2002.

Sanders, Alan J. K. *Historical Dictionary of Mongolia.* 2nd ed. Lanham, MD: Scarecrow, 2003.

———. *Historical Dictionary of Mongolia.* Lanham, MD: Scarecrow Press, 1996.

———. *Mongolia: Politics, Economics and Society.* London: Frances Pinter, 1987.

———. "'Restructuring' and 'Openness'." In *Mongolia Today,* edited by Shirin Akiner. 57–78. London: Kegan Paul International, 1991.

Schaffer, Frederic. *Democracy in Translation: Understanding Politics in an Unfamiliar Culture.* Ithaca, NY: Cornell University Press, 1998.

———. "Political Concepts and the Study of Democracy: The Case of *Demokaraasi* in Senegal." *PoLAR (Political and Legal Anthropology Review)* 20, no. 1 (1997): 40–49.

Schmitter, Philippe C. "More Liberal, Preliberal, or Post-Liberal?" *Journal of Democracy* 6, no. 1 (1995): 15–22.

Schumpeter, Joseph. *Capitalism, Socialism, and Democracy.* (1942) 1975. http://www.amazon.com/Capitalism-Socialism-Democracy-Joseph-Schumpeter/dp/0061330086#reader_0061330086.

Scott, James C. *Seeing Like a State: How Certain Schemes to Improve the Human Condition Have Failed.* New Haven: Yale University Press, 1998.

Sermier, Claire. *Mongolia: Empire of the Steppes*. Hong Kong, China: Airphoto International 2002.

Shane, Scott. "In Russia, Echoes of Revolution." *New York Times*, January 13, 2012. http://www.nytimes.com/2012/01/15/sunday-review/in-moscow-echoes-of-the-91-communist-overthrow.html?pagewanted=all&_r=0. Accessed January 13, 2012.

Shore, Bradd. *Culture in Mind: Cognition, Culture, and the Problem of Meaning*. New York: Oxford University Press, 1996.

Shubin, Sergei. "Networked Poverty in Rural Russia." *Europe-Asia Studies* 59, no. 4 (2007): 591–620.

Smith, Adam. *An Inquiry into the Nature and Causes of the Wealth of Nations*. Chicago: University of Chicago Press, (1776) 1976.

Steiner-Khamsi, Gita and Ines Stolpe. *Educational Import: Local Encounters with Global Forces in Mongolia*. New York: Palgrave, 2006.

Strauss, Claudia. "Models and Motives." In *Human Motives and Cultural Models*, edited by Roy D'Andrade and Claudia Strauss. 1–20. Cambridge: Cambridge University Press, 1992.

Strauss, Claudia and Naomi Quinn. "Schema Theory and Connectionism." In *A Cognitive Theory of Cultural Meaning*, edited by Claudia Strauss and Naomi Quinn. 48–84. Cambridge: Cambridge University Press, 1997.

Tripp, Aili Mari. "Women and Political Change in Post-Soviet Eurasia and Postcolonial Africa." In *Beyond State Crisis? Postcolonial Africa and Post-Soviet Eurasia in Comparative Perspective*, edited by Mark M. Beissinger and Crawford Young. 385–410. Washington, DC: Woodrow Wilson Center Press, 2002.

Tsedenbal, Y. *Mongolian People's Republic on the Road to Socialism*. Ulaanbaatar, Mongolia: Political Literature Publishing House, 1967.

United Nations. *Universal Declaration of Human Rights*. 1948. www.un.org/Overview/rights.html.

United Nations Human Rights Council. "National Report of Mongolia on the Situation of Human Rights." http://www.upr-mongolia.mn/index.php?cmd=Content&menuid=38&/National-Report-of-Mongolia. Accessed March 10, 2012.

United Nations Statistics Division. "Social Indicators: Indicators on Literacy." http://unstats.un.org/unsd/demographic/products/socind/literacy.htm. Accessed March 10, 2012.

United States Supreme Court. "Darin Ryburn, et al. v. George R. Huff, et al. On Petition for Writ of Certiorari to the United States Court of Appeals for the Ninth Circuit, Decided January 23, 2012 "In US Supreme Court *11–208*. Legal Information Institute, Cornell University Law School, 2012. http://www.law.cornell.edu/supremecourt/text/11-208.

US Bureau of Resource Management. "Mission Statement." US Department of State, http://www.state.gov/s/d/rm/index.htm#mission. Accessed July 12, 2012.

US Embassy in Ulaanbaatar. *USAID in Mongolia: Gobi Regional Economic Growth Initiative*. 2003. http://us-mongolia.com/usaidmongolia/gregi.shtml.

USAID. "USAID: Democracy, Human Rights and Governance." http://www.usaid.gov/our_work/democracy_and_governance/. Accessed December 11, 2011.

Verdery, Katherine. "Theorizing Socialism: A Prologue to the 'Transition.'" In *The Anthropology of Politics*, edited by Joan Vincent. 366–86. Oxford, UK: Blackwell, 2002.

———. *What Was Socialism, and What Comes Next?* Princeton, NJ: Princeton University Press, 1996.

Wenar, Leif. "Rights." In *The Stanford Encyclopedia of Philosophy*, edited by Edward N. Zalta, 2007. http://plato.stanford.edu/entries/rights/.

World Bank. "GDP per Capita in Current US$, 1989–2011." http://search.worldbank.org/ data?qterm=GDP%20per%20capita&language=EN. Accessed February 16, 2011.

World Values Survey. *Values Change the World*. 2008. http://www.worldvaluessurvey.org/ wvs/articles/folder_published/article_base_110/files/WVSbrochure6-2008_11 .pdf.

———. "World Value Survey 1981–2008 Official Aggregate." ASEP/JDS Data Archive, http://www.wvsevsdb.com/wvs/WVSIntegratedEVSWVS.jsp?Idioma=I. Accessed December 12, 2011.

Wulff, Robert and Shirley Fiske, eds. *Anthropological Praxis: Translating Knowledge into Action*. Boulder, CO: Westview Press, 1987.

Yadamsuren, Buyanjargal, Mario Merialdi, Ishnyam Davaadorj, et al. "Tracking Maternal Mortality Declines in Mongolia between 1992 and 2007: The Importance of Collaboration." *Bulletin of the World Health Organization* 88, no. 3 (2010): 192–98.

Index

ABOUT THE AUTHOR

Paula L. W. Sabloff is a professor at the Santa Fe Institute. She is a political anthropologist who has conducted research in Mexico, the United States, and Mongolia, and taught at the University of Pittsburgh and the University of Pennsylvania. She curated the exhibition "Modern Mongolia: Reclaiming Genghis Khan" at the National Museum of Natural History (Smithsonian Institution) and is editor of several books, including *Higher Education in the Post-Communist World* (1998), *Modern Mongolia* (2001), and *Mapping Mongolia* (2011).